SCIENTIFIC CREATIONISM

(GENERAL EDITION)

Prepared by the technical staff and consultants
of the
Institute for Creation Research

Edited By

HENRY M. MORRIS, Ph.D.
President, Institute for Creation Research

MASTER BOOKS
EL CAJON, CALIFORNIA

Scientific Creationism

Copyright © 1974

Creation-Life Publishers
P. O. Box 15666
San Diego, California 92115

First printing	*September 1974*
Second printing	*May 1975*
Third printing	*August 1976*
Fourth printing	*December 1977*
Fifth printing	*August 1978*
Sixth printing	*January 1980*
Seventh printing	*September 1980*
Eighth printing	*April 1981*
Ninth printing	*September 1981*
Tenth printing	*December 1982*
Eleventh printing	*January 1984*
Twelfth printing	*April 1985*

ISBN 0-89051-003-2 — Paper
ISBN 0-89051-004-0 — Cloth
Library of Congress Catalog Card No. 74-14160

Cataloging in Publication Data

Institute for Creation Research
   Scientific creationism / prepared by the technical staff and consultants of the Institute for Creation Research ; edited by Henry M. Morris.
   1. Creation.   2. Bible and evolution.
I. Morris, Henry Madison, 1918-   II. Title.

213   74-14160

Printed in the United States of America

CONTENTS

WRITERS AND CONSULTANTS[1]
SCIENTIFIC CREATIONISM
(First Edition)

This book is the result of a cooperative project undertaken by the scientific staff of the Institute for Creation Research, the members of the Technical Advisory Board of the Institute, and a number of other scientists and teachers who assisted in various ways.

The basic text of the manuscript was prepared by the I.C.R. Director, Dr. Henry M. Morris. It has been thoroughly reviewed by the Associate Director, Dr. Duane Gish, and by Professors Harold Slusher and Stuart Nevins. It has been reviewed by the members of the I.C.R. Technical Advisory Board and by the other teachers and scientists listed below. Their corrections and suggestions have all been incorporated in the revised text.

The final manuscript has been tested as a textbook by the I.C.R. staff in a special 14-hour Workshop on Scientific Creationism sponsored by one of the California School Districts for its teachers. Feedback from this course in every way confirmed the suitability of the book for its intended purpose.

The list of writers and consultants follows below:

Thomas G. Barnes, D.Sc. Professor of Physics, University of Texas, El Paso.

William A. Beckman, Ph.D. Professor of Physical Sciences, Christian Heritage College, San Diego.

Edward Blick, Ph.D. Professor of Aerospace, Mechanical and Nuclear Engineering, University of Oklahoma, Norman.

Richard Bliss, M.S. Science Consultant, Unified School District #1, Racine, Wisconsin.

David R. Boylan, Ph.D. Dean, College of Engineering, Iowa State University, Ames.

Larry Butler, Ph.D. Professor of Biochemistry, Purdue University, West Lafayette, Indiana.

Kenneth B. Cumming, Ph.D. Research Biologist, U.S. Consultants Fisheries Service, LaCrosse, Wisconsin.

---

[1]The data shown refer to the degrees and positions held by these men in 1974, when the first edition of this book was published. Although more than half now (1985) hold different positions, and several have been awarded additional degrees, their position on the subject of scientific creationism remains the same.

FOREWORD TO FIRST EDITION

The widespread movement in recent years toward the establishment of new private Christian schools has been stimulated largely by the failure of the public schools to maintain academic and philosophic objectivity. In the name of modern science and of church-state separation, the Bible and theistic religion have been effectively banned from curricula, and a nontheistic religion of secular evolutionary humanism has become, for all practical purposes, the official state religion promoted in the public schools.

The results of two generations of this evolutionary indoctrination have been devastating. Secularized schools have begotten a secularized society. The child is the father of the man and, if the child is led to believe he is merely an evolved beast, the man he becomes will behave as a beast, either aggressively struggling for supremacy himself or blindly following aggressive leaders.

Evolutionist teaching is not only harmful sociologically, but it is false scientifically and historically. Man and his world are *not* products of an evolutionary process but, rather, are special creations of God. According to the Biblical record, God Himself wrote with His own hand these words: "For in six days the Lord made heaven and earth, the sea, and all that in them is. . . ." (See Exodus 20:11; 31:17-19).

That being true, it follows that real understanding of man and his world can only be acquired in a thoroughgoing creationist frame of reference. True education in every field should be structured around creationism, not evolutionism.

Most Christian schools are, therefore, committed to Biblical creationism as a basic premise in their philosophy of education. The Christian school movement is urgently needed in today's world and is already making a vital impact. Fortunate is the child whose parents and church leaders think enough of his future character and his eternal welfare to see that he has a solid and thorough Christian education.

But there are still serious hindrances, even in a Christian school. How can creationism be taught effectively when all

iii

the textbooks are evolution-oriented and when most Christian teachers have been trained in colleges of education where the instruction is based on evolutionism?

Somehow textbooks need to be rewritten and teachers retrained! Such a goal sounds Utopian, but progress *toward* a goal requires a beginning and with God, nothing is impossible.

The Institute for Creation Research was founded for this unique and important purpose. Although it is still young, its teachers' workshops and seminars, as well as its Summer Institutes on Scientific Creationism and its literature programs, have made significant contributions in the lives and ministries of many teachers in both Christian and public schools.

The necessary textbook programs, however, require much greater investments of time and money than do seminars and are being implemented more slowly. In the meantime, until creation-oriented classroom textbooks are available (and, in the case of the public schools, selected textbooks which are at least unbiased on the evolution-creation issue), the best alternative is to provide individual teachers with a sound basic textbook on the subject for their own personal study and use.

This is the purpose of the two new ICR books, *Scientific Creationism* (General Edition) and *Scientific Creationism* (Public School Edition). The latter book deals with all the important aspects of the creation-evolution question from a strictly scientific point of view, attempting to evaluate the physical evidence from the relevant scientific fields without reference to the Bible or other religious literature. It demonstrates that the real evidences dealing with origins and ancient history support creationism rather than evolutionism.

Scientific Creationism (General Edition) is essentially identical with the public school edition, except for the addition of a comprehensive chapter which places the scientific evidence in its proper Biblical and theological context. This section, "Creation According to Scripture," contains a thorough exposition of thé Genesis records of Creation, the Flood and other important events of early history. It also includes the various "theories" that have been proposed (unsuccessfully) for harmonizing the Bible with the evolutionary framework of history.

With this book, the Christian teacher has both Biblical and scientific data at hand to show students the fallacies of evolution and the strong evidences of creation. The teacher can adapt the material to a required subject or grade level as various topics arise in the regular course outline. It also can be taught on an alternate basis as a single coherent unit on scientific Biblical creationism during some appropriate block of time in the annual schedule.

The scientific discussions, are intended to be understandable and usable by teachers with non-scientific backgrounds. The information is well-documented and organized for convenient reference use. The book is careful and courteous in its treatment of the evolutionary viewpoint, as well as properly factual and cautious in its advocacy of creationism and catastrophism. The Biblical discussions, while emphasizing special creation and the so-called "naive literal" approach to Genesis, also include careful and thorough treatment of other viewpoints, and will be found applicable in curricula of all types of Christian schools.

Finally, although the book is written primarily with teachers in mind, it can be used effectively by intelligent laymen in any type of individual or group study situation. So far as is known, this book has the most comprehensive coverage of all major aspects of the question of origins to be found anywhere in a single, small volume.

It is hoped that the book will help restore confidence in special creation as the true explanation of the origin and meaning of the world.

Henry M. Morris
Institute for Creation Research
San Diego, California

July 1974

FOREWORD TO SECOND EDITION

When *Scientific Creationism* was first published in 1974, the modern creationist revival was really just beginning to attract interest from the evolution-dominated scientific/educational establishment. The Creation Research Society was ten years old, and the Institute for Creation Research (under its present name) only two years old. The book was prepared because of the great need at the time for a general text and reference work on all aspects of the creation model of origins, a book which would be scientifically accurate and well documented, yet understandable and persuasive to the non-scientist as well as the scientist.

That it did meet this need is confirmed by its wide use and eleven printings. For over a decade it has served as probably the best known and most influential book in this important field. Many people have been led to sound creationist convictions through reading it, and many schools and colleges have used it as a textbook or required reference. In the meantime, the creation movement has proliferated, with creationist associations now active in every state and many foreign countries.

Many more books on creationism are available now than was the case in 1974. This becomes especially obvious in the greatly expanded bibliographies in this new edition of *Scientific Creationism*. Nevertheless, the demand for this particular book continues to be very strong, so it does seem appropriate to issue it now in a new, updated edition.

There have, of course, been many significant scientific developments bearing on the creation/evolution issue since the publication of the first edition. Not surprisingly, these all seem to strengthen the case for creation and weaken the case for evolution. Many of them, whether by coincidence or otherwise, seem to reflect the influence of the creation movement, with evolutionists coming more and more to acknowledge the validity of the evidences and arguments cited by creationist writers and speakers.

For example, there is the burgeoning influence of the "punctuated equilibrium" .concept in biology and paleontology. Creationists had long argued that there were no true transitional forms in the fossil record, as neo-Darwinians had always maintained. Now we find leading evolutionists saying the same thing. For example:

"The known fossil record fails to document a single example of plyletic evolution accomplishing a major morphologic transition. . . "[1]

"The absence of fossil evidence for intermediary stages between major transitions in organic design . . . has been a persistent and nagging problem for gradualistic accounts of evolution."[2]

Gould defines "punctuated equilibrium" as follows:

"Thus, our model of 'punctuated equilibria' holds that evolution is concentrated in events of speciation and that successful speciation is an infrequent event punctuating the stasis of large populations that do not alter in fundamental ways during the millions of years that they endure."[3]

Thus, there are not even transitional forms to be expected between *species,* let alone genera, families, and higher categories.

Another aspect of neo-Darwinism that is being abandoned by many evolutionists is the concept of natural selection as a "creative" force. Creationists have long argued that natural selection has no predictive value and thus is a mere tautology, stating the obvious fact that organisms that "survive" are thereby decreed to have been the "fittest," but it reveals nothing whatever about how they evolved in the first place. Many evolutionists now agree with this judgment, and are looking for other possible mechanisms. An author of one of the thirty-odd anti-creationist books published in recent years, ackowledges:

"The claim that natural selection is a tautology is

[1]Steven M. Stanley, *Macro-evolution: Pattern and Process* (San Francisco; W. M. Freeman and Co., 1979), p. 39.
[2]Stephen Jay Gould, "Is a New and General Theory of Evolution Emerging?" *Paleobiology* (Vol. 6, No. 1, 1980), p. 127.
[3]Gould, *op cit,* p. 125.

periodically made in the scientific literature itself.''[1]

The remarkable adaptations of organisms to their environments has often been cited as proof of the efficacy of natural selection. Creationists, on the other hand, had always maintained that such adaptations were evidence of design, not chance. Evolutionists now reluctantly admit this to be the case, and argue that *imperfections* in adaptation ("survival of the misfit") is evidence for evolution.

" In fact, as Darwin recognized, a perfect Creator could manufacture perfect adaptations. . . . If there were no imperfections, there would be . . . nothing to favor evolution by natural selection over creation.''[2]

This is an amazing admission of the absence of any real evidence for evolution. Misfits (if there really are such) constitute evidence for *downward* changes (e.g., mutations), not upward changes, as required by any meaningful evolutionary process.

Another extremely significant development is the resurgence of catastrophism in geology. Here, again, creationists have led the way, arguing for years that traditional geological uniformitarianism ("the present is the key to the past") was an impotent dogma, completely incapable of accounting for the great rock beds of the earth's crust, especially the very fossil deposits which had been used as the main evidence of evolution. The neo-catastrophists are now saying the same thing, though they are careful not to credit the creationists. Robert Dott, in his presidential address to the Society of Economic Paleontologists and Minerologists, chooses the term "episodicity" instead of "catastrophism."

"What do I mean by 'episodic sedimentation?' Episodic was chosen carefully over other possible terms. 'Catastrophic' has become popular recently because of its dramatic effect, but it should be purged from our vocabulary because it feeds the neo-catastrophist-

---

[1]D.J. Futuyma, *Science on Trial* (New York: Pantheon Books, 1983), p. 171.
[2]Jeremy Cherfas, "The Difficulties of Darwinism," *New Scientist* (Vol. 102: May 17, 1984), p. 29. Cherfas is here citing arguments developed by the eminent evolutionist, Stephen Jay Gould.

creation cause."[1]

Nevertheless, Dott acknowledges that practically all the geological strata were formed by at least local floods and other such catastrophes.

"I hope I have convinced you that the sedimentary record is largely a record of episodic events rather than being uniformly continuous. My message is that episodicity is the rule, not the exception."[2]

Similarly, James H. Shea, Editor of the *Journal of Geological Education*, has repudiated Lyellian uniformitarianism.

"Furthermore, much of Lyell's uniformitarianism, specifically his ideas on identity of ancient and modern causes, gradualism, and constancy of rate, has been explicitly refuted by the definitive modern sources as well as by an overwhelming preponderance of evidence that, as substantive theories, his ideas on these matters were simply wrong."[3]

This return to catastrophism, of course, does *not* mean *Biblical* catastrophism (centered in the worldwide Flood), but episodic catastrophism, the concept of many regional catastrophes, each separated from the other by long periods of geologic inactivity. In recent years, however, even global catastrophes are again coming into fashion with some geologists, especially the idea of periodic asteroid bombardments, each triggering massive extinctions of flora and fauna.

The Harvard evolutionist, Stephen Jay Gould, has even proposed these intermittent catastrophes and extinctions as a new explanation of evolution!

"Heretofore, we have thrown up our hands in frustration at the lack of expected pattern in life's history— or we have sought to impose a pattern that we hoped to find on a world that does not really display it. . . . If we can develop a general theory of mass extinction, we may finally understand why life

---

[1]Robert H. Dott, "Episodic View Now Replacing Catastrophism," *Geology* (November 1982), p. 16.
[2]*Ibid.*
[3]James H. Shea, "Twelve Fallacies of Uniformitarianism," *Geotimes* (Vol. 10: September 1982), p. 456.

has thwarted our expectations—and we may even extract an unexpected kind of pattern from apparent chaos."[1]

The idea of "evolution by extinction" is surely a fascinating commentary on the wistful search for some kind of mechanism to explain evolution. More significant, however, is Gould's admission that there is really no "pattern in life's history."

"I regard the failure to find a clear 'vector of progress' in life's history as the most puzzling fact of the fossil record."[2]

Gould's admission that there is no clear pattern of progress in the fossil record is significant. The standard geological column has always been assumed to exhibit the evolution of life, from simple to complex, over the geological ages. Creationists, on the other hand, have insisted that this standard column is largely artificial. All the great phyla have existed unchanged since the Cambrian, and this persistence is true right down even to many species (the bacterium *E Coli*, still popular in bacteriological research, has remained the same for a billion years, by evolutionary chronology).

Furthermore, every local column is different from the standard column—always grossly incomplete, frequently with missing ages, often with the ages inverted, and sometimes even with the ages (as deduced from the fossils) mixed together. To the extent that any real order does seem to exist in a local column, creationists have tried to show that such order represents relative elevations of habitat in the ecological communities which were trapped and buried by the sedimentary catastrophe(s) which deposited them.

Geologist David Raup has made extensive studies on these fossil sequences and has come to the following surprising conclusion:

"So the geological time scale and the basic facts of biological change over time are totally independent of evolutionary theory. . . .

In the years after Darwin, his advocates hoped to find

---

[1]Stephen Jay Gould, "The Ediacaran Experiment," *Natural History*, (Vol. 93: February 1984), p. 23.
[2]*Ibid.*

predictable progressions. In general, these have not been found—yet the optimism has died hard, and some pure fantasy has crept into textbooks."[1]

Raup's statistical studies on fossil occurrences have led him not only to the theory of periodic extinctions noted above, but also to the remarkable discovery that the fossils could just as well have been deposited randomly, as far as any order is concerned! He even notes the ironic implications of this for creationists.

"One of the ironies of the evolution-creation debate is that the creationists have accepted the mistaken notion that the fossil record shows a detailed and orderly progression and they have gone to great lengths to accommodate this 'fact' in their Flood geology."[2]

Raup, as Curator of Geology at Chicago's Field Museum, as well as Head of Geology at the University of Chicago, is surely one of the world's most knowledgeable paleontologists. He is also a proponent of neo-catastrophism and punctuated equilibrium, in common with an increasing number of modern evolutionists. One of the top men of the previous generation, a student of the eminent George Gaylord Simpson, has come to a similar conclusion:

" Few paleontologists have, I think, ever supposed that fossils, by themselves, provide grounds for the conclusion that evolution has occurred.'[3]

"The fossil record doesn't even provide any evidence in support of Darwinian theory except in the weak sense that the fossil record is compatible with it, just as it is compatible with other evolutionary theories, and revolutionary theories, and special creationist theories and even ahistorical theories."[4]

No wonder that the Oxford zoologist, Mark Ridley, has concluded that:

---

[1]David M. Raup, "Evolution and the Fossil Record," *Science* (Vol. 213: July 17, 1981), p. 289.
[2]*Ibid.*
[3]David B. Kitts, "Search for the Holy Transformation," *Paleobiology* (Vol. 5: Summer 1979), p. 353.
[4]*Ibid*, p. 354.

"No real evolutionist, whether gradualist or punctua-
tionist, uses the fossil record as evidence in favor of the
theory of evolution over special creation."[1]

Both the ubiquitous evidences of catastrophism in the
geological strata and the ubiquitous absence of transitional
forms in the fossil record can now be combined with the utter
absence of any evidence of evolutionary progression in this
record to make a very strong case for special creation and a
global hydraulic cataclysm as the best model for correlating
the data of geology and paleontology.

Many other developments could be mentioned. Almost
without exception, each new discovery or analysis seems to
weaken the traditional case for evolution and strengthen the
case for creation. Some of these are discussed later on in this
book. The newer data, not only from geology and paleontology,
but also from astronomy, genetics, physics, biochemistry and
other sciences, could be cited in support of scientific creationism. In fact, David Raup has paid an interesting (though
back-handed) compliment to the creationists by noting this
fact:

"I doubt if there is any single individual within the
scientific community who could cope with the full range
of (creationist) arguments without the help of an army of
consultants in special fields."[2]

The inability of evolutionists to cope with the creationist
arguments has been further indicated during the past decade
in the 200 or so creation/evolution debates that have been held
in many places, including most of the leading universities.
Evolutionists have given various excuses why the creationists
usually win these debates (and why most leading evolutionary
scientists now refuse to participate in such debates), but the
real reason is because the scientific evidences support creation
—not evolution!

Consequently, the answer of the evolutionary establishment
to the creationist arguments has not been scientific, but

---

[1]Mark Ridley, "Who Doubts Evolution?" *New Scientist* (Vol. 90: June 25,
1981), p. 831.
[2]David M. Raup, "Geology and Creation," *Bulletin of the Field Museum of
Natural History,* (Vol. 54: March 1983), p. 16.

emotional. Intimidation is evidently the game plan. The A.C.L.U. files or threatens to file lawsuits wherever a two-model approach is considered in a school district. A veritable stream of anti-creationist tirades has poured forth from the liberal news media, as well as the journals and books of the educational/scientific establishment. Evolutionists publicly gloat over the merest suggestion of a misquotation or misrepresentation which they can discover in the copiously documented creationist literature, while their own writings are saturated with out-of-context quotes and flagrant distortions of the creationist arguments.

Evolutionists still cannot seem to comprehend some of the most cogent creationist contentions (e.g., the evidence of the entropy principle against "upward" evolution even in *open* systems). In the absence of any real scientific evidence for real evolution, they have tended to concentrate their polemics on arguments against the Biblical doctrines of recent creation and the worldwide Flood, even though these questions are separate questions from the basic scientific issue of creation versus evolution. At the same time, the scientific evidences for the young earth and flood geology have continued to accumulate rapidly as well.

It is hoped that this new edition of *Scientific Creationism* will stimulate increased interest, both in the scientific and non-scientific communities, on this vital topic. Although most of the book remains unchanged from the first edition, it will be found that the arguments and evidences, with the accompanying documentation, are every bit as valid and relevant today as they were in 1974. A number of new sections have been added, as well as changes in the existing text wherever appropriate. The bibliographies have been greatly expanded, as noted before, but no claim is made as to their completeness. A great many books have been published in this field since 1974, and it is probable that some significant books have been left out. In any case, for those interested in further study, there are obviously many books now available. *Scientific Creationism* is now only one book among many in its field, but it has already made an effective contribution toward the creationist cause, and it is hoped that this new edition will continue to serve in this way in the future.

Henry M. Morris
Institute for Creation Research
June 1985

CHAPTER I

EVOLUTION OR CREATION?

The Importance of Origins

Both parents and teachers know that children are curious creatures. That is, they are insatiably curious about the why's and whences of things. This inborn intellectual alertness, if encouraged and cultivated, leads in adult life to a mature scientific attitude toward the world and the ability to think creatively in solving technological, sociological and personal problems.

Regardless of the subject matter of a particular course of study, it is vital that the student be made aware of origins. If he studies chemistry, he should have an interest in the origin of the elements and the laws that govern chemical reactions. The study of English should give him a sense of the origin of his own language and even of language itself. Biology, of course, should discuss the origin of life and of the various kinds of organisms. A course in government should include discussion of the origin of his own nation and its legal structure, as well as of the origin of nations and laws in general. And so on.

A course of study which does *not* do this may avoid a measure of controversy, but only at the cost of stifling curiosity and inventiveness. Description and techniques are vital in any good course, certainly, but these will only produce skills, not real understanding. This type of instruction, valuable though it is for the immediate goal of making a living, is barren in achieving the broader goal of real *meaning* in living. It is like a bridge without abutments, spanning from nowhere to nowhere, without roots in the past or hope in the future.

The following is a summary of cogent reasons why the study of origins is important in any course:

A. *Scientific Reasons*
    1. Science (i.e., "knowledge") must seek to answer the question "Whence?" as well as "What?"

2. Science is based on cause-and-effect reasoning. Inevitably, therefore, as one assimilates effects to their immediate causes and those causes to *their* causes, one eventually confronts the question of a First Cause.
3. A knowledge of natural laws and processes, without an appreciation of at least the problems associated with their origin, is stultifying to the discovery and comprehension of new scientific principles.

B. *Sociological Reasons*
1. Science has innumerable social implications and applications. Solutions to social problems require a real understanding of the origin of the physical processes which affect them (e.g., nuclear energy, fossil fuels, ecology, genetic engineering, hallucinogenic drugs, etc.).
2. The so-called social sciences themselves require an understanding of the origin of the sociological entities with which they deal (e.g., races, cultures, crime, war, etc.).
3. The milieu of political thought is constantly changing in emphasis. Sociological instruction which emphasizes only the current fad in political activism or social theory, with no foundation in history, will be useless to the student when a new emphasis appears.

C. *Personal Reasons*
1. Each person needs, more than anything, a sense of his own identity and personal goals, and this is impossible without some sense of his origin. What a person comes to believe about his origin will inevitably condition what he believes about his destiny.
2. Lack of a sound scientific understanding of origins and meanings among modern young people has impelled them to seek help in such anti-scientific solutions as "mind-expanding" drugs, witchcraft, astrology, and the like.
3. True mental health, such as teachers desire for their pupils, requires a solid and satisfying philosophy of life, and this certainly demands a mentally-satisfying concept of their personal origin and future.

However, if teachers are to teach creation as a scientifically sound alternative to evolution, they must have available resource information on how to do so. Unfortunately, prac-

2

tically every textbook now available is biased in favor of evolution. A large percentage of teachers, as well as the scientific public, have themselves also been indoctrinated with the evolutionary point of view in their studies in college.

Furthermore, most creationist books treat the subject of origins from the Biblical point of view, as well as the scientific, and, therefore, are not appropriate for instructional purposes in the public schools. There are indeed a number of creationist books which are strictly scientific in their content, but most of these deal with only a few of the relevant topics.

The purpose of *Scientific Creationism* is, first, to treat all of the more pertinent aspects of the subject of origins and to do this solely on a scientific basis, with no references to the Bible or to religious doctrine. The treatment is positive, rather than negative, showing that the creation model of origins and history may be used to correlate the facts of science at least as effectively as the evolution model. Although the book necessarily deals with scientific data, it is written for the non-specialist, and we believe it can be adequately understood and used by most intelligent laymen. It is necessary to use scientific concepts and terminology, but they are all explained as needed, so that the reader should, with at least a little effort on his part, have no great difficulty understanding and using them.

It is our suggestion that every teacher be provided with a copy of *Scientific Creationism* for personal study, and asked to read it in its entirety. If feasible, workshops should be set up by individual school districts to equip their teachers for its use.

Whatever the course being taught, and regardless of the grade level, the teacher will find that the assigned textbook and prescribed supplementary reading are premised on evolution and affected by it in various ways. Whenever a particular subject is encountered which involves origins (e.g., the origin of the solar system, the beginning of the "cave-men," etc.) or the pre-history of the earth and its inhabitants (e.g., the meaning of the dinosaurs, the formation of coal beds, the discovery of the first metals, etc.), the teacher should present the creationist interpretation (as well as the textbook evolutionary interpretation) and, in so far as practicable for the age level involved, the evidence favoring *both* models. The book is conveniently organized and well-

3

indexed to facilitate such use.

Experience has indicated that this approach is more exciting, both to students and teachers, than the one-sided indoctrination in evolutionism which is common today. Teachers and school administrators are urged to give it a fair trial.

This book itself is intended to serve primarily as a source for background information needed by the teacher, rather than as an actual textbook to be used in elementary or secondary school classes. It can thus be adapted as needed, in accordance with the teacher's own preferences, to whatever subject or grade level may be involved. It can also be used, of course, as an actual textbook in formal courses on origins, in either high school or college.

In general, whether as a textbook or as a book for personal study and reference, it is believed that this book will fill the need for a scholarly, yet simple, presentation of all the major evidence and arguments for special creation, as well as the related evidence for a young earth and worldwide flood.

Impossibility of Scientific Proof of Origins

The preceding section has stressed the vital importance of studying the subject of origins. At the same time, it must also be emphasized that it is impossible to *prove* scientifically any particular concept of origins to be true. This is obvious from the fact that the essence of the scientific method is experimental observation and repeatability. A scientific investigator, be he ever so resourceful and brilliant, can neither observe nor repeat *origins!*

This means that, though it is important to have a philosophy of origins, it can only be achieved by faith, not by sight. That is no argument against it, however. Every step we take in life is a step of faith. Even the pragmatist who insists he will only believe what he can see, *believes* that his pragmatism is the best philosophy, though he can't prove it! He also believes in invisible atoms and in such abstractions as the future.

As a matter of observation, belief in something is necessary for true mental health. A philosophy of life is a philosophy, not a scientific experiment. A life based on the whim of

4

the moment, with no rationale, is "a tale told by an idiot, full of sound and fury, signifying nothing."

Thus, one must *believe*, at least with respect to ultimate origins. However, for optimally beneficial application of that belief, his faith should be a reasoned faith, not a credulous faith or a prescribed faith.

To illustrate more exactly what we mean when we say origins cannot be proved, a brief discussion is given below on each of the two basic concepts of origins, creation and evolution:

A. *Creation cannot be proved*

· 1. Creation is not taking place now, so far as can be observed. Therefore, it was accomplished sometime in the past, if at all, and thus is inaccessible to the scientific method.
  2. It is impossible to devise a scientific experiment to describe the creation process, or even to ascertain whether such a process *can* take place. The Creator does not create at the whim of a scientist.

B. *Evolution cannot be proved*

  1. If evolution is taking place today, it operates too slowly to be measurable, and, therefore, is outside the realm of empirical science. To transmute one kind of organism into a higher kind of organism would presumably take millions of years, and no team of scientific observers is available to make measurements on any such experiment.
  2. The small variations in organisms which are observed to take place today (see pp. 51-58) are irrelevant to this question, since there is no way to prove that these changes within present kinds eventually change the kinds into different, higher kinds. Since small variations (including mutations) are as much to be expected in the creation model as in the evolution model, they are of no value in discriminating between the two models.
  3. Even if modern scientists should ever actually achieve the artificial creation of life from non-life, or of higher kinds from lower kinds, in the laboratory, this would not *prove* in any way that such changes did, or even

5

could, take place in the past by random natural processes.

Since it is often maintained by evolutionists that evolution is scientific, whereas creationism is religious, it will be well at this point to cite several leading evolutionists who have recognized that evolution also is incapable of being proved.[1]

Evolution operates too slowly for scientific observation

One of the nation's leading evolutionists, Theodosius Dobzhansky, has admitted:

"The applicability of the experimental method to the study of such unique historical processes is severely restricted before all else by the time intervals involved, which far exceed the lifetime of any human experimenter. And yet, it is just such impossibility that is demanded by anti-evolutionists when they ask for 'proofs' of evolution which they would magnanimously accept as satisfactory."[2]

Note the tacit admission that "the experimental method" is an "impossibility" when applied to evolution.

Evolution is a dogma incapable of refutation

Two leading modern biologists have pointed out the fact that, since evolution cannot in any conceivable way be disproved, therefore, neither can it be proved.

"Our theory of evolution has become . . . one which cannot be refuted by any possible observations. It is thus 'outside of empirical science,' but not necessarily false.

---

[1] It is interesting and encouraging to note that, in the Foreword to the most recent edition of Darwin's *Origin of Species*, a leading British evolutionary biologist, Professor L. Harrison Matthews, F.R.S., recognizes that "Belief in evolution is thus exactly parallel to belief in special creation — both are concepts which believers know to be true but neither, up to the present, has been capable of proof." (London: J.M. Dent & Sons, Ltd., 1971), p. x.

[2] Theodosius Dobzhansky, "On Methods of Evolutionary Biology and Anthropology," *American Scientist*, Vol. 45 (December, 1957), p. 388.

No one can think of ways in which to test it. . . . (Evolutionary ideas) have become part of an evolutionary dogma accepted by most of us as part of our training."[1]

Similarly, Peter Medawar recognized the problem entailed by the fact that no way exists by which to test evolution.

"There are philosophical or methodological objections to evolutionary theory. . . . It is too difficult to imagine or envisage an evolutionary episode which could not be explained by the formulae of neo-Darwinism."[2]

In other words, both the long neck of the giraffe and the short neck of the hippopotamus can presumably be explained by natural selection. A theory which incorporates everything really *explains* nothing! It is tautologous. Those who survive in the struggle for existence are the fittest because the fittest are the ones who survive.

Evolution is an authoritarian system to be believed

"It seems at times as if many of our modern writers on evolution have had their views by some sort of revelation and they base their opinions on the evolution of life, from the simplest form to the complex, entirely on the nature of specific and intra-specific evolution. . . . It is premature, not to say arrogant, on our part if we make any dogmatic assertion as to the mode of evolution of the major branches of the animal kingdom."[3]

"But the facts of paleontology conform equally well with other interpretations. . . . e.g., divine creation, etc., and paleontology by itself can neither prove nor refute such ideas."[4]

Thomas Huxley, probably more responsible than any other one man for the acceptance of Darwinian philosophy, nevertheless recognized that:

---

[1]Paul Ehrlich and L.C. Birch, "Evolutionary History and Population Biology," *Nature*, Vol. 214 (1967), p. 352.

[2]Peter Medawar, *Mathematical Challenges to the Neo-Darwinism Interpretation of Evolution*, (Philadelphia: Wistar Institute Press, 1967), p. xi.

[3]G. A. Kerkut, *Implications of Evolution*, (London: Pergamon, 1965), p. 155.

[4]D. Dwight Davis, "Comparative Anatomy and the Evolution of Vertebrates," in *Genetics, Paleontology and Evolution*, (ed. by Jepsen, Mayr and Simpson, Princeton University Press, 1949), p. 74.

". . .'creation' in the ordinary sense of the word, is perfectly conceivable. I find no difficulty in conceiving that, at some former period, this universe was not in existence; and that it made its appearance in six days . . . in consequence of the volition of some pre-existing Being."[1]

The reason for favoring evolution is not because of the scientific evidence

An outstanding British biologist of a number of years ago made the following remarkable observation:

"If so, it will present a parallel to the theory of evolution itself, a theory universally accepted not because it can be proved by logically coherent evidence to be true but because the only alternative, special creation, is clearly incredible."[2]

The only reason for saying that special creation is incredible would be if one had certain knowledge that there was no God. Obviously, if no Creator exists, then special creation is incredible. But since a universal negative can only be proved if one has universal knowledge, such a statement requires omniscience. Thus, by denying God, Dr. Watson is claiming the attributes of God himself.

There are some scientists, at least, who find it easier to believe in the deity of an omnipotent Creator than in the deity of Professor Watson.

The Two Models of Origins

It is, as shown in the previous section, impossible to demonstrate scientifically which of the two concepts of origins is really true. Although many people teach evolution as though it were a proven fact of science, it is obvious that this is false teaching. There are literally thousands of scientists[3] and other educated intellectuals today who reject evolution, and this would certainly not be the case if evolution were as obvious as many scientists say it is.

---

[1]Leonard Huxley, *Life and Letters of Thomas Henry Huxley,* (London: Macmillan, Vol II, 1903), p. 429.
[2]D.M.S. Watson, "Adaptation," *Nature,* Vol. 123 (1929), p. 233.
[3]The Creation Research Society, for example, numbers over 700 M.S. and Ph.D. scientists on its rolls.

The same is true of creation, of course. Although many believe special creation to be an absolute fact of history, they must believe this for theological, rather than scientific reasons. Neither evolution nor creation can be either confirmed or falsified scientifically.[1]

Furthermore, it is clear that neither evolution nor creation is, in the proper sense, either a scientific theory or a scientific hypothesis. Though people might speak of the "theory of evolution" or of the "theory of creation," such terminology is imprecise. This is because neither can be *tested*. A valid scientific hypothesis must be capable of being formulated experimentally, such that the experimental results either confirm or reject its validity.

As noted in the statement by Ehrlich and Birch cited previously, however, there is no conceivable way to do this. Ideally, we might like to set up an experiment, the results of which would demonstrate either evolution or creation to have been true. But there is no one test, nor any series of tests, which can do this scientifically.

All of these strictures do not mean, however, that we cannot discuss this question scientifically and objectively. Indeed, it is extremely important that we do so, if we are really to understand this vital question of origins and to arrive at a satisfactory basis for the faith we must ultimately exercise in one or the other.

A more proper approach is to think in terms of two scientific models, the *evolution model* and the *creation model*. A "model" is a conceptual framework, an orderly system of thought, within which one tries to correlate observable data, and even to predict data. When alternative models exist, they can be compared as to their respective capacities for correlating such data. When, as in this case, neither can be proved, the decision between the two cannot be solely objective. Normally, in such a case, the model which correlates the greater number of data, with the smallest number of unresolved contradictory data, would be accepted as the more probably correct model.

---

[1] Dr. N. Heribert-Nilsson, Director of the Botanical Institute at Lund University, Sweden, said "My attempt to demonstrate evolution by an experiment carried on for more than 40 years has completely failed. . . . The idea of an evolution rests on pure belief." (*Synthetische Artbildung*, 1953).

When particular facts do show up which seem to contradict the predictions of the model, it may still be possible to assimilate the data by a slight modification of the original model. As a matter of fact, in the case of the evolution model, as Ehrlich and Birch said: "Every conceivable observation can be fitted into it."

The same generalization, of course, is true of the creation model. There is no observational fact imaginable which cannot, one way or another, be made to fit the creation model. The only way to decide objectively between them, therefore, is to note which model fits the facts and predictions with the smallest number of these secondary assumptions.

Creationists are convinced that, when this procedure is carefully followed, the creation model will always fit the facts as well as or better than will the evolution model. Evolutionists may, of course, believe otherwise. In either case, it is important that everyone have the facts at hand with which to consider *both* models, rather than one only. The latter is brainwashing, not brain-using!

Since the rest of this book is devoted primarily to a comparison of these two models, it is important that everyone using it, both teachers and students, clearly understand the formulation of the two models and their implications.

A. *The Evolution Model*

The evolutionary system attempts to explain the origin, development, and meaning of all things in terms of natural laws and processes which operate today as they have in the past. No extraneous processes, requiring the special activity of an external agent, or Creator, are permitted. The universe, in all its aspects, evolves itself into higher levels of order (particles to people) by means of its innate properties.

To confirm that this is the essential nature of the evolution model, several recognized authorities are cited below, giving their own concepts of evolution.

"Most enlightened persons now accept as a fact that everything in the cosmos—from heavenly bodies to human beings—has developed and continues to develop through evolutionary processes."[1]

---

[1] Rene Dubos, "Humanistic Biology," *American Scientist*, Vol. 53 (March 1965), p. 6.

"Evolution comprises all the stages of the development of the universe: the cosmic, biological, and human or cultural developments. . . . Life is a product of the evolution of inorganic nature, and man is a product of the evolution of life."[1]

"Evolution in the extended sense can be defined as a directional and essentially irreversible process occurring in time, which in its course gives rise to an increase of variety and an increasingly high level of organization in its products. Our present knowledge indeed forces us to the view that the whole of reality is evolution — a single process of self-transformation."[2]

"Biological evolution can, however, be explained without recourse to a Creator or a planning agent external to the organisms themselves. There is no evidence, either, of any vital force or immanent energy directing the evolutionary process toward the production of specified kinds of organisms."[3]

Thus evolution entails a self-contained universe, in which its innate laws develop everything into higher levels of organization. Particles evolve into elements, elements into complex chemicals, complex chemicals into simple living systems, simple life forms into complex life, complex animal life into man.

Summarizing, evolution is: (1) naturalistic; (2) self-contained; (3) non-purposive; (4) directional; (5) irreversible; (6) universal; and, (7) continuing.

B. *The Creation Model*

Diametrically opposed to the evolution model, the creation model involves a process of special creation which is: (1) supernaturalistic; (2) externally directed; (3) purposive, and (4) completed. Like evolution, the creation model also applies universally. It also is irreversibly directional, but its

[1] Theodosius Dobzhansky, "Changing Man," *Science*, Vol. 155 (January 27, 1967), p. 409.

[2] Julian Huxley, "Evolution and Genetics," Chap. 8 in *What Is Science?* Ed. J. R. Newman, (New York: Simon & Schuster, 1955), p. 272.

[3] Francisco J. Ayala, "Biology as an Autonomous Science," *American Scientist*, Vol. 56 (Autumn 1968), p. 213.

direction is downward toward lower levels of complexity rather than upward toward higher levels. The completed original creation was perfect and has since been "running down."

The creation model thus postulates a period of special creation in the beginning, during which all the basic laws and categories of nature, including the major kinds of plants and animals, as well as man, were brought into existence by special creative and integrative processes which are no longer in operation. Once the creation was finished, these processes of *creation* were replaced by processes of *conservation*, which were designed by the Creator to sustain and maintain the basic systems He had created.

In addition to the primary concept of a completed creation followed by conservation, the creation model proposes a basic principle of disintegration now at work in nature (since any significant change in a *perfect* primeval creation must be in the direction of imperfection).

The two models may be easily compared by studying the table below:

Evolution Model	*Creation Model*
Continuing naturalistic origin	Completed supernatural origin
Net present increase in complexity	Net present decrease in complexity

The questions of the *date* of creation (old or young) and the nature of cosmic processes *since* creation (dominantly naturalistic and uniform or catastrophic) are separate issues.

It is proposed that these two models be used as systems for "predicting" data, to see which one does so more effectively. To do this, one should imagine that neither the evolutionist nor the creationist knows in advance what data will be found. They do not know what they will find but bravely make predictions, each on the basis of his own model.

The following table indicates the predictions that would probably be made in several important categories.

Category	Basic Predictions of	
	Evolution Model	Creation Model
Galactic Universe	Galaxies Changing	Galaxies Constant
Structure of Stars	Stars Changing into Other Types	Stars Unchanged
Other Heavenly Bodies	Building Up	Breaking Down
Types of Rock Formations	Different in Different "Ages"	Similar in All "Ages"
Appearance of Life	Life Evolving from Non-Life	Life Only from Life
Array of Organisms	Continuum of Organisms	Distinct Kinds of Organisms
Appearance of Kinds of Life	New Kinds Appearing	No New Kinds Appearing
Mutations in Organisms	Beneficial	Harmful
Natural Selection	Creative Process	Conservative Process
Fossil Record	Innumerable Transitions	Systematic Gaps
Appearance of Man	Ape-Human Intermediates	No Ape-Human Intermediates
Nature of Man	Quantitatively Superior to Animals	Qualitatively Distinct From Animals
Origin of Civilization	Slow and Gradual	Contemporaneous with Man

It should be noted that the tabulated predictions are predictions of the *primary* models, as defined in their most general terms as in the foregoing discussion. These primary models may be modified by secondary assumptions to fit certain conditions. For example, the basic evolution model may be extended to include harmful, as well as beneficial, mutations, but this is not a natural prediction of the basic concept of evolution. If the "predictions" of evolution, as listed in the above table, were actually observed in the natural world, they would, of course, in every case be enthusiastically acclaimed as strong confirmations of the evolution model. That fact justifies the conclusion that these are the *basic* predictions of evolution.

The above predictions are merely suggestive of the types of entities that can be used to contrast the two models. Several of these will be discussed in some detail later. At this point, it may be noted that creationists maintain that the predictions of the creation model do fit the observed facts in nature better than do those of the evolution model. The data must be *explained* by the evolutionist, but they are *predicted* by the creationist.

Pedagogical Advantages of the Creation Model

There are great benefits to be derived, for both student and teacher, from a sound exposition of the creation model

13

along with the evolution model. It is strange and disturbing that resistance is encountered from many scientists and teachers to a proposal which is so reasonable and salutary.

Some of these benefits are listed below:

1. It stimulates real thinking on the part of the student, as he is asked to compare these two important models.

2. Creationism is consistent with the innate thoughts and daily experiences of the child and thus is conducive to his mental health. He knows, as part of his own experience of reality, that a house implies a builder and a watch a watchmaker. As he studies the still more intricately complex nature of, say, the human body, or the ecology of a forest, it is highly unnatural for him to be told to think of these systems as chance products of irrational processes.

3. The greatest joy of scientific discovery is to find evidence of beauty and pattern in the processes and structures of nature, especially when, as great scientists[1] such as Newton and Kepler have testified, one senses that he is merely "thinking God's thoughts after Him." This will develop a love and enthusiasm for science in the child more effectively than will anything else.

4. There is no greater stimulus to responsible behavior and earnest effort, as well as honesty and consideration for others, than the awareness that there well may be a personal Creator to whom one must give account. This applies both to student and teacher.

In public schools, both evolution and creation should be taught as equally as possible, since there are children of taxpayers representing both viewpoints in the classes. If people wish *only* evolution to be taught, they should establish private schools with that purpose.

Likewise, an essential purpose of most private Christian schools is to teach creation as the true doctrine of origins

---

[1] It is significant that most of the founding fathers of modern science (Newton, Bacon, Kepler, Galileo, Boyle, Pascal, Faraday, Pasteur, Maxwell, Ray Cuvier, Linnaeus, Agassiz, and a host of others) were creationists, even though they were aware of the various evolutionary concepts of their times.

and they have been established on that basis. This does not mean, however, that students in such schools should not also be instructed concerning evolution. Since they will be living in a world dominated by evolutionary philosophy they should, by all means, be well versed in evolutionary concepts and the supposed evidences for evolution. At the same time they should be informed of the fallacies in those concepts and evidences, as well as the basis for creationism.

The most effective means of accomplishing these goals is probably to evaluate the two models of origins first on a purely scientific basis, following the same procedure in the Christian school as recommended for the public school. Many students in private Christian schools will already have been indoctrinated in evolutionary thinking by previous experiences in the public schools before transferring, and they need first of all to be purged of the ingrained idea that evolution is scientific and creation is "religious." This can best be accomplished by thorough exposure to scientific creationism in a step-by-step comparison with the evolution model.

Accordingly, the next six chapters of this book will deal with the two models of origins on a purely scientific basis with no reference to the Bible or other religious books. It is shown that, at every point, the creation model is superior to the evolution model.

Then, in the final chapter of this book, the general creation model is defined more explicity in terms of Biblical revelation. The whole question of origins and development is brought into its proper Biblical and theological context, and the student can be led into a comprehensive, coherent, and satisfying world-view centered in his personal Creator and Saviour, the Lord Jesus Christ.

It should be emphasized that this order is followed not because the scientific data are considered more reliable than Biblical doctrine. To the contrary, it is precisely because Biblical revelation is absolutely authoritative and perspicuous that the scientific facts, rightly interpreted, will give the same testimony as that of Scripture. It is not creationists who have to distort the facts of science to fit their creation model. It is rather the evolutionists who, in attempting to justify their faith in evolution, are perpetually modifying and expanding the basic concept of evolution in order to explain away all

15

the scientific fallacies and contradictions which it entails.

Evolution as Religion

Since evolution has not been scientifically proved and, in fact, cannot even be tested, in the long-range sense, it must be accepted on faith. Even so-called micro-evolution, or variation, which presumably *can* be tested, has so far failed to exhibit an "upward" trend, and thus has *failed* the test. The mechanism of evolution, if such a mechanism really exists, is still "the central mystery."

Many evolutionists have been highly vocal in contending that creationism (even *scientific* creationism) is inherently religious, since it is a basic tenet of Biblical "fundamentalism." It is, of course, true that religions based on the Bible (whether Protestant, Catholic, Jewish or even Islamic), are monotheistic and thus inherently creationist.

It is equally true, however, that religions which are basically polytheistic, pantheistic, humanistic or atheistic, must be based on some form of evolution. Thus, not only do all atheists and humanists *believe* in evolution, but so do Buddhists, Confucianists, Taoists, Hindus and animists, not to mention Marxists and Nazis, and even the "liberals" in the nominally monotheistic faiths.

Nevertheless, although both creation and evolution have important religious, moral and social implications, they can also each be used to correlate and predict scientific data. The next six chapters will show that the scientific creation model does a better job of this than the evolution model. There are still problems, and more research needs to be done to resolve these, but the problems of the evolution model are far more serious.

As a result, there are today *thousands* of recognized, qualified scientists who have become creationists, in spite of the evolutionary indoctrination which they received in school and the evolutionist intimidation which they now face in organized intellectualism. In a very real sense, creationism is more scientific than evolutionism, and evolutionism is far more religious than creationism.

CHAPTER II

CHAOS OR COSMOS?

Origin of Matter, Energy and Natural Law

The two models of origins can be compared first of all with respect to their explanations of the fundamental nature of the universe and its origin. These are the studies of *cosmology* and *cosmogony*, respectively. Evolution and creation entail complete world-views, and this is the logical place to begin as we compare the two concepts.

The evolution model presupposes[1] that the universe can be completely explained, at least in principle, in terms of natural laws and processes, as a self-contained system, without need of external preternatural intervention. The very laws themselves, therefore, must have somehow developed on the same naturalistic basis. Similarly, energy and matter must have evolved in nature and structure from a primeval chaotic, or randomized, state into its present highly-structured complexity.

The creation model conversely supposes[1] that the universe was simply called into existence by the omnipotence, in accord with the omniscience, of the Creator. Not only the matter and energy of the cosmos, but also the laws controlling their behaviour, were specially created *ex nihilo*, or perhaps better, *ex Deo*.

The rationalist of course finds the concept of special creation insufferably naive, even "incredible." Such a judgment, however, is warranted only if one categorically denies the existence of an omnipotent God.

A more scientific approach is to make comparative predictions from the two models, to test their relative capacity to

---

[1]Anthropomorphic expressions such as this do not accord with strict *scientific* usage, but they do allow emphasis without sacrifice of meaning. Thus, "the evolution model presupposes" really means "those who use the evolution model presuppose."

correlate this realm of the basic laws of nature. It seems obvious that the evolution model would predict that matter, energy and the laws are still evolving since they must have evolved in the past and there is no external agent to bring such evolution to a halt.

Creationists obviously would predict that the basic laws, as well as the fundamental nature of matter and energy, would not now be changing at all. They were all completely created—*finished* in the past, and are being *conserved* in the present.

Cosmologists and cosmogonists of the evolutionary school do recognize this as a legitimate question.

"The naive view implies that the universe suddenly came into existence and found a complete system of physical laws waiting to be obeyed. . . . Actually it seems more natural to suppose that the physical universe and the laws of physics are inter-dependent. This leads us to expect that, if the universe changes in the large, then its laws might also change in a way that could not be predicted; . . ."[1]

The fact is, of course, all observations that have been made to date confirm the straightforward predictions of the creation model; namely, that the basic laws of nature are constant and invariable, and that the basic nature of matter and energy is likewise a constant. There is not as yet the slightest observational intimation that these entities are evolving at all.

That is, the law of gravity, the laws of thermodynamics,[2] the laws of motion, and all other truly basic laws have apparently always functioned[3] in just the way they do now, contrary to a prediction of the basic evolution model.

Similarly, the constancy of matter and energy is so certain that two of the most important laws in science are the *Law*

---

[1] W. H. McCrea, "Cosmology after Half a Century," *Science*, Vol. 160 (June 2, 1968), p. 1297.

[2] "Thermodynamics" — heat energy. The science of thermodynamics deals with the relationships involved in the conversion of heat and other forms of energy into work.

[3] Laws, of course, do not "function," but "are used as descriptions of firmly-demonstrated relationships." Again, however, such anthropomorphisms seem more expressive and less pedantic, and so are used occasionally in this book whenever they do not compromise the meaning.

of Mass Conservation and the *Law of Energy Conservation*. Matter can be changed in state, but cannot be created or destroyed. If one allows for mass-energy interchange, then of course energy can either be regarded as a form of matter or matter as a form of energy, and the conservation principles still apply.

There are other conservation principles in physics (e.g., conservation of momentum, conservation of electric charge, etc.). It seems as certain as science can be certain, that the basic laws of nature are *not* in a process of continuing evolution, but rather of conservation and stability, *exactly as predicted by the creation model!*

These stable aspects of nature can of course be accommodated within the evolution model, but only at the cost of introducing a secondary assumption therein — namely, that the laws completed their own evolution at some time in the past and have been stable since. The point is that this situation *requires explanation* in the framework of the evolution model. The creation model, on the other hand, does not have to explain it, — it *predicts* it!

Therefore, the creation model seems to be the better model, to this point at least. The only objection that could be lodged against it here is that it postulates a supernatural Creator, and the evolutionist often counters with the query: "But, then, who made God?"

But such a question of course *begs* the question. If the evolutionist prefers not to believe in God, he must still believe in some kind of uncaused First Cause. He must either postulate matter coming into existence out of nothing or else matter having always existed in some primitive form. In either case, matter itself becomes its own Cause, and the creationist may well ask: "But, then, who made Matter?"

In either case, therefore, one must simply *believe* — either in eternal, omnipotent Matter or else in an eternal, omnipotent, Creator God. The individual may decide which he considers more reasonable, but he should recognize this is not completely a *scientific* decision either way.

In justification of his own decision, however, the creationist utilizes the scientific law of *cause-and-effect*. This law, which is universally accepted and followed in every field of science, relates every phenomenon as an effect to a cause. No effect is ever quantitatively "greater" nor qualitatively "superior" to its cause. An effect can be lower than its cause but never higher.

Using causal reasoning, the theistic creationist notes that:

The First Cause of limitless Space	must be infinite
The First Cause of endless Time	must be eternal
The First Cause of boundless Energy	must be omnipotent
The First Cause of universal Interrelationships	must be omnipresent
The First Cause of infinite Complexity	must be omniscient
The First Cause of Moral Values	must be moral
The First Cause of Spiritual Values	must be spiritual
The First Cause of Human Responsibility	must be volitional
The First Cause of Human Integrity	must be truthful
The First Cause of Human Love	must be loving
The First Cause of Life	must be living

We conclude from the law of cause-and-effect that the First Cause of all things must be an infinite, eternal, omnipotent, omnipresent, omniscient, moral, spiritual, volitional, truthful, loving, living Being! Do such adjectives describe Matter? Can random motion of primeval particles produce intelligent thought or inert molecules generate spiritual worship? To say that Matter and its innate properties constitute the ultimate explanation for the universe and its inhabitants is equivalent to saying that the Law of Cause-and-Effect is valid only under present circumstances, not in the past.

We might summarize this section by noting the remarkable fact that all the major "conceptual systems of science,"[1] as defined by California's Advisory Committee on Science Education, support the creation model better than they do the evolution model. These conceptual systems, of course, are not limited to California science but are universally accepted. A brief discussion follows on each of these important concepts:

1. *Cause-and-Effect*. This principle has just been discussed. An omnipotent Creator is an adequate First Cause for all observable effects in the universe, whereas evolution is *not* an adequate cause. The universe could not be its own cause.

2. *Relativity*. Einstein emphasized that all frames of reference as to size, position, time and motion in the world

---

[1] *Science Framework for California Public Schools* (Sacramento: Bureau of Publications, California State Department of Education, 1970), 148 pp.

are relative, not absolute. This argues that the universe cannot be an absolute in itself, and therefore can have no independent or absolute existence. Since it could not produce itself, it must be in existence due to the omnipotence of an external Creator, who is Himself its absolute standard.

3. *Motion.* The universe is not static; everywhere in space and time occur phenomena and processes. These manifest omnipresent energy perpetually generating motion. Even matter is composed of particles in constant motion. This fact argues for an omnipotent Cause of such energies and motion, and also for a completed creation in the past, in accord with the creation model. That is, there is a "hierarchy of movements"; one type of movement or dynamic law does not evolve into another.

4. *Energy Conservation.* Energy is the fundamental physical entity and exists in a variety of inter-convertible forms. Everything that exists in space and time *is* energy and everything that *happens* is energy conversion. The Law of Energy Conservation — "energy can be converted from one form into another, but can neither be created nor destroyed" — is the most important and best-proved law in science.

> "This law is considered the most powerful and most fundamental generalization about the universe that scientists have ever been able to make."[1]

Any conservation principle, especially conservation of energy, of course confirms a specific prediction from the creation model. Creation was completed in the past and is being conserved at present.

5. *Mass-Energy Equivalence.* The inter-convertibility of matter and energy is one of the great discoveries of 20th Century science. Thus matter can now be regarded as a form of energy, with the total of mass and energy being conserved in nuclear reactions. Apart from such reactions, matter itself is always conserved, as predicted from the creation model.

6. *Classification and Order.* The fact that categories of natural phenomena can be arranged in orderly classifica-

---

[1] Isaac Asimov, "In the Game of Energy and Thermodynamics You Can't Even Break Even," *Journal of Smithsonian Institute* (June 1970), p. 6.

tion systems (table of chemical elements, biological taxonomy as in the Linnaean system, a hierarchy of star types, etc.) is a testimony to creation. That is, if all entities were truly in a state of evolutionary flux, classification would be impossible. In biological classification, for example, it would be impossible to demark where "cats" leave off and "dogs" begin. Similarities in structure, therefore, do not necessarily imply evolutionary descent from a common ancestor; an alternative and better explanation is that of creation by a common Designer of similar structures for similar functions and different structures for different functions.

7. *Processes.* Every unit of matter in the universe interacts in various ways with other units of matter or energy. The universe is dynamic, forces are interacting, processes are taking place, events are happening, energy is being utilized, and work is being done. All of this activity speaks of orderly and meaningful purpose in the universe, not random stumbling and bumping. Were it not so, there would be no point to scientific study at all. "Meaning" and "purpose" in turn are predictions of the creation model.

8. *Forces and Fields.* Inter-actions in nature depend upon three types of force and the "fields" associated with them; namely, electromagnetic, gravitational and nuclear forces. All three have apparently always acted as they do now, since the beginning of the universe. There is no evidence that these entities have ever "evolved" into their present form. The field action is propagated through free space in the form of wave motion (electromagnetic waves, gravitational waves, etc.) at the same speed as that of light, 300,000,000 meters per second. There is a real mystery in this wave phenomenon because it takes place in the "nothingness" of free space —a vacuum. What vibrates in this wave motion? No one has answered that question. But it is a doubly puzzling problem for evolution. It is unlikely that wave phenomena could evolve in the void of a vacuum where there is nothing to evolve from.

9. *Environmental Interdependence.* In nature, systems normally are integrated with their environments in such marvelous ways as to give the strong appearance, at

least, of creative forethought. In the organic realm, natural selection acts as a conservative mechanism to screen out any novel features which intrude on a previously adjusted system, thus tending to preserve the status quo in nature. On the other hand, if the environment itself changes, there is usually enough variational potential in the created genotype to allow it to adjust to the new environment before it is eliminated. The environment coupled with natural selection, thus constitutes a powerful cybernetic[1] device to conserve the created kinds and the balance of nature. This is exactly what one would predict from the creation model.

10. *Energy Decay.* Finally, there is the remarkable fact that all processes involve energy changes and these changes always tend to go in a "downward" direction, such that there results a net decrease in the "availability" of the converted energy for further useful work. Although the Law of Energy Conservation (the First Law of Thermodynamics) assures us that no energy will be destroyed, this Law of Energy Decay (the Second Law of Thermodynamics) tells us that energy continually proceeds to lower levels of utility.

"What the Second Law tells us, then, is that in the great game of the universe, we not only cannot win; *we cannot even break even!*"[2]

This decay law is so important in its bearing on origins that we shall deal with it at greater length in Chapter IV. At this point we merely note that, once again, the evolution model must find some means of accommodating or explaining it by a secondary assumption. The creation model, on the other hand, *predicts* it! That is, directional changes in an initially perfect system are bound to be in the direction of imperfection.

We conclude this section with an illuminating comment from one of the world's top mathematical physicists:

"It seems to be one of the fundamental features of nature that fundamental physical laws are described in

---

[1] Cybernetics is the study of control devices, as applied both to living organisms and to man-made machines.
[2] Asimov, *op. cit.,* p. 8.

terms of a mathematical theory of great beauty and power, needing quite a high standard of mathematics for one to understand it. You may wonder: why is nature constructed along these lines? One can only answer that our present knowledge seems to show that nature is so constructed. We simply have to accept it. One could perhaps describe the situation by saying that God is a mathematician of a very high order, and He used very advanced mathematics in constructing the universe. Our feeble attempts at mathematics enable us to understand a bit of the universe, and as we proceed to develop higher and higher mathematics we can hope to understand the universe better."[1]

Only a great First Cause who is both omniscient and omnipotent can really account for the physical world as modern science has illumined it. This fact, of course, perfectly supports the creation model.

The Beginning of the Universe

In this section, we wish to discuss the origin of the stellar universe, with its innumerable stars and galaxies. The great variety and complexity of the stars and their varied assemblages lead, more or less, easily to different evolutionary models to explain them. With such diversity in the heavenly bodies, it is not difficult to arrange them into an arbitrary order and then to asume that this arbitrary arrangement actually represents an evolutionary series.

Regardless how reasonable any such model may seem, however, it is obvious that there is no way at all by which it can be experimentally tested. How does one design an apparatus to observe the evolution of a star? It is significant that although one may imagine how one star might evolve into another, or how particles might accumulate to become stars, one never *sees* anything like this happen. As long as men have been observing the stars, they have remained the same, as far as can be observed.

Consider now the implications of the creation model. According to creationism, all major systems and categories

---

[1]P.A.M. Dirac, "The Evolution of the Physicist's Picture of Nature," *Scientific American*, Vol. 208 (May 1963), p. 53.

in nature—including stars and galaxies—were created in the beginning, each with a distinctive structure to serve a distinct purpose. Therefore, the creationist would predict from the creation model that the stars and galaxies would *not* change, certainly not in any manner which would enable them to advance to higher levels in the hierarchy of stars. And the actual fact is that they have *not* so changed, thus conforming perfectly to the expectation of the creation model.

It is well to note at this point, the implications of the First and Second Laws of Thermodynamics with respect to the origin of the universe. It should be stressed that these two Laws are *proven* scientific laws, if there is such a thing. They have been experimentally tested, measured and confirmed, thousands of times, on systems both extremely large and extremely small, and no scientist today doubts their full applicability in the space-time coordinates accessible to us. Therefore the cosmic implications of the two Laws are profound.

1. *The First Law* (*Law of Energy Conservation*) states that nothing is now being either "created" or destroyed. It therefore teaches quite conclusively that the universe did not create itself; there is nothing in the present structure of natural law that could possibly account for its own origin.

2. *The Second Law* (*Law of Energy Decay*) states that every system left to its own devices always tends to move from order to disorder, its energy tending to be transformed into lower levels of availability, finally reaching the state of complete randomness and unavailability for further work. When all the energy of the cosmos has been degraded to random heat energy, with random motion of molecules and uniform low-level temperature, the universe will have died a "heat death."

3. The fact that the universe is not yet dead is clear evidence that it is not infinitely old. Since it will die, in time, if present processes continue, time cannot have been of infinite duration. Our present universe is a *continuum* of space, mass and time, so if one of these entities had a beginning, the other two also must have begun concurrently.

25

4. The Second Law requires the universe to have had a beginning; the First Law precludes its having begun itself. The only possible reconciliation of this problem is that the universe was created by a Cause transcendent to itself.

5. Nothing within the present observable space-mass-time framework is an adequate Cause; therefore the Cause must either be an evolutionary process beyond observable space or prior to observable time (and thus outside the scope of science) or else a creative process which brought space and matter and time into being concurrently and contemporaneously.

   (a) The suggestion that matter evolved into its present structure far out in non-observable space is the so-called *steady-state theory*. That is, to offset the tendency toward universal decay, it is postulated that new matter, in the probable form of hydrogen gas, is continually evolving into existence out of nothing somewhere out in space.

   (b) The suggestion that matter evolved into its present structure far back in non-observable time has been called the *big-bang theory*. That is, a primeval explosion of some kind is supposed to have converted energy into matter; the explosion itself was perhaps caused by a previous gravitational collapse into a super-dense state

6. It is obvious by definition that neither the big-bang theory nor the steady-state theory has any observational basis. In fact, they *contradict* both Laws of Thermodynamics. Therefore, they are philosophical speculations, not science, secondary assumptions to avoid the contradictions implicit in the evolution model.

7. The creation model, on the other hand, in effect *predicts* the two Laws of Thermodynamics, as noted before. A special creation of space, matter and time, by an omnipresent, omnipotent, eternal Creator is the only logical conclusion to be drawn from the two most certain and universal laws in science.

That neither the steady-state nor the big-bang theory of the origin of the universe is really satisfactory is emphasized in the following quotations from first-rate scientific authorities, all of them evolutionists:

"So far as I can judge, the authors of this new cosmology are primarily concerned about the great difficulty that must face all systems that contemplate a changing universe—namely, how can we conceive it to have begun? . . . Nor, for some reason, are they content to suppose that at some period in the distant past something happened that does not continually happen now. It seems to them better to suppose that there was no beginning and will be no ending to the material universe, and therefore, tacitly assuming that the universe must conform to their tastes, they declare that this must have been the case."[1]

"Is it not possible, indeed probable, that our present cosmological ideas on the structure and evolution of the universe as a whole (whatever that may mean) will appear hopelessly premature and primitive to astronomers of the 21st century? Less than 50 years after the birth of what we are pleased to call 'modern cosmology,' when so few empirical facts are passably well established, when so many different over-simplified models of the universe are still competing for attention, is it, we ask, really credible to claim, or even reasonable to hope, that we are presently close to a definitive solution of the cosmological problem?"[2]

One very important unanswered problem in any evolutionary model of the origin of stars and galaxies is the question of the formation of similar particles, elements and molecules throughout the universe.

"In 1875, J. C. Maxwell wrote, 'In the heavens we discover by their light . . . stars so distant that no material thing can ever have passed from one to another; and yet this light . . . tells us also that each of them is built up of molecules of the same kinds that we find on earth. . . .! No theory of evolution can be found to account for the similarity of the molecules. . . . On the

[1] Herbert Dingle, "Science and Modern Cosmology," *Science*, Vol. 120 (October 1, 1954), p. 519.
Although Professor Dingle was referring especially to the steady-state theory, the remarks quoted are equally applicable to the big bang theory.
[2] G. de Vacoleurs, "The Case for a Hierarchical Cosmology," *Science*, Vol. 167 (February 27, 1970), p. 1203.

other hand, the exact equality of each molecule to all others of the same kind gives it . . . the essential character of a manufactured article and precludes the idea of its being eternal and self-existent.' . . . So far as we know, the result is still the same as Maxwell inferred; all electrons are everywhere the same, all protons are the same, and so on. We should expect a sufficiently sophisticated theory to tell us why this is so."[1]

The creation model, of course, does tell us why this is so! The Creator created the entire universe, and He created it a universe, not a multi-verse. Physical entities, as well as biologic entities, were created with similar structures for similar functions, different structures for different functions.

A final note of dissatisfaction with the evolutionary models of the beginning of the universe is seen in the fact that they really beg the question, rather than answering the question, of origins. The Big-Bang theory does not account for the initial super-dense state (except, perhaps, in still another secondary modification, namely, an eternally-oscillating universe). The Steady-State theory does not account for the hydrogen that continually appears out of nowhere. In effect, they answer the question by denying there can be an answer!

Note the wistful suggestion of Isaac Asimov:

"Where did the substance of the universe come from? . . . If $0 = +1 + (-1)$, then something which is 0 might just as well become 1 and -1. Perhaps in an infinite sea of nothingness, globs of positive and negative energy in equal-sized pairs are constantly forming, and after passing through evolutionary changes, combining once more and vanishing. We are in one of these globs in the period of time between nothing and nothing, and wondering about it."[2]

Lest the evolutionist counter with the objection that postulating a personal Creator also explains nothing (who made God?, he will say), we remind him that the creation model *does* predict the laws of Thermodynamics, the

[1] W. H. McCrea, *op. cit.*, p. 1298.
[2] Isaac Asimov, "What is Beyond the Universe?" *Science Digest*, Vol. 69 (April 1971), p. 69.

constancy of natural law, the unity of the universe, and the existence of personality and intelligence in man, all of which pose serious problems to the evolution model.

Origin of the Solar System

School textbooks commonly devote much space to speculations on the origin of the earth and the solar system, even more than to the origin of the universe. Rarely are they honest enough with their young readers, however, to acknowledge that not one of these speculative ideas (whether rotating nebulas, accumulating planetesimals, tidal pluckings, turbulent dust clouds or anything else) is based on any scientific evidence! Each has been in vogue for a while, but has been in turn effectively refuted by other scientists advocating rival theories.

So far as we *know*, in fact, the solar system is quite unique in the universe. There is an almost innumerable quantity of stars, but that does not mean any of them necessarily have planets. Evolutionary astronomers assume that many do, but the only reason for thinking so is what might be called evolutionary statistics. That is, they reason, if our sun somehow evolved a planetary system by natural processes, then surely those same processes must have evolved similar planetary systems around at least a certain number of other stars.

This kind of logic, however, begs the whole question. The only solar system about which we have any information is our own and one does not use statistical analysis when his data consist of only one of a kind. No astronomer has ever yet been able to prove that any real planets exist anywhere outside our solar system. Therefore the question of the origin of our solar system is a unique question to be settled solely on its own merits.

The question is still not answered. Billions of dollars have been spent on the various space probes and lunar landings, and many scientists had hoped that these studies would finally show how the solar system had evolved and would provide evidence that life had also evolved on other planets besides the earth.

Although there have been many valuable "spin-off" effects of the space program, this particular hope has gone unfulfilled. Not only has no evidence been found that life had ever evolved elsewhere in the solar system, but all previous theories of the evolution of the solar system itself have encountered overwhelming problems as new data have come in.

Creationists of course had predicted this all along, on the basis of the creation model. For example, some of the definite predictions from the creation model are as follows:

1. Since the earth, moon and planets were each created for a specific purpose, each would have a distinctive structure. They would not all be of essentially the same composition and structure, as would be the case if they had all evolved together from a common source.
2. Only the earth would be found to have a hydrosphere capable of supporting life as we know it.
3. Only the earth would be found to have an atmosphere capable of supporting life as we know it.
4. No evidence of past or present life would be found anywhere in the solar system except on earth.
5. Evidence would be found of decay and catastrophism on other planets and moons, but not of evolutionary growth in order and complexity.

All of these predictions have been clearly confirmed by the moon landings and by the probes to the various planets and their satellites. Although some scientists still cling to the hope that evidence might yet be found which would support the existence of life in the distant past or distant future on one of these planets, the fact is that no such evidence has been found.

None of the planets has any measurable amount of liquid water and none has an oxygen atmosphere, both of which are absolute essentials for life as we know it. This fact is so well-known and universally accepted that no documentation is necessary.

Similarly, the widely published photographs of the moon's surface, as well as of Mars, clearly show signs of past deterioration, even of a catastrophic nature, from whatever their original forms may have been. The asteroid fragments, meteors and meteorites breaking up, and decaying comets all add their testimony of catastrophism and deterioration. Nowhere in the solar system is found any evidence at all of a building process, either of the planetary bodies themselves or of the complexity of the chemical and physical systems that are found on them.

Finally, the moon landings have permitted man actually to study the composition and structure of some of the materials from at least one extra-terrestrial body. Enough has been found now to permit the firm conclusion that the earth and its moon are of vastly different structure and therefore could not. have the same celestial evolutionary "ancestor."

> "To the surprise of scientists, the chemical makeup of the moon rocks is distinctly different from that of rocks on earth. This difference implies that the moon formed under different conditions, . . . and means that any theory on the origin of the planets now will have to create the earth and the moon in different ways."[1]

This is an extremely important scientific discovery and by all means should be emphasized in the classroom. *The moon and the earth have different structures and therefore different origins!*

Although we do not yet have actual rock materials from the other planets to study, it is easy to predict that they also will be much different from those of the earth. Obviously, if the earth's own satellite did not evolve with or from the earth, it is foolish to think that other planets could have had the same evolutionary origin. This one hard fact of science has rendered quite obsolete all current evolutionary models of the origin of the solar system. The only possible reason for the teacher now to spend time in the classroom on these concepts is for their historical interest and as a commentary on man's persistent attempt to avoid the creationist explanation.

Even before this discovery, of course, a considerable number of serious fallacies in all such evolutionary explanations of the origin of the solar system had been pointed out by various writers. These difficulties included:

1. The concentration of 98% of the angular momentum of the solar system in the planets when 99.8% of the mass of the solar system is concentrated in the sun.

---

[1] Jerry E. Bishop, "New Theories of Creation," *Science Digest,* Vol. 72 (October 1972), p. 42.

2. The extreme inclination of the orbits of Mercury and Pluto, as well as those of asteroids, meteors and comets, from the plane of the sun's ecliptic.
3. The retrograde axial rotations of Uranus and Venus.
4. The fact that one-third of the planetary satellites have retrograde orbits with respect to the rotational direction of their respective planets.

These and other phenomena had proved incapable of reasonable explanation in terms of any of the evolutionary theories. As a result, many astronomers have been frank enough to admit that none of them is satisfactory. The new information about moon structure, however, must be the final blow.

It certainly seems reasonable to conclude that, as of now, the creation model offers the only satisfactory means of accounting for the marvelous structure of the solar system. Not only do the various predictions of the creation model stand up, as noted above, but there is no aspect of the sun or its planets which cannot be explained simply and directly as the product of special creation in the beginning, followed by decay and catastrophe later.

Purpose in Creation

The earth, with its unique hydrosphere, atmosphere, and lithosphere is, so far as all the actual evidence goes, the only body in the universe capable of sustaining higher forms of life such as man. This, of course, is exactly as would be predicted from the creation model. The earth was created specifically to serve as man's home.

The evolutionary model of earth history has to presuppose changing structure over the ages, with its physical features gradually evolving to permit the later evolution of life. There is no evidence of this, however. As will be shown later, rocks of all types can be found in all "ages," and thus there is no evidence that the earth's rock-forming processes have changed over the ages.

Whether considering the origin of matter, of the laws of nature, of the stars and galaxies, of the solar system, or of the earth, we have seen therefore that the creation model correlates all the actual facts of observation much more realistically than does the evolution model. There is no scientific reason to reject the concept that the entire cosmos, with all its infinite variety of systems from atoms to galaxies, was brought into existence at essentially the same time by special creation.

Objections to the creation model are not scientific objections, but philosophic objections. If the creationist points out, for example, the lack of evidence that the various star-types evolve from one into another, the evolutionist responds by saying there is no evidence of creative purpose in the wide variety of these star-types.

Questions regarding *purpose*, however, are not scientific questions, at least not in the usually promoted sense of the term "science." The essential scientific question related to origins has to do simply with whether the evolution model or the creation model provides the more effective vehicle for correlating and predicting scientific facts of observation.

However, in view of the impossibility of ever obtaining actual scientific *proof* of either evolution or creation, and in view of the necessity of making a final choice between the two models on the basis of philosophic or religious preference—faith, if you will—it is not possible to avoid altogether the question of *purpose*.

The creation model does include, quite explicitly, the concept of purpose. The Creator was purposive, not capricious or indifferent, as He planned and then created the universe, with its particles and molecules, its laws and principles, its stars and galaxies, its plants and animals, and finally its human inhabitants.

We can make a scientific choice between evolution and creation on the basis of "best fit" of the observed facts. However, the ultimate *explanation* of these facts and their inter-relationships will be vastly different, depending on which model we choose. The evolutionary explanation must be in terms of random variational processes producing a naturalistic evolutionary chain all the way from particles to people. The creationist explanation will be in terms of primeval planning by a personal Creator and His implementation of that plan by special creation of all the basic entities of the cosmos, each with such structures and such behavior as to accomplish most effectively the purpose for which it was created. The creationist also notes the evidence of decay and catastrophe in the universe, regarding them as temporary intruders and disturbers of the perfect order originally created, and destined ultimately to be removed forever from the creation after they have been allowed to accomplish even *their* purpose.

The conflict between evolution and creation thus inescapably has ultimate theological overtones. However objectively we attempt to compare the factual data of biology or geology in terms of the two scientific models, we eventually confront a non-scientific choice, that is, whether to explain things in terms of evolutionary descent or in terms of creative purpose.

For example, do both fish and men have eyes because man evolved from a fish or because both fish and man needed to see, in order to fulfill their intended creative purpose? Can stars and galaxies be arranged in a logical hierarchy of order from one type to another because they represent different stages in an age-long evolutionary process, or because they were each specially created to serve distinct purposes, such purposes requiring different degrees of size and complexity?

The fact that many evolutionary scientists consciously seek to "eschew teleology" in their approach to the teaching of origins[1] does not prove that teleological explanations are not valid. If, indeed, the creation model provides a more satisfactory framework within which to correlate and predict scientific data, as we are trying to show in this book, then the question of purpose is quite relevant. Rather than seeking to devise explanations in terms of hypothetical evolutionary ancestries, the creationist seeks to ascertain purposes or, as Newton, Kepler and many other outstanding scientists of the past have phrased it, to "think God's thoughts after Him."

Admittedly it may be difficult at this stage of inquiry to comprehend the Creator's purpose in making pulsars or spiral nebulae or dinosaurs or bed-bugs. We can make "reasoned guesses," however, and such guesses are *no less scientific* than the guesses that others make about the imagined evolutionary development of pulsars, spiral

---

[1] A. J. Bernatowicz, "Teleology in Science Teaching," *Science*, Vol. 128 (December 5, 1958), pp. 1402-1405.

nebulae, dinosaurs, and bed-bugs. At least the concept of an omnipotent, purposive Creator provides an adequate Cause to produce these and all other observable effects in the universe, whereas random matter does not.

In the creationist concept, man is the highest of all creatures, and thus all other created systems must in some way be oriented man-ward, as far as purposes are concerned. Even the evolutionist recognizes that man is the highest product of the cosmic process.

"In man is a three-pound brain which, as far as we know, is the most complex and orderly arrangement of matter in the universe."[1]

The creationist believes that only an omnipotent Creator could design and construct the human brain! He cannot prove such a fact scientifically, of course, but neither can the evolutionist prove that random particles can organize themselves into a human brain, or into anything else but random particles.

The creationist explanation not only is far more in keeping with the law of causality, the laws of thermodynamics, and the laws of probability, but also gives assurance that there is real meaning and eternal purpose to existence. This conclusion is worth everything in the developing life of a child or young person.

Evolution out of Nothing

In recent years, evolutionary cosmogonies have themselves evolved in an almost unbelievable fashion. To all intents and purposes, the steady-state theory has been completely abandoned, even by its chief originator and proponent, Sir Fred Hoyle. Furthermore, Sir Fred and many others have also rejected the big-bang theory. As Weisskopf has said:

"No existing view of the development of the cosmos is completely satisfactory, and this includes the standard

---

[1] Isaac Asimov, "In the Game of Energy and Thermodynamics You Can't Even Break Even," *Smithsonian Institute Journal* (June 1970), p. 10.

model, which leads to certain fundamental questions and problems."[1]

The oscillating-universe idea is also being abandoned.

"We now appreciate that, because of the huge entropy generated in our Universe, far from oscillating, a closed universe can only go through one cycle of expansion or contraction."[2]

As what appears to be a desperate attempt to escape the creationist implications of genuine cosmogony, a new wave of cosmo-physicists has offered what they call the *inflationary universe*. This notion suggests that the universe (including all of space and time) began as an infinitesimal particle which inflated to grapefruit size in its first instand (10^{-35} seconds) of existence. This initial "cold big whoosh"[3] was then supposedly followed by the standard "hot big bang."

And what about the initial particle-sized universe? Two of the originators of this concept have an answer:

"It is then tempting to go one step further and speculate that the entire universe evolved from literally nothing."[4]

Tryon conjectures:

"...that our Universe had its physical origin as a quantum fluctuation of some pre-existing true vacuum, or state of nothingness."[5]

Thus one's choice of cosmogonies finally boils down to the following: *Evolution ex nihilo* or *Creation ex Deo*. The choice used to be: "Eternal Matter" or "Eternal God." Now it has become: "Omnipotent Nothingness" or "Omnipotent Creator."

[1]Victor P. Weisskopf, "The Origin of the Universe," *American Scientist*, Vol. 71 (Sept./Oct. 1983), p. 474.

[2]S.A. Bludman, "Thermodynamics and the End of the Closed Universe," *Nature*, Vol. 308 (March 22, 1984), p. 322.

[3]Edward P. Tryon, "What Made the World?" *New Scientist*, Vol. 101 (March 8, 1984), p. 16.

[4]Allan H. Guth and Paul J. Steinhardt, "The Inflationary Universe," *Scientific American*, Vol. 250 (May 1984), p. 128.

[5]Edward P. Tryon, *op cit*, p. 15.

CHAPTER III

UPHILL OR DOWNHILL?

The Laws of Thermodynamics

Having considered the origin of the universe and its basic structure, we next examine the characteristics of the laws which govern it and the processes which take place in it. We have already noted the importance of the First and Second Laws of Thermodynamics in this connection, and we now wish to consider more fully the powerful evidence which these Laws offer in support of the creation model.

1. *Predictions of the Evolution Model Relative to the Basic Laws*

If the evolution model were really an effective framework for predicting scientific data, it should certainly predict the basic principles by which nature functions. If it is really true that random matter has evolved, through successive stages, into elements, stars, chemical polymers, living cells, worms, fishes, amphibians, reptiles, mammals and, finally, man, then there must obviously be some powerful and pervasive principle which impels systems toward higher and higher levels of complexity. This is surely the most fundamental and important prediction of the evolution model—namely, a basic law of increasing organization, which introduces new systems into nature and which develops existing systems into higher systems. To give it an identifying name, let us call it the *Principle of Naturalistic Innovation and Integration*. It seems clear there must really be some such principle operating in nature if the evolution model of origins and development is valid.

If an evolutionist had no prior knowledge of nature's laws, and had only his evolution model to go by, he would surely have to predict this kind of fundamental principle operating in nature, and would expect to find it experimentally operating when he proceeded to make actual measurements of specific processes. No one would ever, on the basis of evolutionary assumptions, predict any such laws as the First and Second Laws of Thermodynamics.

2. *Predictions of the Creation Model Relative to the Basic Laws*

The creation model, on the other hand, explicitly predicts the Two Laws. Since it postulates a primeval creation which was both complete and perfect, as well as purposeful, it is evident, first, that a principle of conservation would be established to assure the accomplishment of the purpose of the created entities and, second, any changes which come in and intrude, as it were, on the perfect creation are bound to be harmful. Thus the creation model predicts a basic principle in nature which might be called the *Principle of Naturalistic Conservation and Disintegration.* This predicted principle is exactly the converse of that predicted by the evolution model—conservation instead of innovation, and disintegration instead of integration!

The question is which prediction fits the observed facts? The answer is that the creationist prediction is confirmed exactly by the Laws of Thermodynamics, which are now accepted universally by scientists as the two Laws which govern all natural processes. The principle of conservation is the First Law and the principle of disintegration is the Second Law. The evolutionist predictions of innovation and integration exist only in the realm of evolutionary philosophy, not in the realm of observable scientific data.

"The two laws of thermodynamics are, I suppose, accepted by physicists as perhaps the most secure generalizations from experience that we have."[1]

The *Second* Law of Thermodynamics is particularly important in this discussion, since it states that there exists a universal principle of change in nature which is downhill, not uphill, as evolution requires. It can be defined in various ways, in different contexts, as follows:

(1) *Classical Thermodynamics*
"In any physical change that takes place by itself the entropy always increases." (Entropy is "a

---

[1] P. W. Bridgman, "Reflections on Thermodynamics," *American Scientist*, Vol. 41 (October 1953), p. 549.

measure of the quantity of energy *not* capable of conversion into work").[1]

(2) *Statistical Thermodynamics*

"The equivalence of entropy in the classical and statistical contexts is implied in the following: 'Each quantity of energy has a characteristic quality called entropy associated with it. The entropy measures the degree of disorder associated with the energy. Energy must always flow in such a direction that the entropy increases'."[2]

"As far as we know, all changes are in the direction of increasing entropy, of increasing disorder, of increasing randomness, of running down." [3]

(3) *Informational Thermodynamics*

In connection with systems for the processing and transmission of information (e.g., computers, automation, television, newspapers, etc.), a highly sophisticated new science known as information theory has incorporated the concept of entropy as a measure of the "noise," or degree of uncertainty, in the communication of the information. It is an interesting testimony to the unity of nature that the same mathematical concepts and equations apply to this type of thermodynamics as to the others.

"It is certain that the conceptual connection between information and the second law of thermodynamics is now firmly established."[4]

"(There are many ways) of stating what is called the Second Law of Thermodynamics . . . all of them are equivalent although some very sophisticated mathematics and physics is involved in showing the equivalence."[5]

---

[1] Isaac Asimov, "In the Game of Energy and Thermodynamics, You Can't Even Break Even," *Journal of the Smithsonian Institute*, (June 1970), p. 8.

[2] Freeman J. Dyson, "Energy in the Universe," *Scientific American*, Vol. 224 (September 1971), p. 52.

[3] Isaac Asimov, "Can Decreasing Entropy Exist in the Universe?" *Science Digest*, (May 1973), p. 76.

[4] Myron Tribus and Edward C. McIrvine, "Energy and Information," *Scientific American*, Vol. 224 (September 1971), p. 188.

[5] Isaac Asimov, "In the Game of Energy and Thermodynamics, You Can't Even Break Even," *Journal of the Smithsonian Institute*, (June 1970), p. 8.

It is therefore possible to regard any natural process in any of several ways: (1) as an energy conversion system, in which work is being accomplished; (2) as a structured system which is undergoing a change in structure; (3) as an information system, in which information is being utilized and transmitted. Entropy is a measure of: in the first case, the unavailability of the energy for further work; in the second case, the decreased order of the system's structure; in the third case, the lost or distorted information.

Whichever is the more useful in a given case, it is obvious that all such explanations describe a downhill trend. Energy becomes unavailable, disorder increases, information becomes garbled.

For the evolution of a more advanced organism, however, energy must somehow be gained, order must be increased, and information added. The Second Law says this will not happen in any natural process unless external factors enter to make it happen.

"It is one of this law's consequences that all real processes go irreversibly. . . . Any given process in this universe is accompanied by a change in magnitude of a quantity called the entropy. . . . All real processes go with an increase of entropy. The entropy also measures the randomness or lack of orderliness of the system, the greater the randomness the greater the entropy."[1]

It seems obvious that the Second Law of Thermodynamics constitutes a serious problem to the evolution model. Creationists are puzzled as to why evolutionists give so little attention to this problem. Most books promoting evolution never mention it at all, and many competent evolutionary scientists have been inclined to dismiss it as of no importance to the problem. When pressed, however, for a means of reconciling the entropy principle with evolution, one of the following answers is usually given:

1. *"The Second Law does not apply to living systems."*
"In the complex course of its evolution, life exhibits a remarkable contrast to the tendency expressed in the Second Law of Thermodynamics. Where the Second

---

[1] Harold F. Blum, *Time's Arrow and Evolution* (Princeton, N.J.: Princeton University Press, 1962), p. 14.

Law expresses an irreversible progression toward increased entropy and disorder, life evolves continually higher levels of order. The still more remarkable fact is that this evolutionary drive to greater and greater order also is irreversible. Evolution does not go backward."[1]

However, merely stating that evolution contradicts the Second Law (which is all the above-cited author does) hardly justifies him in assuming it doesn't apply! He is simply assuming, without question, that evolution is true. The fact is, of course, that the processes of life are fundamentally very complex chemical processes, and the laws of thermodynamics do apply to chemical processes. One of the most competent biochemists, a thoroughgoing evolutionist himself, Dr. Harold Blum, has devoted much effort to convincing his fellow biologists that entropy *does* apply to life processes.

"No matter how carefully we examine the energetics of living systems we find no evidence of defeat of thermodynamic principles, but we do encounter a degree of complexity not witnessed in the non-living world."[2]

2. *"The Second Law is only a statistical statement, and exceptions are possible."*
But as Angrist[3] points out:

"It is only that the odds against such an event are extraordinarily large. . . . The chemist, Harry A. Bent, has calculated the odds against a local reversal of entropy, specifically the possibility that one calorie of thermal energy could be converted completely into work. His result can be expressed in terms of a familiar statistical example, the probability that a group of monkeys hitting typewriter keys at random could produce the works of Shakespeare. According to Bent's calculation, the likelihood of such a calorie conversion is about the same as the probability that the monkeys could produce Shake-

---

[1] J. H. Rush, *The Dawn of Life* (New York: Signet, 1962), p. 35.
[2] Harold F. Blum, *op. cit.*, p. 119.
[3] Stanley W. Angrist, "Perpetual Motion Machines," *Scientific American*, Vol. 218 (January 1968), p. 120.

speare's works 15 quadrillion times in succession without error."

3. *"Perhaps the Second Law was not operating long ago."*

Well, maybe there was a different principle operating in the past, during the supposed ages when evolution was taking place—maybe the "Principle of Naturalistic Innovation and Integration," as predicted by the evolution model. But this assumption would be tantamount to the denial of the basic assumption of evolutionism, namely, that *present* processes suffice to account for the origin of things. In effect, this device would acknowledge the validity of the creationist approach, acknowledging that special creative processes operating only in the past are necessary to explain the world of the present.

4. *"Perhaps the Second Law doesn't apply to other parts of the universe."*

Even such a competent scientist as Isaac Asimov suggests this:

"We don't know all the kinds of things that are happening in the universe. The changes we do observe are all in the direction of increasing entropy. Somewhere, though, there may be changes under unusual conditions that we can't as yet study which are in the direction of decreasing entropy."[1]

Such speculation may be interesting, but it has no relation to science. There is no evidence, and very few scientists believe, that the laws are different in other parts of the universe (it is a *uni*-verse, not a *di*-verse!). Anyway, we are discussing the question of origins as it applies to the earth and to terrestrial life, and the Second Law *does* apply on earth.

5. *"The Second Law does not apply to open systems."*

By far the most common response by evolutionists to the problem posed by the Second Law is to deny its applicability to open systems such as the earth. Since there is enough energy reaching the earth from the sun to more than offset

---

[1] Isaac Asimov, "Can Decreasing Entropy Exist in the Universe?" *Science Digest*, (May 1973), p. 76.

the loss of energy in its processes due to entropy, they say, the problem is irrelevant.

However, this response is itself irrelevant, since it confuses *quantity* of energy (of which there is certainly enough) with *conversion* of energy. The question is not whether there is enough energy from the sun to sustain the evolutionary process; the question is *how* does the sun's energy sustain evolution?

Although it is true that the two laws of thermodynamics are defined in terms of isolated systems, it is also true that in the real world there is no such thing as an isolated system. *All* systems in reality are open systems and, furthermore, they are all open, in greater or lesser degree, directly or indirectly, to the energy from the sun. Therefore, to say that the earth is a system open to the sun's energy does not explain anything, since the same statement is true for every other system as well!

In *all* systems, the Second Law describes a *tendency* to go from order to disorder; in *most* systems, time produces an *actual* change from order to disorder.

There do exist a few types of systems in the world where one sees an apparent increase in order, superficially offsetting the decay tendency specified by the Second Law. Examples are the growth of a seed into a tree, the growth of a fetus into an adult animal, and the growth of a pile of bricks and girders into a building.

Now, if one examines closely all such systems to see what it is that enables them to supersede the Second Law locally and temporarily (in each case, of course, the phenomenon is only ephemeral, since the organism eventually dies and the building eventually collapses), he will find in every case, at least two essential criteria that must be satisfied:

(a) *There must be a program to direct the growth.*

A growth process which proceeds by random accumulations will not lead to an ordered structure but merely a heterogeneous blob. Some kind of pattern, blueprint, or code must be there to begin with, or no ordered growth can take place. In the case of the organism, this is the intricately complex genetic program, structured as an information system into the DNA molecule for the particular organism. In the case of the building, it is the set of plans prepared by the architects and engineers.

(b) *There must be a power converter to energize the growth.*

The available environmental energy is of no avail unless it can be converted into the specific forms needed to organize and bond the components into the complex and ordered structure of the completed system. Unless such a mechanism is available, the environmental energy more likely will break down any structure already present.

"We have seen that organization requires work for its maintenance and that the universal quest for food is in part to provide the energy needed for the work. But the simple expenditure of energy is not sufficient to develop and maintain order. A bull in a china shop performs work, but he neither creates nor maintains organization. The work needed is particular work; it must follow specifications; it requires information on how to proceed."[1]

In the case of a seed, one of the required energy conversion mechanisms is the marvelous process called *photosynthesis*, which by some incompletely understood complex of reactions converts sunlight into the building of the plant's structure. In the animal numerous complex mechanisms—digestion, blood circulation, respiration, etc.—combine to transform food into body structure. In the case of the building, fossil fuels and human labor operate numerous complex electrical and mechanical devices to erect the structure. And so on.

Now the question again is, not whether there is enough energy reaching the earth from the sun to support evolution, but rather *how* this energy is converted into evolution? The evolutionary process, if it exists, is by far the greatest growth process of all. If a directing code and specific conversion mechanism are essential for all lesser growth processes,

---

[1] George G. Simpson and W. S. Beck, *Life: An Introduction to Biology* (2nd Ed.; New York: Harcourt, Brace & World, 1965), p. 466.

then surely an infinitely more complex code and more specific energy converter are required for the evolutionary process.

But what are they? The answer is that no such code and mechanism have ever been identified. Where in all the universe does one find a plan which sets forth how to organize random particles into particular people? And where does one see a marvelous motor which converts the continual flow of solar radiant energy bathing the earth into the work of building chemical elements into replicating cellular systems, or of organizing populations of worms into populations of men, over vast spans of geologic time?

The mechanisms of mutation and natural selection are, to put it kindly, inadequate for such a gigantic task. Mutation is not a code, but a random phenomenon. Neither can it assimilate energy into a more highly organized form of the structure it affects. Natural selection is not a code which directs the production of anything new; it serves merely as a screen which sieves out unfit variants and defective mutants. It certainly is not an energy conversion device.

Thus neither mutation nor natural selection is either a directing program or an energy converter. If neither is either, they can't both be both! And evolution must have both to produce growth!

Until evolutionists can not only speculate, but demonstrate, that there does exist in nature some vast program to direct the growth toward higher complexity of the marvelous organic space-time unity known as the terrestrial biosphere (not to mention that of the cosmos), as well as some remarkable global power converter to energize the growth through converted solar energy, the whole evolutionary idea is negated by the Second Law.

We are warranted, then, in concluding that the evolutionary process (the hypothetical Principle of Naturalistic Innovation and Integration) is completely precluded by the Second Law of Thermodynamics. There seems no way of modifying the basic evolutionary model to accommodate this Second Law.

But even if evolutionists do eventually come up with some ingenious modification of their model which permits both evolution and the Second Law to function, this would still constitute at best only an evolutionist rationalization of the

Second Law. In other words, maybe someday (though it is hard to see how) the evolutionary model might be able to *explain* the Laws of Thermodynamics. The creation model, on the other hand, does not have to explain them, for it *predicts* them!

The Origin of Life

No doubt one of the most difficult stages in the evolutionary process would be the transition from non-life to life, from non-replicating chemicals to self-replicating systems. Nevertheless, if the evolution model is valid, this transition must have occurred, and it must have occurred by natural processes which can be explained in terms of the same laws of nature which operate today.

That being true, it should be expected as a basic prediction from the evolution model that the processes themselves still operate today and therefore that the evolution of life from non-life also is taking place today. When empirical observations show that such evolution is *not* occurring today, then the evolution model must be modified with another secondary assumption, namely, that there were different conditions in the earth's primeval atmosphere and hydrosphere than those which exist at present.

Again the simplicity and potency of the creation model is apparent. It does not have to *explain* why life is not evolving from non-life today; it *predicts* this situation. Life, according to creationism, was a unique work of the creation period and is therefore not being created today.

The creation model obviously corresponds more directly to the present-day facts associated with this question of life's origin than does evolution. But now let us look more critically at these secondary assumptions of evolutionism which ostensibly allow life to appear in the past when conditions were different. Nobody knows, of course, that past conditions *were* different, and the geologic evidence is against this idea, but we can assume for the sake of argument that they might have been.

Biochemists interested in this field have tried to approach the problem both analytically and experimentally, trying to learn enough of the structure of living materials to see how life could get started on its own and then to try to duplicate

46

this imaginary abiogenesis in the laboratory under conditions simulating those which presumably existed on the primitive earth.

Although many such scientists have expressed great confidence in the ultimate solution of this problem, the fact is that a solution is nowhere in sight and will probably never be attained. This is because of the overwhelming difficulties involved in synthesizing by natural means, either analytically or experimentally, a structure of such astounding complexity as even the simplest living thing. Let us look briefly at both the analytical and experimental barriers.

1. *Analytical complexity of living material.*

Higher organisms are composed of a tremendous number of specialized cells, and within each cell is an intricate complex of specialized protein molecules. Each protein molecule is a particularly organized structure composed of about twenty different amino acids, and each amino acid is made up of the four elements hydrogen, oxygen, nitrogen and carbon (in two cases a sulfur atom is also present).

These complex systems are all, in the case of every known organism, reproduced and assembled on the basis of the "instructions" built into the DNA molecular system. DNA (deoxyribonucleic acid) is composed of six simpler molecules; these consist of four bases, the arrangement of which specifies the message, made up of nitrogen, oxygen, hydrogen and carbon, along with a deoxyribose sugar molecule and a phosphate molecule which hold the bases in place.

The DNA molecule not only has information required for the synthesis of the specific protein molecules needed by the cell, but also that needed for its own replication. Thus reproduction and inheritance depend directly on this remarkable molecule, as organized differently and specifically for each kind of organism.

Thus, the problem of abiogenesis devolves upon the method by which the first replicating system evolved. The insuperable barrier, however, is that DNA can only be replicated with the specific help of certain protein molecules (enzymes) which, in turn, can only be produced at the direction of DNA. Each depends on the other and both must be present for replication to take place.

47

Really, it seems only special creation can account for the initiation of this process. Many serious investigators have recognized this problem.

"Directions for the reproduction of plans, for energy and the extraction of parts from the current environment, for the growth sequence, and for the effector mechanism translating instructions into growth—all had to be simultaneously present at that moment. This combination of events has seemed an incredibly unlikely happenstance, and has often been ascribed to divine intervention."[1]

Although the above was written in 1955, just two years after the discovery of the structure of DNA by James Watson and Francis Crick, this mystery is no nearer solution today than it was then. A recent reviewer discussed this intriguing subject in almost the same vein.

"But the most sweeping evolutionary questions at the level of biochemical genetics are still unanswered. . . . The fact that in all organisms living today the processes both of replication of the DNA and of the effective translation of its code require highly precise enzymes and that, at the same time, the molecular structures of those same enzymes are precisely specified by the DNA itself, poses a remarkable evolutionary mystery.

"Did the code and the means of translating it appear simultaneously in evolution? It seems almost incredible that any such coincidence could have occurred, given the extraordinary complexities of both sides and the requirement that they be coordinated accurately for survival. By a pre-Darwinian (or a skeptic of evolution after Darwin) this puzzle surely would have been interpreted as the most powerful sort of evidence for special creation."[2]

We shall consider in more detail the tremendous complexity of even the simplest protein molecule in the next

---

[1] Homer Jacobson, "Information, Reproduction and the Origin of Life," *American Scientist*, (January 1955), p. 121.
[2] Caryl P. Haskings, "Advances and Challenges in Science in 1970," *American Scientist*, Vol. 59 (May-June 1971), p. 305.

chapter. But even if such a molecule could ever be formed by chance, it could never reproduce itself. The fact that the DNA molecule is necessary for reproduction and that it can only operate in the presence of proteins which it had previously specified and organized seems to be an impenetrable barrier to this vital phase of evolution.

Again, however, this is no problem to the creationist. The creation model predicts that life can come only from life.

2. *Experimental Barriers to Synthesizing Life*

Because of misleadingly enthusiastic newspaper accounts, many people have the impression that scientists have actually been able to "create life in a test tube." However, this most certainly is not the case. The day when biochemists can take the basic chemicals (carbon, oxygen, etc.) and from these construct amino acids, and then protein molecules, and then the DNA molecules which can specify their reproduction and future organization, all without benefit of any pre-existing living material, is yet a long way off. In fact, the problem is so enormously complex that it almost certainly will *never* be done.

But even if, someday, it *is* accomplished, that achievement will not prove that the same thing happened by chance three billion years ago. Rather, it will prove, if anything, that an exceedingly high concentration of intelligent planning and precisely controlled laboratory apparatus were necessary for the accomplishment.

We do not disparage in any way the impressive achievements of biochemists working in this field. The results of these experiments have not created life, however. In order to put this matter in proper perspective, a brief review of the major experiments of this sort is in order here.

(a) *Synthesis of amino acids.* Various experimenters, beginning with Stanley Miller, have produced certain amino acids with specialized apparatus and conditions which were supposed to correspond to the imagined conditions on the primitive earth. However, amino acids are not living things in any sense at all. Furthermore, Miller's apparatus included a trap to separate them as soon as they were formed, otherwise they would have quickly been broken down by the same "atmospheric" conditions which produced them. Such protection would not have been available on the primitive earth.[1]

(b) *Linking of amino acids.* Sidney Fox and others have been able, by very special heating techniques and certain conditions which could never have existed on the hypothetical primeval earth to bond the amino acids together to form what he called "proteinoids." These were not in any sense the highly ordered specific proteins found in living substances, however. They were mere "blobs," with no order and no utility. Even these would quickly have been destroyed if they had ever been actually produced on the primeval earth.

(c) *Copying genes, DNA, etc.* A great deal of newspaper publicity attended the so-called "synthesis of DNA" by Arthur Kornberg in 1967. Severo Ochoa and others have likewise attained fame by synthesizing viral DNA, a gene, or other biologically active molecules, and no doubt these are all remarkable and praiseworthy achievements. Without discussing details, however, every such case involved *copying* the template DNA molecule, simulating those under which such copies are made in actual cells. Furthermore, in every case, the appropriate enzymes must be present.[3] Thus in no case has a gene or DNA molecule or any other such entity been synthesized unless similar entities were already present to start from.

(d) *Synthesizing cells.* In 1970, J. P. Danielli was reported actually to have synthesized a living cell. Once again, however, he started with living cells, then disassembled them, then refabricated a cell from parts of the dismantled cells. Again this is a notable accomplishment, but it can by no means be called the creation of life.

Creationists believe that this continued emphasis on the naturalistic or artificial production of living organisms is

---

[1] S. L. Miller, "Production of Amino Acids under Possible Primitive Earth Conditions," *Science*, Vol. 117 (1953), p. 528.

[2] S. W. Fox, K. Harada, G. Krampitz, and G. Mueller, "Chemical Origin of Cells," *Chemical and Engineering News*, (June 22, 1970), p. 80

[3] M. Goulian, A. Kornberg, and R. L. Sinsheimery, "Enzymatic Synthesis of DNA, XXIV. Synthesis of Infectious Phage ϕX174 DNA," *Proceedings, National Academy of Science*, Vol. 58 (1967), p. 2321.

highly misleading. None of these phenomena would ever occur under natural conditions. Teachers can do a much greater service to their pupils by stressing the uniqueness and complexity and wonder of life. There is no slightest *scientific* evidence that life can come from non-life. The creation model emphasizes the unique origin of life, at the creative word of a *living* Creator. The scientific law of cause and effect requires the First Cause of life to be living!

Variation and Selection

When Charles Darwin first published his theory of the origin of species by natural selection, it was his idea that the continual small variations between individuals of a species, that are observed in nature, would confer differing degrees of advantage or disadvantage in the struggle for existence. Those with significant advantages would be favored by natural selection and thus would survive longer to transmit these characteristics by inheritance to their descendants. Thus, gradually, completely new and higher types of organisms would emerge.

Normal variations were later found to be subject to the rigid Mendelian laws of inheritance, representing nothing really novel but only characters already latent within the genetic system. Modern molecular biology, with its penetrating insight into the remarkable genetic code implanted in the DNA system, has further confirmed that normal variations operate only within the range specified by the DNA for the particular type of organism, so that no truly novel characteristics, producing higher degrees of order or complexity, can appear. Variation is horizontal, not vertical!

It is normal variation of this sort, unfortunately, which is still commonly offered as evidence of present-day evolution. The classic example of the *peppered moth* of England, "evolving" from a dominant light coloration to a dominant dark coloration, as the tree trunks grew darker with pollutants during the advancing industrial revolution, is the best case in point. This was not evolution in the true sense at all but only variation. Natural selection is a conservative force, operating to keep kinds from becoming extinct when the environment changes.

51

"The (peppered moth) experiments beautifully demonstrate natural selection—or survival of the fittest—in action, but they do not show evolution in progress, for however the populations may alter in their content of light, intermediate, or dark forms, all the moths remain from beginning to end *Biston betularia.*"[1]

In other words, the phenomenon of variation and natural selection, rather than explaining evolution in the way Darwin thought it did, is really a marvelous example of the creationist's principle of conservation in operation. That is, a fundamental prediction from the creation model is that, since the Creator had a purpose for each kind of organism created, He would institute a system which would not only assure its genetic integrity but would also enable it to survive in nature. The genetic system would be such as to maintain its identity as a specific kind while, at the same time, allowing it to adjust its characteristics (within limits) to changes in environment. Otherwise, even very slight changes in its habitat, food supply, etc., might cause its extinction.

Natural selection thus cannot produce any real novelties. It is a passive thing, a sort of sieve, through which pass only the variants which fit the environment. Those which do not fit are stopped and discarded by the sieving process. However, it can only act on variants which come to it via the genetic potentialities implicit in the DNA structure for its particular kind; it cannot generate anything new itself. The reshuffling, or recombination, of characters already implicitly present in the germ cell certainly does not create anything really new in an evolutionary sense. Nevertheless, this phenomenon of recombination followed by natural selection is somehow regarded by evolutionists as a very important aspect of their model.

"Recombination is by far the most important source of genetic variation, that is, of material for natural selection."[2]

---

[1] L. Harrison Matthews, "Introduction" to Darwin's *Origin of Species* (London: J. M. Dent & Sons, Ltd., 1971), p. xi.

[2] Ernst Mayr, *Populations, Species and Evolution* (Cambridge, Mass.: Harvard University Press, 1970), p. 103.

As the term itself suggests, recombination does not generate something new, certainly not something of a higher order of complexity. In effect, it is merely another name for variation.

But even if variation, or recombination, really could produce something truly novel, for natural selection to act on, this novelty would almost certainly be quickly eliminated. A new structural or organic feature which would confer a real advantage in the struggle for existence—say a wing, for a previously earth-bound animal, or an eye, for a hitherto sightless animal—would be useless or even harmful until fully developed. There would be no reason at all for natural selection to favor an incipient wing or incipient eye or any other incipient feature. Yet, somehow, if the evolution model is valid, wings have "evolved" four different times (in insects, flying reptiles, birds and bats) and eyes have "evolved" independently at least three times. Salisbury has recently commented on this remarkable fact as follows:

"My last doubt concerns so-called parallel evolution. . . . Even something as complex as the eye has appeared several times; for example, in the squid, the vertebrates, and the arthropods. It's bad enough accounting for the origin of such things once, but the thought of producing them several times according to the modern synthetic theory makes my head swim."[1]

Which comment reminds us that Charles Darwin said that the thought of the eye, and how it could possibly be produced by natural selection, made him ill.

Natural selection, acting upon the variational potential designed into the genetic code for each organism, is thus a powerful device for permitting *horizontal* variation, or *radiation*, to enable it to adapt to the environment and thus to survive. It is useless, however, in generating a *vertical* variation, leading to the development of higher, more complex kinds of organisms. In fact, it acts to *prevent* such vertical variation, since incipient novelties would be useless at best until truly developed and functional. In most cases, in fact, such novelties would be positively harmful. It is

---

[1] Frank B. Salisbury, "Doubts about the Modern Synthetic Theory of Evolution," *American Biology Teacher*, (September 1971), p. 338.

significant that evolutionists have never yet been able to document, either in the living world or the fossil world, an incipient organ or structure leading to a future useful feature.

All of which is a specific confirmation of the predictions of the creation model.

Genetic Mutations

Since it is obvious that neither ordinary variations, nor recombinations of existing characters, can account for "upward" evolution, some extraordinary mechanism must be found for this purpose. In the modern synthetic theory of evolution, or neo-Darwinism, the mechanism universally adopted for this purpose is that of *mutation.*

A mutation is assumed to be a real structural change in a gene, of such character that something novel is produced, not merely a reworking of something already there. In some way, the linkages in a segment of the DNA molecule are changed, so that different "information" is conveyed via the genetic code in the formation of the structure of the descendant.

"It must not be forgotten that mutation is the ultimate source of all genetic variation found in natural populations and the only new material available for natural selection to work on."[1]

The phenomenon of mutation, therefore, is a most important component of the evolution model. The evolution model must postulate *some* mechanism to produce the required upward progress in complexity which characterizes the model in its broadest dimension. Mutation is supposedly that mechanism.

The basic evolution model would predict, therefore, that mutations must be primarily beneficial, generating a "vertical" change upward toward higher degrees of order. Each such change must be positively helpful in the environment if it is to be preserved by natural selection and contribute to evolutionary progress.

The creation model, on the other hand, would predict that, if there are any such things as real mutations, causing

[1]Ernst Mayr, *op. cit.*, p. 102.

"vertical" changes in complexity and order of the kinds, they will be harmful, not beneficial.

With these two models in mind, let us now consider some of the actual experimental facts relative to mutations.

1. *Mutations are random, not directed.*

"It remains true to say that we know of no way other than random mutation by which new hereditary variation comes into being, nor any process other than natural selection by which the hereditary constitution of a population changes from one generation to the next."[1]

There is no way to control mutations to make them produce characteristics which might be needed. Natural selection must simply take what comes.

2. *Mutations are rare, not common.*

"It is probably fair to estimate the frequency of a majority of mutations in higher organisms between one in ten thousand and one in a million per gene per generation."[2]

3. *Good mutations are very, very rare.*

The man who has probably devoted more study than any other man to experimental observation of mutations, said:

"But mutations are found to be of a random nature, so far as their utility is concerned. Accordingly, the great majority of mutations, certainly well over 99%, are harmful in some way, as is to be expected of the effects of accidental occurrences."[3]

The man probably more responsible than any other for the modern view of evolution known as neo-Darwinism, which says evolution proceeds by the accumulation of small mutations preserved by natural selection, is even less confident in the frequency of beneficial mutations.

"A proportion of favorable mutations of one in a thousand does not sound much, but is probably generous,

[1]C. H. Waddington, *The Nature of Life* (New York: Atheneum, 1962), p. 98.
[2]Francisco J. Ayala, "Teleological Explanations in Evolutionary Biology," *Philosophy of Science*, Vol. 37 (March 1970), p. 3.
[3]H. J. Muller, "Radiation Damage to the Genetic Material," *American Scientist*, Vol. 38 (January 1950), p. 35.

since so many mutations are lethal, preventing the organism living at all, and the great majority of the rest throw the machinery slightly out of gear."[1]

As a matter of fact, the phenomenon of a truly beneficial mutation, one which is *known* to be a mutation and not merely a latent characteristic already present in the genetic material but lacking previous opportunity for expression, and one which is permanently beneficial in the natural environment, has yet to be documented. Some evolutionists doubt that they occur at all:

"Accordingly, mutations are more than just sudden changes in heredity; they also affect viability, and, to the best of our knowledge, invariably affect it adversely. Does not this fact show that mutations are really assaults on the organism's central being, its basic capacity to be a living thing?"[2]

4. *The Net Effect of All Mutations is Harmful*

Even if the mutations are not harmful enough to cause their carriers to be eliminated completely by natural selection, the over-all effect is to gradually lower the viability of the population.

"The large majority of mutations, however, are harmful or even lethal to the individual in whom they are expressed. Such mutations can be regarded as introducing a 'load,' or genetic burden, into the pool. The term 'genetic load' was first used by the late H. J. Muller, who recognized that the rate of mutations is increased by numerous agents man has introduced into his environment, notably ionizing radiation and mutagenic chemicals."[3]

That the net effect of mutations is harmful, rather than beneficial, to the supposed progress of evolution, is made transparently clear by the zeal with which evolutionists for decades have been trying to get mutation-producing radiations removed from the environment!

---

[1] Julian Huxley, *Evolution in Action* (New York: Harper Bros., 1953), p. 41.
[2] C. P. Martin, "A Non-Geneticist Looks at Evolution," *American Scientist*, (January 1953), p. 102.
[3] Christopher Wills, "Genetic Load," *Scientific American*, Vol. 222 (March 1970), p. 98.

"The most important actions that need to be taken, however, are in the area of minimizing the addition of new mutagens to those already present in the environment. Any increase in the mutational load is harmful, if not immediately, then certainly to future generations."[1]

It does seem that, if evolutionists really believed that evolution is due to mutations, they would favor all measures which could increase the rate of mutations and thus facilitate further evolution. Instead, they have consistently for decades opposed nuclear testing for the very purpose of *preventing* mutations!

5. *Mutations affect and are affected by many genes.*

The mutation concept is no longer as simple as it once was. Instead of a given characteristic being controlled by a specific gene, it now appears that each gene affects many characteristics and every characteristic is controlled by many genes.

"Moreover, despite the fact that a mutation is a discrete, discontinuous effect of the cellular, chromosome or gene level, its effects are modified by interactions in the whole genetic system of an individual."[2]

"This universal interaction has been described, in deliberately exaggerated form, in this statement: *Every character of an organism is affected by all genes, and every gene affects all characters.* It is this interaction that accounts for the closely knit functional integration of the genotype as a whole."[3]

It would seem obvious that if any one mutation is highly likely to be deleterious, then since a changed characteristic requires the combined effects of many genes, and therefore many concurrent mutations, the probability of harmful effects is multiplied manyfold. Conversely, the probability of simultaneous good mutations in all the genes which control a given character is reduced to practically zero.

---

[1] *Ibid*, p. 107.
[2] George G. Simpson, "Uniformitarianism," Chap. 2 in *Essays in Evolution and Genetics*, Ed. by Max A. Hecht & Wm. C. Steeres (New York: Appleton-Century Crofts, 1970), p. 80.
[3] Ernst Mayr, *op. cit.*, p. 164. Emphasis is his.

Misfits and Extinctions

For many years, Darwinian evolution was supposed to generate organisms of beautiful complexity, perfectly adapted to their respective environments. "Survival of the fittest" was the watchword. Never mind, as noted above, that mutations almost always generate misfits which soon die out.

Evolutionists more recently have reversed themselves on this subject, recognizing that perfect adaptations really constitute evidence of design. Now they consider the misfits to be better evidence for evolution!

"If there were no imperfections, there would be no evidence of history, and therefore nothing to favor evolution by natural selection over creation."[1]

Similarly, evolutionists somehow imagine that the large array of extinct animals in the fossil record (e.g., trilobites, dinosaurs) somehow constitutes an evidence of evolution. This is strange logic. The evidence that dinosaurs have become extinct tells us nothing at all about how they came into existence in the first place.

As a matter of fact, many species of plants and animals have become extinct in recent times.

"As in the past, new life forms will arise, but not at a fraction of the rate they are going to be lost in the coming decades and centuries. We are surely losing one or more species a day right now out of the five million (minimum figure) on Earth."[2]

It is significant that not one new species of plant or animal is known to have evolved on Earth during recorded history, but large numbers have become extinct. If the present is the key to the past, then how on Earth could men ever have evolved the idea of evolution!

To the creationist, of course, misfits and extinctions constitute still further evidence of the universal entropy principle, which in turn points up the necessity of primeval special creation.

---

[1]Jeremy Cherfas, "The Difficulties of Darwinism," *New Scientist*, Vol. 102 (May 17, 1984), p. 29. Cherfas is here discussing the evidence cited by S.J. Gould.

[2]Norman Myers, "The End of the Lines," *Natural History*, Vol. 94 (February 1985), p. 2.

CHAPTER IV

ACCIDENT OR PLAN?

The Complexity of Living Systems

The evolutionary model attributes all of the systems and structures of the universe to the operation of natural processes operating under the impetus of the innate properties of matter and the laws of nature. It assumes that no external supernatural agent plans and directs these processes; the universe is self-contained and self-evolving by random actions of its components.

On the other hand, the creation model attributes the systems and structures of the cosmos to a planned, purposive creation of all things in the beginning by an omniscient Creator. The creationist maintains that the degree of complexity and order which science has discovered in the universe could never be generated by chance or accident.

This issue can actually be attacked quantitatively, using simple principles of mathematical probability. The problem is simply whether a complex system, in which many components function unitedly together, and in which each component is uniquely necessary to the efficient functioning of the whole, could ever arise by random processes. The question is especially incisive when we deal with living systems. Although inorganic relationships are often quite complex, living organisms are immensely more so. The evolution model nevertheless assumes all of these have arisen by chance and naturalism.

1. *Probability of a complex system arising instantly by chance.*

Assume a "sea" of freely available components, each uniquely capable of performing a specific useful function. What is the probability that two or more of them can come together by chance to form an integrated functioning organism?

As long as the number of components in the organism is small, the chance association in this way is a reasonable possibility. For example, consider two components, A and B. If they happen to link up in the form A-B, say, the combined system will work, but B-A will not work. Thus, there is one chance out of two that these two components will combine into a functioning system. That is, there is a 1/2 probability of "success."

If there are three components, — A, B and C — there are six possible ways these can link up, ABC, ACB, BAC, BCA, CAB, and CBA. Since it is assumed that only one of these will work, there is a 1/6 probability of success. The number of combinations is calculated by multipying each factor in the series together. Thus:

No. of combinations for 2 components = 1 x 2 = 2
No. of combinations for 3 components = 1 x 2 x 3 = 6
No. of combinations for 4 components = 1 x 2 x 3 x 4 = 24
No. of combinations for 5 components = 1 x 2 x 3 x 4 x 5 = 120
No. of combinations for n components = 1 x 2 x 3 x . . . x n

The shorthand way of identifying such products is as the "factorial" of the specified number of components, written as "!". For example, 1 x 2 x 3 x 4 is equal to 4! ("four factorial"), or 24.

The "factorials" become exceedingly large as the number of components increases.

6! = 720	10! = 3,628,800	$(1,000,000)! \cong 10^{3,000,000}$
7! = 5,040	$100! \cong 10^{158}$	etc.
8! = 40,320	$200! \cong 10^{375}$	
9! = 362,880		

Consider, for example, an organism composed of only 100 integrated parts. Remember that each of these parts must fulfill a unique function in the organism and so there is only one way in which these 100 parts can be combined to function effectively. Since there are 10^{158} different ways in which 100 parts can link up, the probability of a successful chance linkage is only one out of 10^{158} (Note that 10^{158} is equal to a number written as "one" followed by 158 "zeros").

This number is too large to comprehend properly. To give a rough idea, however, one may note there are only approximately 10^{80} electrons in the entire universe! Assuming that this represents the number of particles available to serve as potential components in our 100-part organism, this means that 10^{78} such groups of 100 parts each could be formed at any one time. To be sure to get the one that works, however, there must be 10^{158} such groups formed. It is, therefore very unlikely that one of the 10^{78} actual groups would be the one needed.

However, in event none of the first trial groups work, assume that they unlink, mix around, and then try again. Then, let them all try again, and again, and keep on trying, as long as possible.

The universe is said by astronomers to be less than 30 billion years old. One can calculate that, in 30 billion years, there would be 10^{18} seconds. Now let us assume that each of the above cycles of linking, unlinking and reshuffling, occupies only a billionth part of a second, so that a billion (10^9) trials can be made each second.

Thus the maximum number of trial combinations that could be made in all the universe in 30 billion years, even under such absurdly generous conditions, is still only 10^{78} x 10^9 x 10^{18}, or 10^{105} combinations. There need to be 10^{158} such combinations, however, to be certain of getting the one which will work.

Finally, then, the chance that one of these 10^{105} possible combinations will be the correct one is one chance in $10^{158}/10^{105} = 1$ in 10^{53}.

This is still an almost infinitesimally small number, actually one chance out of a hundred million billion billion billion billion billion. For all practical purposes, there is no chance at all!

And yet an organism composed of only 100 parts is impossibly simple. Research sponsored in part by NASA[1] (for the purpose of enabling astronauts to recognize even the most rudimentary forms of life on other planets) has shown that the simplest type of protein molecule that could be said to be "living" is composed of a chain of at least 400 linked amino acids, and each amino acid is a specific combination of four or five basic chemical elements, and each chemical element is a unique assemblage of protons, electrons and neutrons.

---

[1] Harold J. Morowitz, "Biological Self-Replicating Systems," *Progress in Theoretical Biology*, Ed. F. M. Snell (New York: Academic Press, 1967), pp. 35ff. See discussion in James F. Coppedge *Evolution: Possible or Impossible* (Grand Rapids: Zondervan, 1973), pp. 95-115.

It is thus inconceivable (to anyone but a doctrinaire evolutionist) that a living system could ever be formed by chance. Yet, if a Creator is excluded from the problem, there is no other way that at least the *first* living system could have been formed.

2. *Probability of Synthesis of DNA Molecule*

The problem discussed in the preceding section is really oversimplified. A simple linked protein molecule, or any other such system, could never reproduce itself. In the world of living organisms, as discussed in the preceding chapter, the phenomena of reproduction and inheritance are always directed by the DNA molecule. The evolution of life therefore must have involved somehow the accidental synthesis of the first such DNA molecule. Frank Salisbury, who is himself an evolutionary biologist, discusses this riddle as follows:

"Now we know that the cell itself is far more complex than we had imagined. It includes thousands of functioning enzymes, each one of them a complex machine itself. Furthermore, each enzyme comes into being in response to a gene, a strand of DNA. The information content of the gene (its complexity) must be as great as that of the enzyme it controls."

"A medium protein might include about 300 amino acids. The DNA gene controlling this would have about 1,000 nucleotides in its chain. Since there are four kinds of nucleotides in a DNA chain, one consisting of 1,000 links could exist in 4^{1000} different forms. Using a little algebra (logarithms) we can see that $4^{1000} = 10^{600}$. Ten multiplied by itself 600 times gives the figure 1 followed by 600 zeros! This number is completely beyond our comprehension."[1]

It seems beyond all question that such complex systems as the DNA molecule could never arise by chance, no matter how big the universe nor how long is time. The creation model faces this fact realistically and postulates a great Creator, by whom came life.

---

[1] Frank B. Salisbury, "Doubts about the Modern Synthetic Theory of Evolution," *American Biology Teacher*, (September 1971), p. 336.

3. *Probability of Synthesis by Gradual Accretion*

Some evolutionists suggest that it is not necessary to suppose that complex molecules arose all at once. They might have been slowly and gradually synthesized by some process analogous to natural selection. That is, a system might advance from one part to a two-part system, then from two parts to three parts, and so on. At each step, if the combination turned out to be advantageous in its immediate environment, it would survive and then be ready to undertake the next step.

On the other hand, if a particular trial step turned out to be harmful, as it normally would (since a random change in a well-functioning system normally would decrease its efficiency), then presumably the molecule would be destroyed, or at least would be inhibited from further advance. Furthermore, many environmental pressures would continually be operating which would tend to break it back down into a simpler form.

In order to continue toward higher and higher order, therefore, each trial step would have to be immediately beneficial; there could be no failures or backward steps. This chain of unbroken successful trials would have to be continued until the molecule arrived at a degree of order or information which enabled it to reproduce itself, at which point, presumably, it would have attained the stage of life.

We can examine this process probabilistically by assigning an arbitrary probability to each step of the process. All would agree, surely, that a probability of 1/2 for each change would be quite optimistic. That is, we shall assume it is just as likely that each change will be successful as that it will be unsuccessful. Undoubtedly the actual probability of success is far less than that.

With this assumption, however, the probability of ultimately becoming a living system is obtained by multiplying the probabilities of every step together. If n steps are necessary to build the required degree of order, then the probability becomes equal to $(1/2)^n$, or one chance out of $(2)^n$.

Now the question is how many such steps are needed—what is the value of n? The problem is analogous to designing a machine capable of building a duplicate machine. A prominent scientist in the field of information theory analyzes this problem as follows:

"Suppose we wanted to build a machine capable of reaching into bins for all of its parts, and capable of assembling from these parts a second machine just like itself. What is the minimum amount of structure or information that should be built into the first machine? The answer comes out to be of the order of 1500 bits— 1500 choices between alternatives which the machine should be able to decide. This answer is very suggestive, because 1500 bits happens to be also of the order of magnitude of the amount of structure contained in the simplest large protein molecule which, immersed in a bath of nutrients, can induce the assembly of those nutrients into another large protein molecule like itself, and then separate itself from it."[1]

According to these studies (and other more recent studies have given about the same result), the number of such steps needed to build the first machine (or protein molecule) by chance is 1500. The probability of this being achieved by chance is therefore $(1/2)^{1500}$, or one chance out of $(2)^{1500}$, which number is equal to $(10)^{450}$.

This number is again almost incalculably great. Even if we were to assume the complete set of trials up to the point of failure (or 1500 in the event of success) could be accomplished in a billionth of a second, and even if we assume there are 10^{80} systems attempting these trials (10^{80} equals the total number of particles in the universe), and that they keep trying for 30 billion years (10^{18} seconds), there could still be only the following number of attempts to achieve such a replicating molecule in all the universe in all time:

$$\text{No. attempts} = 10^{80} \ (10^{18})(10^9) = 10^{107}$$

This number is immensely smaller than the number of attempts $(10)^{450}$ that would be required to be sure that one of them would work. Thus the step-by-step process of trying to achieve through a natural selection technique the encoding of sufficient "information" to synthesize a replicating molecule seems beyond all plausibility.

A further instructive comparison of the amount of information contained in this imaginary simplest replicating

---

[1] Marcel J. E. Golay, "Reflections of a Communications Engineer," *Analytical Chemistry*, Vol. 33 (June 1961), p. 23.

molecule is with the amount of information contained in all the books of the world. Let us assume every word in every book is a unit of information. Now make the following reasonable additional assumptions (each one is actually unreasonably generous):

Average number of words per page = 500
Average number of pages per book = 500
Average number of copies printed of each book = 10,000
Average number of books published per year = 10,000,000
Total number of years during which books have been
  published = 4000

Multiplying all these numbers together, the total number of meaningful words ever published equals

$$500 \times 500 \times 10{,}000 \times 10{,}000{,}000 \times 4{,}000 = 10^{20}.$$

This number is also equal to $(2)^{66}$, and so would represent only 66 successive, successful choices between equally probable alternatives. This number is, obviously, tremendously smaller than the 1500 successful choices required to synthesize a replicating molecule. There is far more information in the simplest living system than in all the copies of all the books ever written!

This amazing fact is easily explained by the creation model but poses a gigantic problem to the evolution model. Dr. Larry Butler, professor of biochemistry at Purdue University, indicates[1] that he likes to issue the following challenge to his students and biochemist colleagues:

"Assume any primordial soup you wish, with all the organic chemicals you specify—including enzymes, nucleic acids, sugars, or whatever you like, as long as they are not living. The mixture must be sterile, of course, to prevent bacterial contamination. Assume also any kind of atmosphere you wish, including any compounds known to be present anywhere in the solar system. Then assume any kind of energy source you wish—electrical sparks, heat, ultraviolet light, or any known form of energy. Now show, either analytically or experimentally, that a truly living organism will arise out of this set of materials."

---

[1] Personal Communication.

So far, no one has accepted his challenge!

4. *Probability of Increasing Complexity of Living Systems*

The problem of life's origin is "solved" by evolutionists by ignoring the difficulties. Consider the following remarkable statement by Harvard professor George Wald:

"The important point is that since the origin of life belongs in the category of at-least-once phenomena, time is on its side. However improbable we regard this event, . . . given enough time it will almost certainly happen at least once. . . . Time is in fact the hero of the plot. . . . Given so much time, the 'impossible' becomes possible, the possible probable, and the probable virtually certain. One has only to wait: time itself performs miracles."[1]

But we have already shown there is not nearly enough time available to perform such a miracle.

At any rate, ignoring this problem, let us go on and assume we do have, somehow, functioning living organisms. The problem is how can a population of living organisms structured at one degree of complexity be elevated by random processes to a higher degree of complexity?

The accepted explanation, of course, is that of random mutation and natural selection. As a matter of fact, however, this kind of problem is essentially the same as that of "inorganic natural selection" operating on molecular systems changing randomly. We have just shown this process to be utterly inadequate from a probabilistic point of view, and there is no reason to suppose natural selection will be any more successful in producing increased order in the organic realm.

Nevertheless, evolutionists have a tremendous faith in the efficacy of natural selection to do just this. Julian Huxley has a fascinating discussion of this in one of his books. He says:

"A proportion of favorable mutations of one in a thousand does not sound much, but is probably generous. . . . And a total of a million mutational steps sounds a great deal but is probably an understatement. . . . However, let us take these figures as being reasonable estimates.

---

[1]George Wald, "The Origin of Life," in *The Physics and Chemistry of Life* (New York: Simon & Schuster, 1955), p. 12.

With this proportion, but without any selection, we should clearly have to breed a million strains (a thousand squared) to get one containing two favorable mutations; and so on, up to a thousand to the millionth power to get one containing a million. Of course this could not really happen, but it is a useful way of visualizing the fantastic odds against getting a number of favorable mutations in one strain through pure chance alone. A thousand to the millionth power, when written out, becomes the figure 1 with three million noughts after it; and that would take three large volumes of about 500 pages each, just to print! . . . No one would bet on anything so improbable happening. And yet it has happened! It has happened, thanks to the working of natural selection and the properties of living substance which make natural selection inevitable!"[1]

Natural selection must indeed be a wonderful thing, if it can thus convert an impossibility into an inevitability! Creationists, however, point out that all *observed* instances of natural selection involve conservative adaptations to environment (e.g., the peppered moth), not generation or preservation of mutants of higher order. Mutations are harmful, not helpful, and natural selection acts to try to prevent their getting established in the population as a whole.

Again, however, let us be as generous as possible, and assume that each successive evolutionary step has a probability of success of 1/2. That is, a given population representing, say, n degrees of order (information content in its genetic code) has as great a probability of changing to a population of $(n + 1)$ degrees of order as it does of slipping back to $(n - 1)$ degrees of order or lower.

Actually it is far more probable that the population will slip backward. There are far more harmful mutations than good ones and, although many of the more harmful ones would be eliminated altogether by natural selection, those that are only slightly harmful will persist and gradually build up the "genetic load" in the population, as discussed in Chapter III.

---

[1] Julian Huxley, *Evolution in Action* (New York: Harper and Brothers Co., 1953), p. 41.

"The somatic effects of mutations vary from great to barely perceptible or, quite likely, to imperceptible by usual methods of observation. The probabilities that a mutation will survive or eventually spread in the course of evolution tend to vary inversely with the extent of its somatic effects. Most mutations with large effects are lethal at an early stage for the individual in which they occur and hence have zero probability of spreading. Mutations with small effects do have some probability of spreading and as a rule the chances are better the smaller the effect."[1]

Consequently, a probability of 1/2 for the successful accomplishment of each successive evolutionary advance seems quite generous. Even if an individual *does* experience a good mutation ("good" in the sense of a higher degree of order), it would be ineffective unless it could somehow be transmitted through the population by an inbreeding mechanism which would cause the inbreeding sub-group to predominate in the population before deleterious mutations cause its elimination. The process of having such a good mutation spread through the population to elevate the entire population to a higher degree of order seems extremely difficult and unlikely.

Futhermore, when we deal with the evolution of higher kinds of organisms such as, say, the vertebrates, the degree of complexity is tremendously higher than the "simple" protein and DNA molecules we have been considering heretofore. Each such animal is an organized system of trillions of living cells, each one of which is uniquely equipped for a specific job in the organism of which it is a part. Then, each one of these cells is a highly organized system in itself, containing vast numbers of component protein molecules, each one in its own unique place. And all of this complexity is directed and controlled in its construction by the many thousands of DNA molecules in the germ cells.

For one kind of animal to evolve into a distinctly higher kind of animal would require a tremendous number of

---

[1] George Gaylord Simpson, "Uniformitarianism: An Inquiry into Principle Theory and Method in Geohistory and Biohistory," Chap. 2 in *Essays in Evolution and Genetics*, Ed. by Max A. Hecht & Wm. C. Steeres (New York: Appleton-Century Crofts, 1970), p. 80

mutational steps. Huxley's example, previously quoted, mentioned a "million mutational steps," for the assumed evolution of a horse. Considering that mutations must be small, each one probably imperceptible, a million seems small indeed.

Obviously, from our previous discussion, a million successive, successful mutational steps, each with a probability of one-half, is almost as inconceivable as the instantaneous chance assemblage of a million components into an integrated whole. The chance of success in this case becomes one out of $(2)^{1,000,000}$, or one out of $(10)^{300,000}$.

Such numbers are so large as to convey no real understanding of their magnitude. The universe of 5-billion light-years radius contains only 10^{80} particles of electron size. If there were no empty space at all, with the entire universe solid-packed with electrons, it could still hold only 10^{130} electrons. If each such electron were a mutating system, going through the required million mutations a billion times every second for the 10^{18} seconds in 30 billion years, the total number of attempts that could be made is only 10^{157}. There is not the remotest possibility that one of these would be successful, since the chance of one success is only one out of $10^{(300,000 - 157)}$ or one out of $10^{(299,843)}$.

The probabilities become more and more infinitesimal as we ascend the scale of complexities in the living world. Meditate, for example, upon the ten billion integrated cells in the cerebral cortex of the human brain!

The creation model is not embarrassed by such complexities, as all of them simply reflect the omniscient, omnipotent Creator. The evolutionist who rejects the concept of special creation as "incredible" seems willing to exercise a highly credulous faith in natural selection and all its statistical incredibilities. The faith of the creationist seems at least as reasonable as the faith of the evolutionist.

Similarities and Differences

In the organic realm, there are many similarities between different kinds of plants and animals, and evolutionists have interpreted these as evidence of common ancestry. Creationists, on the other hand, interpret the same similarities as evidence of common creative planning and design. The evolutionist has to assume all such characteristics have developed by chance mutations and natural selection. Creationists explain them as structures designed by the Creator for specific purposes, so that when similar purposes were involved, similar structures were created.

One might write this issue off as an impasse, since similarities are expected in both the evolution and creation models. However, we also have *differences* to account for!

For example, cats and dogs are somewhat similar, but they have many differences as well. The creation model says that similar structures on both were created for similar functions for both, and that different structures were created for their different functions.

The evolution model, on the other hand, encounters a real problem. If the cat and dog evolved from a common ancestor in the same environment by the same process, how did they ever get to be different? It would seem there ought rather to be an integrated series of animals between cats and dogs, so that one could never tell where "cats" stop and "dogs" begin.

Dr. W. R. Thompson, for many years the director of the Commonwealth Institute for Biological Control in Ottawa, Canada, in his comments written for the special Centennial Edition of Charles Darwin's *Origin of Species*, commented on these ubiquitous differences between organisms as follows:

". . . but taking the taxonomic system as a whole, it appears as an orderly arrangement of clearcut entities, which are clearcut because they are separated by gaps. . . . The general tendency to eliminate, by means of unverifiable speculations, the limits of the categories nature presents to us, is the inheritance of biology from the *Origin of Species*. To establish the continuity required by theory, historical arguments are invoked, even though historical evidence is lacking. Thus are engendered those fragile towers of hypotheses based on hypotheses, where fact and fiction intermingle in an inextricable confusion."[1]

---

[1] W. R. Thompson, "Introduction" to *Origin of Species* (New York: Everyman's Library, Dutton, 1956).

As Dr. Thompson points out, a "continuity" of organisms is required by the theory, but there is no evidence that it exists now or has ever existed. The evolution model implies that all organisms have come from a common ancestor. Since they all live in a continuity of environments in the same world and have developed by the same natural processes, the primary prediction from the evolution model must be that of a continuum of organisms, rather than distinct kinds separated by gaps. To explain the gaps, numerous secondary assumptions have to be introduced into the model—the "towers of hypotheses based on hypotheses" noted by Dr. Thompson.

The creation model, once again, does not have to "explain" the data by introducing such secondary assumptions. To the contrary, it *predicts* the data. That is, an array of distinct kinds of organisms, separated by gaps, with *both* similarities and differences.

In view of the foregoing facts, it is strange that evolutionists constantly place such strong emphasis on similarities as evidence of evolution. In every case the similarities are better explained by creation and the differences are predicted by creation. Consider the following superficial similarities, cited commonly as evidence for evolution.

1. *Similarities in Morphology* (*Comparative Anatomy*)

Similarities in structure are considered one of the main evidences of evolution. To some extent, since the standard Linnaean classification scheme is arbitrary and man-made, such similarities may actually indicate common ancestry. This is certainly true at the level of varieties, and possibly also at the species level and occasionally at the level of higher categories. It should be remembered, however, that no observational or experimental evidence exists for ancestral relationships in these higher categories. This is purely an evolutionary assumption.

Probably the leading American taxonomist (*taxonomy* is the science of classification) is Ernst Mayr, of Harvard. Professor Mayr emphasizes that all such higher categories (genera, families, orders, etc.) are quite arbitrary, since no experimental proof can be offered to demonstrate any such relationships. A reviewer of Mayr's most authoritative work, *Principles of Systematic Zoology* (New York, McGraw-Hill, 1969, 434 pp.), makes the following illuminating comment:

"According to the author's view, which I think nearly all biologists must share, the species is the only taxonomic category that has at least in more favorable examples a completely objective existence. Higher categories are all more or less a matter of opinion."[1]

The fact that men are able to arrange plants and animals in a classification table on the basis of their morphologic features, certainly is no proof that those more closely associated in the table are more directly related by evolutionary descent. All such an arrangement proves is that man has the ability to devise methods for classifying and categorizing assemblages of data.

As a matter of fact, the classification table is a much better support for the creation model. If an evolutionary continuum existed, as the evolution model should predict, there would be no gaps, and thus it would be impossible to demark specific categories of life. Classification requires not only similarities, but differences and gaps as well, and these are much more amenable to the creation model.

2. *Similarities in Embryology*

Even before the time of Charles Darwin, evolutionists were claiming that similarities in embryonic development indicated a common ancestry. Textbooks today still show sketches of embryos of such animals as chickens, rabbits and lizards, along with those of men, noting striking similarities between them as presumed evidence of common ancestry.

This type of similarity proves common ancestry no more clearly than it proves common design. On the assumption of creation, since most higher animals were designed to reproduce their own kinds by the same type of reproductive process, it would be expected that embryonic development would be similar for all such animals.

Since the embryonic animal begins its existence in each case as a single-celled union of two parental cells, and the following cell multiplication must operate for some time in

---

[1] G. W. Richards, "A Guide to the Practice of Modern Taxonomy" *Science*, Vol. 167 (March 13, 1970), p. 1477.

the same type of environment, and since furthermore many of the structures to be developed must be somewhat similar (limbs, head, etc.), it would be natural that the developing embryos would look much alike for the initial stages of their development.

At such time, however, as it becomes necessary for specialized characters to begin to form, corresponding to the parental kinds, then these superficial resemblances give way to the appropriate distinctive characteristics. Actually, these significant differences show up quite early in the embryonic development.

The differences, even at the initial stages, are again much more important than the similarities. The DNA for the chicken is utterly different from that for the lizard, even though the difference is not obvious visually. The distinctive genetic code programmed for each kind of animal assures that only that kind will develop from the embryo. Superficial brief similarities are irrelevant to the evolution-creation question; the intricately designed differences constitute the greater reality.

3. *Similarities in Biochemistry*

Now that we have mentioned DNA, it is noteworthy that even this has been offered as evidence of evolution. That is, the fact that the DNA molecule is basic in the reproductive mechanisms for all kinds of organisms is assumed to suggest common ancestry. The infinitely more significant fact that each specific kind of organism has its *own* DNA molecular structure, different from that of every other kind, is ignored. The tremendous complexity of DNA molecules has already been discussed; such a system could never have evolved itself by chance. Neither could one type of DNA evolve into the DNA for another type of organism; its structure is designed to prevent that very thing. It is hard to imagine a more solid evidence for special creation than the mere existence and function of DNA.

Other chemicals in living organisms have likewise been studied on a comparative basis, especially such proteins as gamma globulin, insulin, cytochrome C, hemoglobin and others. Various techniques have been used to test these molecules on a comparative basis for a wide variety of organisms. In general (though with a great many exceptions) the respective similarities in these biochemical systems align themselves in about the same way as do the more traditional similarities based on anatomical and other gross morphological features.

This, of course, is exactly what would be expected on the basis of the creation model, so it certainly cannot be used as legitimate evidence for evolution. These studies in *molecular taxonomy* can actually prove helpfully supplemental to older studies in *morphological taxonomy*, with a view to eventual determination of the true boundaries of the original created kinds, beyond which variation and mutation cannot go.

4. *Similarities in Behavior*

Occasionally, similarities in animal behavior have been cited as evidence of relationship. Examples are difficult to find, however, and the much more typical situation is that of different behavior patterns. Even closely related kinds are often found to have drastically divergent habits or instincts. Once again, such similarities in behavior as may actually exist can be well explained in a creationist context.

5. *Deceptive Similarities*

There are many cases of what appear to be striking similarities which even evolutionists do not believe came from a common ancestor. They attribute these either to convergence or mimicry.

Convergence, or parallelism, is the assumed parallel and independent evolutionary development of similar features in unrelated animals. Wings, for example, are believed to have evolved completely independently four different times (in insects, flying reptiles, birds and bats) from four different non-winged ancestors. The eye of the squid is believed to have been evolved independently from the eye of the fish, even though both types of eyes are structurally very similar. The whale is believed to have evolved from a land mammal, even though its shape is like that of a fish. There are numerous other examples of convergence.

Mimicry is a phenomenon in which one type of organism appears as though it were imitating another type—for example, in coloration—in order to achieve the same type of environmental protection. The main examples of mimicry are found among insects.

Evolutionists use the explanations of either convergence or mimicry to explain superficial similarities which, for some reason (usually other more significant similarities—e.g., the mammalian features of the whale) do not lend themselves to the direct evolutionary explanation.

The point is, however, if there are actually numerous similarities among organisms which cannot be attributed to common ancestry, how then can we be sure which, if any, similarities *are* due to common ancestry?

The creation model, remember, does not encounter such problems. It suggests an array of similarities and differences, so that similarities simply suggest similar purposes (e.g., both birds and bats needed to fly, so the Creator created wings for both of them). This concept would apply equally well to so-called convergent evolution and cases of mimicry. All were created as distinct kinds, with similar structures for similar purposes and different structures for different purposes.

Vestiges and Recapitulations

A long-cited evidence of evolution, used even before Darwin, is that certain vestigial remnants of assumed former evolutionary changes can still be seen in the structures of organisms living today. These remnants are of two main types, the so-called vestigial organs and recapitulating embryos. These are assumed to have significance as a record of former evolution but no longer to have utility in living organisms today.

If these features really exist, the creation model could explain them in terms of the decay principle associated with the Second Law of Thermodynamics. At most, they would not testify of evolution into higher order but rather of decay into lower order. In this case the creation model would not actually *predict* such features, but at least it could explain them as well as the evolution model (which would not have predicted them either).

As a matter of fact, however, it is very doubtful that such phenomena exist at all. We consider them each briefly below:

1. *Vestigial Organs*

Certain organs on man, as well as on various animals, have long been described as useless vestiges of structures which were useful in a former evolutionary stage. However, this evidence is no longer offered with the confidence which once accompanied it. Practically all the so-called "vestigial" organs, especially those in man, have been proved in recent years to have definite uses and not to be vestigial at all. At one time, evolutionists claimed there were about 180 such vestigial organs in man, but practically none are claimed now. Some of these were the thyroid gland, the thymus, the coccyx, the pineal gland, the ear muscles, the tonsils and the appendix. All of these are now known to have useful, and often essential, functions.

In view of the history of this subject, it would seem the better part of wisdom not to claim any organs at all as vestigial. The ignorance of scientists about the specific functions of such structures does not prove they have none. It is more likely than not that in the very few cases remaining more intensive study will, as it often has in the past, reveal specific functions actually accomplished by these supposedly useless organs.

The small residuum of what may be true atrophies are surely poor examples of evolution! They are degenerative changes, if anything, possibly the result of harmful mutations.

2. *The Recapitulation Theory*

The hoary evolutionary cliche, "Ontogeny recapitulates phylogeny," is a popular definition of what used to be called the "biogenetic law." *Ontogeny* is the development of the embryo, and *phylogeny* is the imagined evolutionary development of the kind of animal. In the case of man, for example, it was taught that the human embryo began life as a marine protozoan, developed in a watery environment into a worm with a pulsating-tube heart, then into a fish with gill-slits and a two-chambered heart, then into an amphibian with a three-chambered heart and a mesonephros kidney, then into a mammal with a four-chambered heart, metanephros kidney, and a tail, and finally into a human being. In this way, the human embryo actually retains "vestiges" of its former evolution by recapitulating its major phases.

The rationale of this strange idea apparently was that new evolutionary stages of the kind of adult animal were acquired by a sort of extension of the embryonic development corresponding to its previous stage, but that the embryo always had to go through all its previous stages first to get to the new stage.

76

Modern studies in molecular genetics have shown the impossibility of such concepts. The DNA for a man is not the DNA for a fish, nor is it the DNA for a fish with something new added. The DNA for each kind is uniquely programmed to produce its own kind, not to produce a temporary replica of some other kind.

Furthermore, embryologic studies have shown that there are so many omissions, additions, and inversions in the embryologic sequences, as compared to the supposed evolutionary sequences, that the idea of recapitulation could certainly not be called a *law*! Even the few apparent parallels are quite superficial and in no sense could represent an actual recapitulation.

The most famous and impressive of these parallels has undoubtedly been the supposed development of "gill slits" in the "fish stage" of human embryonic growth. This supposed recapitulation was entirely superficial; the human embryo never at any time develops gills or gill slits, and therefore is never a fish. It has no fish tail, fins, or any other fish structures.

The human embryo does develop pharyngeal pouches, as does the fish embryo. In the fish, these later become the site of the gills. In the human, they become the eustachian tubes, the thymus and parathyroid glands. In the meantime, as they are developing, they serve as essential guides for the developing blood vessels, and are thus not useless vestiges at all.

The same applies to the developing kidneys, heart and other features. A great deal of evidence exists now that all aspects of all stages of the development of all embryos have vital roles in the progress of the embryonic growth of each specific creature. There are no redundant vestiges of former evolutionary stages; all steps are necessary components of the present organism. The creation model would, in fact, expect them all to reflect careful planning and design, and this is exactly what they do.

Consequently, very few modern embryologists place any confidence today in the recapitulation theory. It is surprising that so many prominent evolutionists continue to refer to this idea as evidence for evolution. Those who are knowledgeable, either in embryology or paleontology, do not. For example, a Columbia University biologist, in a recent review

77

of the work of Haeckel (the contemporary of Charles Darwin who popularized the recapitulation theory) has stressed that the theory has ". . . been demonstrated to be wrong by numerous subsequent scholars."[1]

Systematic Gaps in the Fossil Record

It is significant that the same array of similarities and differences between organisms is found in the realm of the fossils as in the realm of the living. The same types of gaps between kinds exist in the fossil record as in the Linnaean classification system for plants and animals in the present world.

As we have seen, if the evolution model were valid, one would expect to find a horizontal continuum of living organisms, rather than clearcut categories. Gaps between kinds can only be explained by a series of secondary assumptions, postulating special environments and selection histories for the various gaps.

Gaps in the fossil record require still more secondary assumptions. In this case, there must have been at least a "vertical" continuum between each fossil organism and its evolutionary ancestors, so that the absence of such transitional fossils is certainly not a primary prediction of the evolution model, as it is for the creation model. The gaps in this case cannot be explained by assuming the transitional forms never developed at all, as is done for the living array of organisms. They must somehow be explained instead as due to special conditions which prevented the transitional forms which did exist from being fossilized or those which were fossilized from being found.

The creation model, on the other hand, requires no such secondary assumptions. It predicts that there would be systematic gaps in the fossil record and that these would be essentially the same gaps as in the present world. The same plan of creation, with similar structures for similar purposes

---

[1] Walter J. Bock, "Evolution by Orderly Law," *Science*, Vol. 164 (May 4, 1969), p. 684. Similarly, Professor C. H. Waddington, of the University of Edinburgh, has said "The type of analogical thinking that leads to theories that development is based on the recapitulation of ancestral stages or the like no longer seems at all convincing or even very interesting to biologists." (*Principles of Embryology*, 1965, p. 10).

and different structures for different purposes applies to all organisms, whether living or extinct. The fossil record can no more be a random collection of chance products of random processes than can the living world. Even animals which have become extinct (and extinction is an example of decay, not development) must have been a part of the original created categories.

If evolution were true, one would suppose that the classification system itself would evolve over the ages. If all animals and plants are randomly changing, the categories of classification should likewise be changing. The fact is, however, that it has been the same since the beginning, even assuming the geological ages are as taught in orthodox geology. Note the following:

1. All kingdoms and subkingdoms are represented in the geologic record from the Cambrian onward.
2. All phyla of the animal kingdom are represented from the Cambrian onward.
3. All classes of the animal kingdom are represented from the Cambrian onward, except:
   (a) Moss-corals (Ordovician onward)
   (b) Insects (Devonian onward)
   (c) Graptolites (Cambrian to Carboniferous)
   (d) Trilobites (Cambrian to Permian)
4. All phyla of the plant kingdom are represented from the Triassic onward, except:
   (a) Bacteria, algae, fungi (Precambrian onward)
   (b) Bryophytes, pteridophytes (Silurian onward)
   (c) Spermophytes (Carboniferous onward)
   (d) Diatoms (Jurassic onward)
5. All orders and families (as well as kingdoms, phyla and classes) appear suddenly in the fossil record, with no indication of transitional forms from earlier types. This is true even of most genera and species.

The following statements from leading evolutionists confirm the fact that most of the forms of plants and animals have arisen suddenly in the fossil record. There is no evidence that there have ever been transitional forms between these basic kinds.

"In spite of these examples, it remains true, as every paleontologist knows, that *most* new species, genera and families, and that nearly all categories above the

79

level of families, appear in the record suddenly and are not led up to by known, gradual, completely continuous transitional sequences."[1]

"There is no need to apologize any longer for the poverty of the fossil record. In some ways it has become almost unmanageably rich, and discovery is outpacing integration. . . . The fossil record nevertheless continues to be composed mainly of gaps."[2]

"So far as we can judge from the geologic record, large changes seem usually to have arisen rather suddenly, in terms of geologic time . . . fossil forms intermediate between large subdivisions of classification, such as orders and classes, are seldom found."[3]

To be more specific, we continue to document in more detail the fact that the transitions between major kinds are missing in every case. Consider the significant gaps enumerated below:

1. *From Protozoans to Metazoan Invertebrates*
One of the most important fossil gaps is that between the questionable, one-celled microorganisms found in Precambrian strata and the abundant complex marine invertebrate life of the Cambrian, as well as the strange "Ediacaran" fossils of the Precambrian.

"The introduction of a variety of organisms in the early Cambrian, including such complex forms of the arthropods as the trilobites, is surprising. . . . The introduction of abundant organisms in the record would not be so surprising if they were simple. Why should such com-

[1] George Gaylord Simpson, *The Major Features of Evolution* (New York: Columbia University Press, 1953), p. 360.
[2] T. Neville George, "Fossils in Evolutionary Perspective," *Science Progress*, Vol. 48 (January 1960), pp. 1, 3.
[3] Paul A. Moody, *Introduction to Evolution* (New York: Harper and Row, 1962), p. 503. N. Heribert-Nilsson, of Lund University in Sweden, after 40 years of study in paleontology and botany, finally was forced to conclude: "It is not even possible to make a caricature of an evolution out of paleobiological facts. The fossil material is now so complete that . . . the lack of transitional series cannot be explained as due to the scarcity of the material. The deficiencies are real; they will never be filled." (*Synthetische Artbildung*, 1953).

plex organic forms be in rocks about six hundred million years old and be absent or unrecognized in the records of the preceding two billion years? . . . If there has been evolution of life, the absence of the requisite fossils in the rocks older than the Cambrian is puzzling."[1]

"One of the major unsolved problems of geology and evolution is the occurrence of diversified multicellular marine invertebrates in Lower Cambrian rocks and their absence in rocks of greater age. These early Cambrian fossils included porifera, coelenterates, brachiopods, mollusca, echinoids, and arthropods. Their high degree of organization clearly indicates that a long period of evolution preceded their appearance in the record. However, when we turn to examine the pre-Cambrian rocks for the forerunners of these Early Cambrian fossils, they are nowhere to be found."[2]

"Granted an evolutionary origin of the main groups of animals, and not an act of special creation, the absence of any record whatsoever of a single member of any of the phyla in the Precambrian rocks remains as inexplicable on orthodox grounds as it was to Darwin."[3]

There is obviously a tremendous gap between one-celled microorganisms and the high complexity and variety of the many invertebrate phyla of the Cambrian. If the former evolved into the latter, it seems impossible that no transitional forms between any of them would ever be preserved or found. A much more likely explanation for these gaps is that they represent permanent gaps between created kinds. Each organism has its own structure, specifically designed for its own purpose, not accidentally evolved by random processes.

2. *From Invertebrates to Vertebrates*

The evolutionary transition from invertebrates to vertebrates must have involved billions of animals, but no one has

---

[1]Marshall Kay and Edwin H. Colbert, *Stratigraphy and Life History* (New York: John Wiley & Sons, 1965), p. 102.

[2]Daniel I. Axelrod, "Early Cambrian Marine Fauna" *Science*, Vol. 128 (1958), p. 7.

[3]T. Neville George, "Fossils in Evolutionary Perspective," *Science Progress*, Vol. 48 (January 1960), p. 5.

ever found a fossil of one of them. Invertebrates have soft inner parts and hard outer shells; vertebrates have soft outer parts and hard inner parts—skeletons. How did the one evolve into the other? There is no evidence at all.

The "earliest" vertebrates are certain orders of fish, the Osteostraci and the Heterostraci. Concerning these, one of the nation's leading vertebrate paleontologists, Dr. Alfred Romer of Harvard, has written:

> "In sediments of late Silurian and early Devonian age, numerous fishlike vertebrates of varied types are present, and it is obvious that a long evolutionary history had taken place before that time. But of that history we are mainly ignorant."[1]

Which means, simply, that there are no fossils yet available of incipient forms leading up to these fish from their assumed invertebrate ancestors. Surely it is more reasonable to believe that vertebrates and invertebrates were separate creations from the beginning.

3. *From Fishes to Amphibians*

The next major evolutionary advance must have been from fish to amphibian. Somehow the fin of the fish must have been transformed into the foot of the amphibian, not to mention the myriad of other necessary changes. To date, however, no fossil of a "fishibian," with fins partly converted into feet (or any other transitional characters) has ever been found.

The chief candidate for such a transitional form was long supposed to have been the coelacanth, a crossopterygian fish, which was supposed to have certain limb-like characters on its fins indicating initial advance toward amphibianhood. Ultimately it was destined, so it was believed, to become a primitive amphibian known as a labyrinthodont. The coelacanth was believed to have finished this transition

---

[1] A. S. Romer, *Vertebrate Paleontology* (Chicago: University of Chicago Press, 1966), p. 15. Similarly, F. D. Ommanney, in his book *The Fishes* (Life Nature Library, 1964, p. 60) says: "How this earliest chordate stock evolved, what stages of development it went through to eventually give rise to truly fishlike creatures we do not know. Between the Cambrian when it probably originated, and the Ordovician when the first fossils of animals with really fishlife characters appeared, there is a gap of 100 million years which we will probably never be able to fill."

sometime in the Mesozoic, since no fossils have been found subsequent to that era.

Evolutionists were embarrassed when it was discovered in 1938 that these fish are still alive and well, living in the waters near Madagascar.

"Throughout the hundreds of millions of years the coelacanths have kept the same form and structure. Here is one of the great mysteries of evolution."[1]

It is hard to see how these fish could have become amphibians when they are still the same as they were a hundred million years ago when they began to make the transition. There seem, however, to be no other candidates. The lungfish, the "walking catfish," and other fish that seem to have certain resemblances to land animals, have all been ruled out by evolutionists for various other reasons.

4. From Amphibians to Reptiles to Mammals

The fossil record throws very little light on the hypothetical evolution of amphibians into reptiles, or that of reptiles into mammals. All of them are four-legged vertebrates with similar skeletal structures and thus their fossilized remains provide little basis for distinguishing between them. Among animals living today, there are certain reptiles whose bony parts closely resemble those of certain amphibians and others that closely resemble certain mammals. The external characters and appearance, as well as the physiological functions, of amphibians, reptiles and mammals, are all vastly different from each other, but these differences need not show up in the fossil record.

The fact that it may be difficult to tell, for example, whether a certain fossil was a reptile or a mammal does not mean at all that it was transitional between the two in an evolutionary sense. If we could see the whole animal, and not just its skeleton, it would quickly be apparent which it was.

Of much more significance is the fact that each of the various orders of amphibians, reptiles and mammals appears suddenly in the fossil record, without incipient forms leading

---

[1] Jacques Millot, "The Coelacanth, " *Scientific American*, Vol. 193 (December 1955), p. 37. Dr. Millot was the Director of Madagascar's Institute of Scientific Research, and also associated with the Paris Museum of Natural History.

up to it and without transitional forms between it and any other order.

For example, the paleontologist George Gaylord Simpson notes that each of the 32 orders of mammals in the classification system appears suddenly in the fossil record with all its distinct ordinal characteristics fully expressed. Concerning this, he says:

"This regular absence of transitional forms is not confined to mammals, but is an almost universal phenomenon, as has long been noted by paleontologists."[1]

To take one example of these mammalian orders, consider the rodents. In number of species and genera, the rodents exceed all other mammals combined, so they would be most likely of all to show evidence of intermediate forms. The paleontologist Alfred Romer says, however:

"The origin of the rodents is obscure. . . . Presumably, of course, they had arisen from some basal, insectivorous, placental stock, but no transitional forms are known."[2]

The most unique mammal is probably the bat, with its wings. To produce a bat from whatever its mammalian or reptilian ancestor may have been, there must have been innumerable transitional forms, but none has ever been found.[3]

5. *From Reptiles to Birds*

Evolutionists universally maintain that reptiles are the evolutionary ancestors of birds. Again, however, there is no fossil evidence of this, despite the famous *Archaeopteryx*. W. E. Swinton has admitted:

"The origin of birds is largely a matter of deduction. There is no fossil evidence of the stages through which

---

[1] George Gaylord Simpson, *Tempo and Mode in Evolution* (New York: Columbia University Press, 1944), p. 106.

[2] Alfred S. Romer, *Vertebrate Paleontology* (Chicago: University of Chicago Press, 1966, p. 303.

[3] A remarkable photo of what is called the "oldest known bat," quite indistinguishable from modern bats, is shown on the cover of *Science*, Vol. 154 (December 9, 1966); Photo taken by G. L. Jepsen.

the remarkable change from reptile to bird was achieved."[1]

The interesting fossil, *Archaeopteryx*, however, had certain characteristics (e.g., teeth) which were deemed to be reptilian and others (e.g., wings and feathers) which were deemed avian. Consequently, this is always the most emphasized example, in evolutionary textbooks, of evolution between two major classes of animals. If there is any transitional form at all, *Archaeopteryx* is the one. As Dunbar says:

"It would be difficult to find a more perfect 'connecting link' between two great groups of animals, or more cogent proof of the reptilian ancestry of the birds."[2]

Yet this same author, in the very same paragraph, recognizes that *Archaeopteryx* is not part reptile at all, but 100 per cent bird. He says it is:

". . . because of its feathers distinctly to be classed as a bird."[3]

The fossilized impressions of the feathers on the wings of *Archaeopteryx* have been found and this shows it was warm-blooded, not a reptile with scales and cold blood.

Thus, *Archaeopteryx* is a bird, not a reptile-bird transition. It is an extinct bird that had teeth. Most birds don't have teeth, but there is no reason why the Creator could not have created some birds with teeth. Not all reptiles have teeth, though some do. The same is true of fishes, amphibians and mammals. Some have teeth and some don't. The same evidently was true of the original birds. For some reason, those that were created with teeth have since become extinct.

At the very least, there must have been a tremendous number of transitional forms between *Archaeopteryx* and its imaginary reptilian ancestor. Why does no one ever find a fossil animal with half-scales turning into feathers, or half-forelimbs turning into wings? Such animals must have lived in great numbers over long periods of time, but no fossils of

---

[1] W. E. Swinton, *Biology and Comparative Physiology of Birds*, A. J. Marshall, Ed., (New York: Academic Press, 1960), Vol. I, p. 1.
[2] Carl O. Dunbar, *Historical Geology* (New York: John Wiley and Sons, 1961), p. 310.
[3] *Ibid.*

them have ever been found. There are not even any fossils of forms intermediate between the flying reptiles (pterosaurs) and *their* non-winged reptilian ancestors. All of this is very strange in the context of the evolution model, but is directly predicted by the creation model.

6. *Origin of Insects*

If the evolutionary origin of the higher animals is obscure, the origin of insects is completely blank. Insects occur in fantastic number and variety, but there is no fossil clue to their development from some kind of evolutionary ancestor.

Of course, it is remarkable that insect fossils are found at all. Nevertheless, they have been found fossilized in considerable numbers, preserved in amber, coal, volcanic ash, or such materials. All such deposits must have been formed rapidly, of course, or the insect fossils could not have endured so long.

The most remarkable feature about such fossil insects as are known is that they are very similar to those living now. In many cases, however, they are much larger than their modern relatives. There are giant dragonflies, giant cockroaches, giant ants, and so on. But their form is no different in essence from that of modern insects.

". . . by and large, the insect population of today remains remarkably similar to that of the earlier age. All the major orders of insects now living were represented in the ancient Oligocene forest. Some of the specific types have persisted throughout the 70-million years since then with little or no change."[1]

7. *Origin of Plants*

The study of paleobotany has been even more disappointing to evolutionists than that of ancient animal life. One of the outstanding paleobotanists of modern times was Professor C. A. Arnold, of the University of Michigan. In his authoritative treatment of this subject he noted this fact as follows:

"It has long been hoped that extinct plants will ultimately reveal some of the stages through which existing

---

[1] C. T. Brues, "Insects in Amber," *Scientific American*, Vol. 185 (November 1951), p. 60.

groups have passed during the course of their development, but it must be freely admitted that this aspiration has been fulfilled to a very slight extent, even though paleobotanical research has been in progress for more than one hundred years. As yet we have not been able to trace the phylogenetic history of a single group of modern plants from its beginning to the present."[1]

Likewise, Professor Corner of the Botany Department of Cambridge University, though an evolutionist himself, has said:

". . . but I still think that to the unprejudiced, the fossil record of plants is in favor of special creation."[2]

8. *Persistence of Kinds through Geologic Time*

We have already noted that all the kingdoms, phyla and classes in the organic world have been essentially unchanged since life began, and that even the orders and most of the families, genera, and even species appear suddenly in the fossil record, with no incipient forms leading up to them.

This constancy of the classification system and persistence of the major categories of organisms is of course contrary to what one would expect from the evolution model, but is a prediction of the creation model. It is a testimony to creative purpose and design, rather than chance variation and natural selection.

To point up the essential identity of the fossil world of organisms with the world of living organisms, the following list may be helpful, especially in emphasizing in the classroom the fact that, after all, animals today are not too much different than in the past.

Examples of Persistence of Fossil Communities
(among many others)

Precambrian:	Algae, bacteria, fungi
Cambrian:	Sponges, snails, jellyfish
Ordovician:	Clams, starfish, worms
Silurian:	Scorpions, corals
Devonian:	Sharks, lungfish

---

[1] C. A. Arnold, *An Introduction to Paleobotany* (New York: McGraw-Hill Publ. Co., 1947) p. 7.

[2] E. J. H. Corner, *Evolution in Contemporary Botanical Thought*, ed. by A. M. MacLeod and L. S. Cobley (Chicago: Quadrangle Books), 1961.

Carboniferous:	Ferns, cockroaches
Permian:	Beetles, dragonflies
Triassic:	Pines, palms
Jurassic:	Crocodiles, turtles
Cretaceous:	Ducks, pelicans
Paleocene:	Rats, hedgehogs
Eocene:	Lemurs, rhinoceroses
Oligocene:	Beavers, squirrels, ants
Miocene:	Camels, wolves
Pliocene:	Horses, elephants
Pleistocene:	Man

The list above could easily be greatly expanded; the examples given are typical, not exhaustive. It is obvious even from this limited summary that while there may have been many changes within the kinds (as provided by creative forethought, through adaption to changing environments facilitated by the created genetic variational potential in each kind), the kinds have apparently not varied since the beginning, except for those that have become extinct.

9. *Living Fossils*

A number of modern organisms have been found *only* in ancient strata. Until their unexpected discovery in recent years, still living, it was thought that they had been extinct for, in some cases, over a hundred million years. They were actually used previously as "index fossils," dating the strata in which they were found. The use of these "living fossils" as index fossils, of course, immediately had to cease as soon as they were found still living. Though they had not been preserved in the strata representing the imagined intervening aeons, they must have been there somewhere!

There has been so little change in these "living fossils" that it is hard to believe the evolution model is really valid. What makes an organism evolve into a high degree of complexity (with no evidence of this evolution in the fossil record) and then stop evolving? Perhaps the most anomalous of all situations is that among these "living fossils" are those one-celled organisms which are supposed to have started the evolutionary process in the first place.

"Among single-celled organisms, the discovery, during the past decade, of survivors from a very remote past has been equally remarkable, though here it is a matter of finding essentially modern forms as Precambrian fossils. The most remarkable of these and also one extraordinary form first known as a fossil and then discovered living today, came from the Gunflint Iron Formation of Southern Ontario, which is about 1.9 billion years old."[1]

This is a remarkable testimony to evolutionary stagnation! Other living fossils include the following, among others:

Tuatara (beakhead reptile):	"extinct" since Cretaceous
Coelacanth (crossopterygian fish):	"extinct" since Cretaceous
Neopilina (segmented mollusk):	"extinct" since Devonian
Lingula (brachiopod shellfish):	"extinct" since Ordovician
Metasequoia (dawn redwood):	"extinct" since Miocene

Since most index fossils are small marine organisms, and since the depths of the ocean are relatively unexplored, it is not at all impossible that some of these (trilobites, graptolites, ammonites, etc.) will be found still living someday.

Now the question is how does the evolutionary model account for these systematic, regular, ubiquitous gaps in the fossil record? It does not predict such gaps, as does the creation model and so must try to accommodate them by various secondary assumptions. In view of the wealth of fossils now available, it is impossible to say any longer, as Darwin did in his day, that the gaps will be filled in by further fossil collecting.

The usual assumption is that: (1) evolution took place in small segregated populations, and (2) the mutation rate was accelerated due to temporarily increased environmental radiation.

"It seems likely that the dominant core of a population or species is rarely primarily involved in the evolutionary process."[2]

"Inasmuch as evolutionary changes are at least in part the result of genetic mutations, an increase in the flux of ionizing radiation, however small, will act to accelerate the evolutionary process."[3]

---

[1] G. Evelyn Hutchinson, "Living Fossils," *American Scientist*, Vol. 58 (September 1970), p. 534.

[2] John J. Christian, "Social Subordination, Population Density, and Mammalian Orders," *Science*, Vol. 168 (April 3, 1970).

[3] John F. Simpson, "Evolutionary Pulsations and Geomagnetic Polarity," *Bulletin, Geological Society of America*, Vol. 77 (February 1966), p. 200.

"The boundaries between eras, periods and epochs on the geological time scale generally denote sudden and significant changes in the character of fossil remains. . . . Researchers have sometimes come up with drastic explanations for these changes such as an increase in mutation rates due to cosmic rays."[1]

The combination of small populations and rapid evolution is offered in lieu of the missing transitional forms. This is clearly a case of special pleading and is both untestable and unlikely. Evolutionists in effect are saying we can never hope to *see* evidence of evolution; it went too fast in the past and is senescent in the present!

Punctuated Equilibrium

A colorful new term coined by Niles Eldredge and Stephen Jay Gould to denote this mysterious hypothetical process of rapid evolution in small populations is "punctuated equilibrium." Steven M. Stanley calls it "quantum speciation." Older writers (e.g., Richard Goldschmidt) called it "hopeful monsters."

Such an imaginary process might help explain the universal absence of transitional structures in the fossil record, but there is no *genetic* evidence of any such process. Keith S. Thomson, Professor of Biology and Dean of the Graduate School at Yale, says the mechanism of evolution is still the "central mystery."[2]

The really central mystery is why, after 150 years of futile searching for some genetic mechanism that could generate real "vertical" evolution, evolutionists still believe in evolution at all!

---

[1] "Fossil Changes: 'Normal Evolution' " *Science News,* Vol. 102 (Report on the International Geological Congress at Montreal), (September 2, 1972), p. 152.

[2] Keith Stewart Thomson, "The Meanings of Evolution," *American Scientist,* Vol. 70 (Sept./Oct. 1982), p. 529.

CHAPTER V

UNIFORMITARIANISM OR CATASTROPHISM?

The Message of the Fossils

In the preceding chapter, we have shown that the regular and systematic gaps in the fossil record are inconsistent with the evolution model of earth history. But if the fossils do not teach evolution, then what exactly is their message? How and when were formed the tremendous beds of sedimentary rocks which contain those fossils?

This question immediately raises the issue of uniformitarianism or catastrophism.

This is really a different question altogether than the basic issue of creation versus evolution, as far as purely scientific models are concerned. Each of the two issues could be discussed independently of the other. They are closely related issues, however, and it is well now to look at this topic also.

That is, were the fossils and the rocks and the other features of the earth's crust formed slowly over vast aeons of time by the same processes now at work in the earth? This idea, known as *uniformitarianism,* is almost always assumed in the textbook treatment of subjects related to earth structure and history. Or is it more likely that many or most of such deposits were formed rapidly in a relatively short period of time? This idea is *catastrophism.*

Now the evolution model is usually associated with uniformitarianism and the creation model with catastrophism. This association does not preclude the possibility that *local* catastrophes can occur within the broad framework of evolutionary uniformitarianism. Nor does it suggest that catastrophism rejects the normal uniform operation of natural laws and processes during most of earth history. Creationists believe in general uniformitarianism as an evidence of the Creator's providential maintenance of the laws He created in the beginning. On the other hand, certain catastrophists actually deny the existence of a Creator, attributing past cataclysms to purely natural causes. Thus the two terms are flexible and to some extent indicate differences in degree rather than kind.

Nevertheless, it is true that the evolution model is fundamentally tied to uniformitarianism, since it assumes that present natural laws and processes suffice to explain the origin and development of all things. The creation model is fundamentally catastrophic because it says that present laws and processes are *not* sufficient to explain the phenomena found in the present world. It centers its explanation of past history around both a period of special *constructive* processes and one or more periods of special *destructive* processes, both of which operated in ways or at rates which are not commensurate with present processes.

The association of evolution with uniformitarianism is also required by the fact that evolution obviously requires an immensity of time. The same is true of earth features which are to be explained by uniformitarianism.

". . . the Scottish geologist, James Hutton, . . . maintained that *the present is the key to the past* and that, given sufficient time, processes now at work could account for all the geologic features of the Globe. This philosophy, which came to be known as the doctrine of *uniformitarianism*, demands an immensity of time; it has now gained universal acceptance among intelligent and informed people."[1]

Professor Dunbar, who wrote those words a good many years ago, might be surprised to learn that there are today thousands of intelligent and informed *scientists*, and many times more other intelligent and informed people from other fields who reject the doctrine of uniformitarianism. The present is *not* the key to the past!

Even among orthodox evolutionary geologists, there are many today who are seriously questioning or altering the traditional application of uniformitarianism to geology. Statements from a number of these are given below.

1. *Uniformitarianism contradicts the actual data.*
   "Conventional uniformitarianism, or 'gradualism,' i.e., the doctrine of unchanging change, is verily contradicted by all post-Cambrian sedimentary

---

[1] Carl O. Dunbar, *Historical Geology* (2nd ed. New York: John Wiley & Sons, 1960), p. 18.

data and the geotectonic histories of which these sediments are the record."[1]

2. *One must distinguish between uniformity of natural laws and uniformity of the rates of particular processes*

"Uniformitarianism is a dual concept. Substantive uniformitarianism (a testable theory of geologic change postulating uniformity of rates or material conditions) is false and stifling to hypothesis formation. Methodological uniformitarianism (a procedural principle asserting spatial and temporal invariance of natural laws) belongs to the definition of science and is not unique to geology.... Substantive uniformitarianism as a descriptive theory has not withstood the test of new data and can no longer be maintained in any strict manner."[2]

3. *Many geologists today are turning away from uniformitarianism.*

"The doctrine of uniformitarianism has been vigorously disputed in recent years. A number of writers, although approaching the subject from different directions, have agreed that this doctrine is composed partly of meaningless and erroneous components and some have suggested that it be discarded as a formal assumption of geological science. . . . It seems unfortunate that uniformitarianism, a doctrine which has so important a place in the history of geology, should continue to be misrepresented in introductory texts and courses by 'the present is the key to the past,' a maxim without much credit."[3]

4. *Uniformitarianism has been misused by teachers of geology.*

"Often, I am afraid, the subject is taught superficially, with Geikie's maxim 'the present is the key

---

[1]P.D. Krynine, "Uniformitarianism is a Dangerous Doctrine," *Paleontology,* Vol. 30 (1956), p. 1004.

[2]Stephen Jay Gould, "Is Uniformitarianism Necessary?" *American Journal of Science,* Vol. 263 (March 1965), pp. 223, 227.

[3]James W. Valentine, "The Present is the Key to the Present, *Journal of Geological Education,* Vol. 14 (April 1966), pp. 59, 60.

to the past' used as a catechism and the imposing term 'uniformitarianism' as a smokescreen to hide confusion both of student and teacher."[1]

5. *Unusual geologic phenomena should be included in interpretation.*
   "Accepting the principle of the rare event as a valid concept makes it even more desirable to retire the term 'uniformitarianism.' If further investigations should prove that singular events of great importance have indeed taken place in the past, then the term 'uniformitarianism' not only becomes confusing but outright erroneous."[2]

6. *Many unusual events have, in fact, affected the strata.*
   "There are many other reasons why we should not blindly accept the doctrine of uniformitarianism, without at least qualifying the concept. . . . We find certain rock types in the geologic column that are not being seen to form, at least in quantity, anywhere on earth today."[3]

Surely, with so much authoritative opinion (and much more could be cited, if necessary), we are warranted in considering catastrophism as an alternative interpretation of the geologic strata. We shall find not only that there is no type of geologic feature which cannot be explained in terms of rapid formation but that there are in fact a great many such features which can *only* be explained that way. Furthermore, we shall show reason for believing that all these features were formed essentially consecutively and continuously, so that the entire complex known as the *geologic column* can be understood in terms of relatively rapid formation. The "immensity of time" demanded by uniformitarianism and evolutionism is by no means demanded by the actual facts of the geologic strata.

This conclusion is abundantly warranted by the fossils themselves, which are the most important components of

[1]Stephen Jay Gould, "Is Uniformitarianism Useful?" *Journal of Geological Education,* Vol. 15 (October 1967), p. 150.
[2]P.E. Gretener,"Significance of the Rare Event in Geology," *Bulletin, American Assoc. of Petroleum Geologists,* Vol. 51 (November 1967), p. 2205.
[3]Edgar B. Heylmun, "Should We Teach Uniformitarianism?," *Journal of Geological Education,* Vol. 19 (January 1971), p. 36.

the strata. It is the fossils which "date" the rocks, and which distinguish one "geologic age" from another. It is the fossils which provide the main evidence for evolution. Yet it is the fossils which speak most clearly of rapid formation! Note the following documented facts.

1. *The fossils are the means by which rocks are assigned a geologic age.*

   "The only chronometric scale applicable in geologic history for the stratigraphic classification of rocks and for dating geologic events is furnished by the fossils."[1]

   "In each sedimentary stratum certain fossils seem to be characteristically abundant: these fossils are known as *index fossils*. If in a strange formation an index fossil is found, it is easy to date that particular layer of rock and to correlate it with other exposures in distant regions containing the same species."[2]

   "Thus it appears that the only presently available rational geochronological indices are biostratigraphically based — i.e., biochronologic."[3]

2. *The assumption of evolution is the basis upon which fossils are used to date the rocks.*

   "This book tells of the search that led to the development of a method for dividing pre-historic time based on the evolutionary development of organisms whose fossil record has been left in the sedimentary rocks of the earth's crust."[4]

   "Vertebrate paleontologists have relied upon 'stage-of-evolution' as the criterion for determining the chronologic relationships of faunas."[5]

---

[1] O.H. Schindewolf, "Comments on Some Stratigraphic Terms," *American Journal of Science*, Vol. 225 (June 1957), p. 394.

[2] J.E. Ransom, *Fossils in America* (New York, Harper and Row, 1964) p. 43.

[3] T.G. Miller, "Time in Stratigraphy," *Paleontology*, Vol. 8 (February 1965), p. 119.

[4] W.B.N. Berry, *Growth of a Prehistoric Time Scale* (San Francisco, W.H. Freeman Co., 1968) p. 5.

[5] J.F. Evernden *et al*, "K/A Dates and the Cenozoic Mammalian Chronology of North America," *American Journal of Science*, Vol. 262 (February 1964), p. 166.

3. *The fossils, on the other hand, provide the main evidence for evolution.*

"The most important evidence for the theory of evolution is that obtained from the study of paleontology. Though the study of other branches of zoology, such as Comparative Anatomy or Embryology, might lead one to suspect that animals are all inter-related, it was the discovery of various fossils and their correct placing in relative strata and age that provided the main factual basis for the modern view of evolution."[1]

"Although the comparative study of living plants and animals may give very convincing circumstantial evidence, fossils provide the only historical, documentary evidence that life has evolved from simpler to more and more complex forms."[2]

Thus, although the fossil record has been interpreted to teach evolution, the record itself has been based on the assumption of evolution. The message is a mere tautology. The fossils speak of evolution, because they have been *made* to speak of evolution. Furthermore, the universal prevalence of gaps, instead of transitional forms, in the fossil record shows that even *this* message is only a skeleton outline, with no substance.

And now, finally, we begin to recognize the *real* message of the fossils. There is no truly objective time sequence to the fossil record, since the time connections are based on the evolutionary assumption, which is the very point in question. The relative positioning of the fossiliferous strata, therefore, must be strictly a function of the sedimentary and other processes which deposited them. Apart from the time requirements of the evolutionary assumption, there is no objective reason why we cannot seriously consider whether these strata were deposited rapidly and massively, rather than slowly and sporadically.

---

[1] G.A. Kerkut, *Implications of Evolution* (Oxford, Pergamon Press, 1960) p. 134.

[2] C.O. Dunbar, *Historical Geology* (2nd ed. New York, John Wiley and Sons, Inc., 1960), p. 47.

In fact the very existence of fossils necessarily speaks of rapidity of formation! Fossils are not produced by slow uniformitarian rates of sediment deposition.

"To become fossilized a plant or animal must usually have hard parts, such as bone, shell or wood. It must be buried quickly to prevent decay and must be undisturbed throughout the long process."[1]

There are a number of different ways by which fossils can be produced and preserved. In every case, they must be formed rapidly, or else the forces of erosion, bacterial decay, weathering, or other disintegrative processes will destroy them before the fossilization process is complete. Fossil-forming processes include: (1) preservation of bones or soft parts by induration (compact burial); (2) formation of casts or molds; (3) petrifaction; (4) cementation of tracks or other impressions; (5) freezing; (6) carbonization (e.g., coal).

Although some have visualized fossilization as a slow process, brought about by gradual application of heat, pressure, chemical replacement, etc., it should be obvious that the actual formation of potential fossils in the first place, before other processes can start to work on them at all, requires rapid and compact burial of the organisms concerned, and this requires catastrophism.

If one doubts this, let him try to think of places where fossils are being formed today by uniformitarian processes. Consider, for example, the vast beds of fossilized herring in California, in Miocene-age shales.

"The numbers of fossils may be so great as to suggest abnormal conditions, possibly a catastrophe of some sort. Such an example was described by D.S. Jordan from the Miocene of California. Enormous numbers of the herring *Xyne grex* were found crowded on a bedding plane in the 'Monterey shale.' Jordan estimated that more than a billion fish, averaging 6 to 8 inches in length, died on 4 square miles of bay bottom. Catastrophic death in the sea on a comparable scale occurs today,

---

[1] F.H.T. Rhodes, H.S. Zim and P.R. Shaffer, *Fossils* (New York, Golden Press, 1962) p. 10.

due in many instances, to the development of 'red water'."[1]

The author failed to note, however, that while a 'red tide' may produce vast numbers of dead fish, it does not produce *fossil* fish! The fish decay on the shore, or are eaten by scavengers, but they don't become fossils.

And what about the great beds of dinosaur bones, found on practically every continent? Dr. Edwin Colbert is probably the chief authority on dinosaurs, and the following are typical quotations from his writings:

1. *In New Mexico*

"As the layer was exposed (the workers cut a large scallop into the hillside) it revealed a most remarkable dinosaurian graveyard in which there were literally scores of skeletons one on top of another and interlaced with one another. It would appear that some local catastrophe had overtaken these dinosaurs, so that they all died together and were buried together."[2]

2. *In Wyoming*

"At this spot the fossil hunters found a hillside literally covered with large fragments of dinosaur bones. . . . In short, it was a veritable mine of dinosaur bones. . . . The concentration of the fossils was remarkable; they were piled in like logs in a jam."[3]

3. *In Alberta*

"Innumerable bones and many fine skeletons of dinosaurs and other associated reptiles have been quarried from these badlands, particularly in the 15-mile stretch of river to the east of Steveville, a stretch that is a veritable dinosaurian graveyard."[4]

[1] Harry S. Ladd, "Ecology, Paleontology and Stratigraphy," *Science*, Vol. 129 (January 9, 1959), p. 72.

[2] Edwin Colbert, *Men and Dinosaurs* (New York, E.P. Dutton and Co., 1968) p. 141.

[3] *Ibid*, p. 151.

[4] Edwin Colbert, *The Age of Reptiles* (New York, W.W. Norton and Co., 1965) p. 169.

4. *In Belgium*

"Thus it could be seen that the fossil boneyard was evidently one of gigantic proportions, especially notable because of its vertical extension through more than a hundred feet of rock."[1]

Similar dinosaur graveyards are found on every continent, all over the world. Again the uniformitarian is challenged to point to any such phenomena occurring anywhere in the world today.

There are also great beds of fossil mammal remains (e.g., the elephant beds of Siberia, the hippopotamus beds of Sicily, etc.), great beds of amphibians (e.g., the masses of extinct amphibians in the Permian beds of Texas, etc.), tremendous beds of plant fossils (e.g., the coal measures), and so on. Practically all the kinds of organisms living in the present world have been also found in the fossil world, more often than not in the form of fossil graveyards containing large numbers of fossils.

The most extensive fossil deposits, however, are of marine invertebrates. It is these which have provided most of the "index fossils" for geologic dating. Many animals of this sort live in modern oceans, of course, and their shells and other remains are produced in great abundance today. At first thought, one would suppose that the remains of such organisms, continually dropping down upon the sea bottom and mixing with the sediments there, are gradually becoming fossilized.

Proof of this is hard to come by, however. The sediments at the bottom of the ocean are still soft sediments, not solid rock. Seashells are found in abundance along the sea shore, but these do not grade into sea-shell-bearing rock formations anywhere. The latter seem to have been produced in the past by some process of rapid lithification which one cannot see going on today.

Fossil-bearing rocks containing such invertebrates are found all over the world, and they often contain such fossils in great abundance, and yet it is very difficult, if not impossible, to find such rocks in process of formation today. Occasionally fossiliferous rocks are found in which the

---

[1]Edwin Colbert, *Men and Dinosaurs*, p. 58.

process of burial and lithification was so rapid that even the soft parts of the animals were preserved.

"The discovery of soft parts of Paleozoic fossils is a very rare event. During an extended X-ray investigation of Devonian fossils from the famous localities of Bundenbach and Wissenbach (Lower and Middle Devonian, West Germany) many unprepared slates were found in which soft parts and extremely fine structures of the embedded fossils are preserved."[1]

These fossils (trilobites, etc.) are some of the most important of the presumably extinct marine invertebrates used to date ancient strata, which in this case, amazingly, are supposed to be about 300 million years old.

It would be easy to give further illustrations of fossil-bearing rocks from every "age" and from every part of the world, which must have been formed rapidly in order to have been formed at all. The very existence of fossils, especially in large numbers, is evidence of catastrophism on at least a local scale. Since fossil-bearing strata are ubiquitous, and in fact make up the entire "geologic column," there is therefore evidence of catastrophism everywhere!

"There is no need to apologize any longer for the poverty of the fossil record. In some ways it has become almost unmanageably rich, and discovery is outpacing integration."[2]

Fossils thus clearly give evidence of rapid burial and therefore catastrophism. They support the catastrophist model more directly and obviously than the uniformitarian model. The latter is forced to incorporate at least local catastrophes into its basic framework of uniformitarianism in order to explain the data.

The question then becomes one of whether catastrophism is only an occasional interruption in the normal system of uniformitarianism, or whether catastrophism must actually

---

[1] Wilhelm Stuermer, "Soft Parts of Cephalopods and Trilobites: Some Surprising Results of X-Ray Examinations of Devonian Slates," *Science*, Vol. 170 (December 18, 1970), p. 1300.

[2] T. Neville George, "Fossils in Evolutionary Perspective," *Science Progress*, Vol. 48 (January 1960), p. 1.

be taken as the rule itself, in interpreting geologic formations. Before we decide this question, it is necessary to examine other geologic features and formations, in addition to the fossils. Were these formed rapidly in short periods of time, or gradually over long ages? The next section explores this question.

Rapid Formation of Geologic Deposits

In view of the widespread lip-service which geologists pay to the doctrine of uniformitarianism, it is surprising to find that practically none of the earth's geologic features and types of formations can be explained this way. That is, present-day geologic processes, acting at the same rates as at present, cannot possibly account for the geologic events of the past. The present is *not* the key to the past!

Consider first the main types of rocks found in the earth's crust, and how they were formed.

1. *Igneous Rocks*

Igneous rocks (granites, basalts, etc.) apparently were formed rapidly. They were formed by the upwelling of magmas (rock materials heated to the liquid state) from deep in the earth's mantle, below the crust. As the magmas cooled, either as *intrusives*, below the surface, or *extrusives*, on the surface, they became the solid rocks with which we are familiar. Magmas don't remain liquid very long after reaching the earth's relatively cool crust, so it is clear that these rocks were formed rapidly. Each igneous formation (including the giant batholiths and laccoliths, as well as the dikes, sills, etc.) therefore must have formed quickly once the material emerged from the mantle. Not even modern volcanism is meaningful in respect to such structures as these.

2. *Metamorphic Rocks*

The process of metamorphism, by which sedimentary rocks are converted into metamorphic rocks (e.g., limestone into marble, etc.) is very poorly understood, for the obvious reason that it does not seem to be taking place today. Some geologists even attribute certain granites to a supposed metamorphic process called "granitization" which converts sedimentary rocks into apparent granites. In any case, tremendous heat and stress must be involved in the metamorphism, and this presupposes abnormal conditions, at least in comparison to modern sediment-forming processes.

3. Sedimentary Rocks

The sedimentary rocks are the most important from the point of view of historical geology, not only because they cover most of the earth's surface, but also because they contain the fossils. It is to sedimentary rocks that uniformitarianism is assumed to be particularly applicable, since we can easily observe modern sedimentary processes at work and then presumably extrapolate them into the past to explain the sedimentary rocks.

The problem is that this doesn't work!

"It has long been assumed that preserved sedimentary rocks record primarily normal or average conditions for past epochs but this uniformitarian assumption must be challenged."[1]

There are of course many different kinds of sedimentary rocks. The most important of these are discussed below. Each one, as we examine it in turn, will be seen to be inexplicable on uniformitarian premises.

4. Sandstones

Sandstones once were loose sands, transported and then deposited by moving water.[2] Sands, of course, are transported and deposited along river beds and beaches today by hydraulic action, but they only become sand*stone* under very unusual conditions. The primary requisite is the presence of a cementing agent, which would in turn require previous erosion and dissolution of materials containing such chemicals. If such a cementing agent were available, however, the transformation of a sand into sandstone could be accomplished in a few hours (e.g., production of a cement sidewalk from sand, water and Portland cement), not at all requiring a million years of compaction!

---

[1] R.H. Dott and R.L. Batten, *Evolution of the Earth* (New York, McGraw-Hill Publ. 1971) p. 226.
[2] Some sandstones may have formed from windblown sand, rather than water-transported sand, although this is doubtful. If so, however, the provision of the needed cement on any uniformitarian basis becomes an even greater mystery.

Furthermore it is significant to note that sandstone formations frequently cover wide regions. For example, the so-called "St. Peter Sandstone" and its correlative formations cover practically all of the United States from California to Vermont and from Canada to Tennessee. Nothing like this is being formed today and it would seem that only a continent-wide flood could accomplish it.

5. *Shales*

Rocks which have been formed from small-sized particles such as silt and clay are called shales, siltstones or mudstones. They are very extensive in the geologic column and are often quite fossiliferous. Like sandstone, they require the presence of some kind of cement to become rock. Similarly, like the sandstones, they are often found spread in continuous layers over wide regions, far too extensive to be considered a normal delta or lake deposit. They must have in most cases been formed by massive transportation of mud from some unknown far-away source, held in suspension by turbulent waters, and then dumped over wide regions as the waters decelerated and became quiescent. Shales are often found vertically above sandstones, as would be expected in hydraulic deposition. A watery matrix containing and transporting particles of various sizes would tend to deposit the gravels (conglomerates) first, then sand and then silt. Chemical materials in solution would tend to be deposited last. This type of order is often found over large regions.

6. *Conglomerates*

Cemented gravels and boulders, with interstitial sands and pebbles, are called conglomerates. It is obvious that the hydraulic transportation of this type of sediment requires very strong current velocities, in fact nothing less than flood conditions.

Thus, when vast region-wide blankets of conglomerate rocks are found, only region-wide floods can explain them. And such phenomena are not at all uncommon in the geologic column. The Shinarump conglomerate of the Colorado Plateau, for example, spreads over an area of 125,000 square miles. Nothing like this is being formed in the world today, as uniformitarianism should require. There is even evidence of a blanket conglomerate of Miocene stratigraphy covering an area from Alberta to New Mexico and Utah to Kansas, containing boulders of granite and limestone in a matrix of silt.[1]

7. *Limestones and Dolostones*

Limestones are chemical sediments composed largely of calcium carbonate ($CaCO_3$) and dolostones are composed largely of dolomite, $CaMg (CO_3)_2$. The two are thus somewhat similar, except for the element magnesium found in dolomite.

Many marine organisms secrete calcite and aragonite, both of which chemically are calcium carbonate, so these materials are common in modern sediments. Calcite is an effective cementing agent, so it seems that limestone rocks could be forming today, possibly enclosing shells and other organic remains as fossils. A specific example would be a growing coral reef.

On the other hand, there are in the geologic column many massive limestones which are of such extent and such uniformity as to defy explanation in terms of any modern parallel. Nothing less than massive precipitation from solution in chemical-rich waters, when conditions of pH, temperature, etc., changed suddenly, seems adequate to account for them. This phenomenon is explicable in the context of a hydraulic cataclysm, but difficult to explain otherwise.

The dolomite rocks are even more difficult to explain on uniformitarian principles, since no dolomite sediments are being produced today at all. A standard textbook on stratigraphy says:

"Although dolostone is by no means uncommon among the sedimentary rocks of the geologic record, its origin is still uncertain. Probably the chief reason for this uncertainty is that, unlike the other major types of sediments, it is nowhere known to be forming today, and therefore the present fails us as a key to the past."[2]

Dolostones are often found associated with limestones, yet clearly distinct from them. Again it seems that only direct

---

[1] Stuart E. Nevins, "Stratigraphic Evidence of the Flood," in *Symposium on Creation #III* (Grand Rapids, Baker Book House, 1971) p. 59.

[2] C.O. Dunbar and John Rodgers, *Principles of Stratigraphy* (New York, John Wiley & Sons, Inc., 1957) p. 237.

precipitation from magnesium-rich flood waters can explain them.

8. Chert

Chert is a chemical sedimentary rock composed mostly of silica (SiO_2). Again uniformitarianism fails, for no bedded chert seems to be forming today. The best authorities explain it on the basis of direct precipitation from silica-bearing waters.

"The origin of the bedded cherts is a very controversial subject; . . . . Most students of bedded chert . . . regard them as primary precipitates of silica gel."[1]

Such processes are not occurring today, but would seem to require some kind of catastrophic volcanic outpouring, followed by a vast Flood to distribute the materials over wide areas.

9. Evaporites

A special type of rock that uniformitarians have often claimed as proving long periods of time is the evaporite. These are beds of either common salt, gypsum or anhydrite. The term "evaporite" itself is prejudicial, because it implies that the beds were formed by long-continued evaporation from inland seas or lakes containing saline waters.

The fact is, however, that there are no modern lakes or seas which are forming evaporite beds which are in any way comparable to many of the great thicknesses of such beds in the geologic column. Not only are the ancient evaporite beds far too thick, they are also much too pure to have been formed over millions of years by an evaporating relict sea. Almost certainly, they were formed either tectonically or by direct precipitation, not by evaporation at all.

The possibility of direct precipitation of evaporites has been shown by recent laboratory experiments:

"The following conclusions are based on the results of three brine experiments and their relations to a geologic model.

1. Salt precipitation can occur in a marine evaporite basin by mixing brines of different composition and specific gravity.

---

[1] F.G. Pettijohn, *Sedimentary Rocks* (2nd ed. New York, Harper and Row, 1957), p. 442.

2. Precipitation occurs without further loss by evaporation.

3. Precipitation can occur from brines that were undersaturated before mixing."[1]

In the context of a global hydraulic cataclysm, it is easy to visualize conditions which would result in this kind of precipitation.

Probably even more significant in this connection are the studies of the Russian geophysicist Sozansky, who has shown almost conclusively that "evaporite" deposits are actually in most cases the product of juvenile origin through tectonic movements.

"The absence of remains of marine organisms in ancient salts indicates that the formation of the salt-bearing sections was not related to the evaporation of marine water in epicontinental seas.

"Other geologic data, such as the great thickness of salt deposits, the rapid rate of formation of salt-bearing sections, the presence of ore minerals in salts and in the caprocks of salt domes do not conform with the bar hypothesis."

"The analysis of recent geologic data, including data on the diapirs found in ocean deeps, permits the conclusion that these salts are of a juvenile origin — that they emerged from great depths along faults during tectonic movements. This process is often accompanied by the discharge of basin magmas."[2]

The complete absence of organic material in "evaporites" is especially significant.

"It is well known that salts are chemically pure formations which are void of the remains of marine organisms. If salt-bearing sections were formed in lagoons or marginal seas by the evaporation of seawater, then organic matter, chiefly plankton, would have to enter the salt-forming basin together with the waters. As a

---

[1] Omer B. Roup, "Brine Mixing: An Additional Mechanism for Formation of Basin Evaporites," *Bulletin, American Association of Petroleum Geologists,* Vol. 54 (December 1970), p. 2258.

[2] V.I. Sozansky, "Origin of Salt Deposits in Deep-Water Basins of Atlantic Ocean," *Bulletin, American Association of Petroleum Geologists,* Vol. 57 (March 1973), p. 590.

result, the bottom sediments would be rich in organic matter."[1]

Thus, instead of supporting uniformitarianism and the concept of long ages, evaporite beds actually constitute a serious problem to the uniformitarian model. There is no present-day process at all capable of producing such formations. Evaporites clearly favor the cataclysmic model.

We have discussed all the more important types of rocks and have seen that each is incommensurate with modern processes and strongly suggests rapid formation. This fact of course supports our previous conclusion that the fossil deposits found in these rocks also require processes of rapid formation.

This fact is still further confirmed by a consideration of those geologic deposits which are of special economic interest, namely coal, oil and metallic ores. There is a widespread conception that long ages are required to produce these materials, but this is incorrect. Let us consider each of them briefly:

1. *Coal*

All agree that coal is composed of carbonized remains of great masses of plant remains. However, coal seams are regularly found interbedded with strata of shale, limestone or sandstone. Furthermore they are sometimes very thick and also are repeated dozens, sometimes scores, of times in a vertical section.

There is obviously no such phenomenon being produced in the present world. There are many existing peat bogs, of course, but none of these grade vertically downward into a series of coal seams. The uniformitarian peat-bog theory of coal seam origin seems quite unrelated to the real world.

A very obvious proof that coal beds must have been formed rapidly is the existence of "polystrate" fossil tree trunks, as well as other polystrate fossils (that is, fossils extending through several strata of coal and the other rock units) in the coal beds.

"In 1959 Broadhurst and Magraw described a fossilized tree, in position of growth, from the Coal Measures at Blackrod near Wigan in Lancashire. This tree was preserved as a cast, and the evidence available suggested

---

[1] *Ibid*, p. 589.

that the cast was at least 38 feet in height. The original tree must have been surrounded and buried by sediment which was compacted before the bulk of the tree decomposed so that the cavity vacated by the trunk could be occupied by new sediment which formed the cast. This implies a rapid rate of sedimentation around the original tree."[1]

This is not at all an unusual phenomenon, but is quite common. N. A. Rupke, of Princeton, has given numerous examples.[2] Broadhurst also says:

"It is clear that trees in position of growth are far from being rare in Lancashire (Teichmuller, 1956, reaches the same conclusion for similar trees in the Rhein-Westfalen Coal Measures), and presumably in all cases there must have been a rapid rate of sedimentation."[3]

There are many other evidences that coal seams were formed rapidly, probably by transportation of massed plant accumulations by flooding waters, interspersed by alternative flows of sand or silt or lime mud from other directions. These are listed as follows, without comment or documentation (although such could be provided, if needed)[4]:

a. Fossil trees are sometimes found standing on an angle and even upside down in the coal seams.

b. Coal seams occasionally split into two seams separated by transported marine sediments.

c. Marine fossils — tubeworms, sponges, corals, mollusks, etc., — are often found in coal beds.

d. Many coal seams have no sign of a fossil soil under them. The "underclays" sometimes cited are not true soils, with a soil profile, and most authorities now believe they are transported materials.

e. Large boulders are often found in coal beds.

f. The so-called *stigmaria*, sometimes cited as roots of the

---

[1] F.M. Broadhurst, "Some Aspects of the Paleoecology of Non-Marine Faunas and Rates of Sedimentation in the Lancashire Coal Measures," *American Journal of Science*, Vol. 262 (Summer 1964), p. 865.

[2] N.A. Rupke, "Prolegomena to a Study of Cataclysmal Sedimentation," *Quarterly of the Creation Research Society*, Vol. 3 (May 1966), pp. 16-37.

[3] F.M. Broadhurst, *op cit*, p. 866.

[4] See S.E. Nevins, *op cit*, pp. 44-46.

coal-seam trees, have been shown by Rupke to be fragments unattached to specific trees and actually transported into place by water currents.[1]

But probably the most conclusive evidence against the
uniformitarian concept of coal origin is the very concept
itself — namely that there could be scores of cycles of peat
bog growth, subsidence, transgression of marine strata,
uplift, renewed peat bog growth, and so on, each such cycle
lasting for vast ages. For example, consider the following:

"In the case of the Permo-Carboniferous of India, the
Barakar Series of the Damuda Series, overlying the
Talchir Boulder Bed, includes numerous coal seams,
some up to 100 feet thick, occurring in a well-developed
and oft-repeated cycle of sandstone, shale, coal. . . . The
vegetation is considered to be drift accumulation.

"The concept of periodic epirogeny is a reasonable one,
but a more or less complete cessation of clastic sedimentation in the lacustrine basin during coal accumulation is difficult to account for on a wholly diastrophic
origin. As an explanation for the fifty to sixty cycles of
the Damuda system, it has an element of unreality."[2]

We suggest that the flood model of coal vegetation
accumulation is much more realistic. The conversion of the
vegetation into coal, through adiabatic[3] compression, heating, and shearing stresses, is much more easily visualized in
terms of catastrophism than slow vertical accumulation of
sediments.

2. *Oil*

Just as coal is fossil plant material, so most geologists
believe oil to be the converted remains of millions of trapped
and buried marine animals, mostly the soft parts of invertebrates (though there is evidence that buried fishes may also
have contributed). The exact manner of origin of oil is quite
obscure and, of course, this very fact militates against
uniformitarianism. Oil is not being formed today, nor is it

---

[1]N.A. Rupke, "Sedimentary Evidence for the Allochthonous Origin of
Stigmaria, Carboniferous, Nova Scotia," *Bulletin, Geological Society of America,* Vol. 80 (1969), pp. 2109-2114.
[2]S.E. Hollingsworth, "The Climatic Factor in the Geological Record."
Quarterly Journal, Geological Society of London, Vol. 118 (March 1962), p. 13.
[3]i.e. without gain or loss of heat.

found even in Pleistocene (Ice-Age) deposits. It almost certainly was formed by some kind of catastrophic burial of vast numbers of marine organisms.

The subsequent conversion of this organic matter into hydrocarbons and then into petroleum is a function more of temperature and pressure than of time. That long ages need not be required has been strikingly indicated by recent laboratory manufacture of oil from garbage!

"There is great promise in a system being developed by government scientists that converts organic material to oil and gas by treating it with carbon monoxide and water at high temperature and pressure. . . .

"By using the waste-to-oil process, 1.1 billion barrels of oil could be gleaned from the 880 million tons of organic wastes suitable for conversion (each year)."[1]

3. *Metals*

The formation of ore deposits is likewise inexplicable in terms of any slow, uniformitarian process. Their mode of formation is not at all certain, so far as geologists are concerned, but is generally believed to have been associated with flows of magma. Igneous rock flows are, as already noted, rapid and of short duration, so the same must likewise be true of the metallic flows associated with them. In any case, nothing of the sort is taking place now, so far as known, even in volcanic lava flows. The uniformitarian model once again seems inadequate. The cataclysmic model seems more likely to be productive, but as yet there is no specific explanation in this framework either. In any event, since the uniformitarian approach which has been followed heretofore has been so notably unproductive in either locating or explaining metal deposits, a systematic analysis in terms of cataclysmic processes would be at least worth a try.

There are many other types of deposits which seem incapable of explanation in uniformitarian terms.

"We find certain rock types in the geologic column that are not being seen to form, at least in quantity, anywhere on earth today. Where can granite be observed

---

[1] Larry L. Anderson, "Oil Made from Garbage," *Science Digest*, Vol. 74 (July 1973), p. 77.

forming? Where can dolomite or siliceous iron formations be seen to form in quantity? Yet we have thousands of cubic miles of these rock types in the crust of the earth. The Paleozoic Era was marked by carbonate rock deposition, yet carbonate types are quite subordinate in modern sequences of sediments. Herz (1969) attributes the formation of anorthosite to the 'anorthosite event,' which was possibly a great cataclysm in the Precambrian history of the earth. It is possible that other rock types were created during and following catastrophic events on earth."[1]

We do not claim that the cataclysmic model encounters no problems, or that more research is unnecessary. It does seem, however, that it has fewer and less serious problems than uniformitarianism.

Contemporaneity of the Fossil World

We have shown that the fossil deposits required rapid burial in each case and also that all the major types of rock formations are best understood in terms of rapid deposition. Since each particular deposit was formed rapidly, the question naturally arises as to whether the entire series of deposits, representing the whole geologic column, may have been formed rapidly.

The evolution model, of course, cannot possibly allow a rapid formation of the entire column. If evolution functions at all, it requires aeons of time in earth history. Thus the geologic column, which ostensibly represents this history, must at all costs be interpreted in terms of vast ages. Therefore, even though each segment of the column must be interpreted in terms of rapid formation, somehow the whole system must be made to fit the uniformitarian assumption of long ages. This means that there must be extensive time gaps in the column, when no deposition was occurring.

The creation model, on the other hand, can interpret the column in terms of essentially continuous deposition, all accomplished in a relatively short time—not instantaneously, of course, but over a period of months or years, rather than

---

[1] Edgar B. Heylmun, "Should We Teach Uniformitarianism?" *Journal of Geological Education*, Vol. 19 (January 1971), p. 36.

millions of years. In effect, this means that the organisms represented in the fossil record would all have been living contemporaneously, rather than scattered in separate time-frames over hundreds of millions of years.

In other words, the fossil world was much like our own world. If the present is really the key to the past, as uniformitarians allege, why should this be surprising? In the present world are found one-celled organisms, marine invertebrates, fishes, amphibians, reptiles, birds, mammals and men. The only reason to think that all should not have been living contemporaneously in the past is the assumption of evolution. Apart from this premise, there is no reason to doubt that man lived at the same time as the dinosaurs and trilobites.

We need, therefore, to consider two questions: (1) Is there evidence in the stratigraphic column of continuous deposition from beginning to end; (2) Is there evidence that fossils from different "ages" in the column may actually have been living at the same time?

The answer to both questions is "yes." The geologic column does not represent the slow evolution of life over many ages, as the evolution model alleges, but rather the rapid destruction and burial of life in one age, in accordance with the contemporaneous catastrophism model.

Consider first the question of the continuity of the strata. The major portion of the geologic column is of course composed of stratified rocks, in most cases originally deposited as sediments by moving water. These are grouped in units called "formations," each of which consists of a considerable number of strata, or layers, and extends over a certain regional area, of greater or lesser extent.

To properly evaluate the time factor in the deposition of these sedimentary strata, one must consider the nature of the hydraulic processes which deposited them. This requires some knowledge of the mechanics of sedimentation.

Each stratum may be from a fraction of an inch to several inches in thickness. It is distinguished from the strata above and below by "stratification planes" at the interface. The adjacent strata may be of the same material, contain the same types of fossils and look very much like it. The planes between them, however, indicate that some slight difference must have intervened to denote a break — either a brief time-lapse in deposition, or a slight change in one or more of the characteristics of the sediment-forming flow.

The phenomenon of sediment transportation and deposition is quite complex and depends upon many different factors — flow velocity, flow direction, flow volume, flow depth, flow width, channel slope, channel roughness, water temperature, character of material in stratum bed, supply of sediment to stream, dissolved chemicals, and others. If any one of these factors changes, then the sedimentary characteristics of the flow will change. Consequently a stratification plane would form at any area of deposition and a new stratum would begin to form with slightly different characteristics.

Suppose, however, that there is a long period of interruption of the depositional process at the top of a certain stratum. If water continues to flow, the stratum may begin to be eroded, or at least the ripples and other irregularities on its surface will be eroded. If the water flow itself stops, then subaerial erosion will take place. Possibly the strata may even be uplifted and tilted, so that the period of erosion will "truncate"[1] the beds. The resulting surface in either case will become an erosional surface. If the surface of truncation is parallel to the stratification planes, it is called a "disconformity" or "paraconformity"; if at an angle, it is called an "unconformity."

When an unconformity exists between two sets of strata, it is obvious that there has been a period of erosion in between. A paraconformity, however, is difficult or impossible to distinguish from a normal stratification plane, except possibly by the absence of the normal surficial irregularities at the bedding plane, or possibly by a change in the mineralogical or paleontological contents of the beds above and below.

Now an unconformity may conceivably indicate a long period of erosion. One might at first suppose that major unconformities could be used to note a time break — perhaps the end of one geological epoch and the beginning of another. The problem with this, however, is that *there is no worldwide unconformity!* A time break in one region may not be noted in another region at all.

---

[1] i.e., cut off.

"The employment of unconformities as time-stratigraphic boundaries should be abandoned. Because of the failures of unconformities as time indices, time-stratigraphic boundaries of Paleozoic and later age must be defined by time — hence by faunas."[1]

The above quotation points out that the only way to tell when one age has ended and another begun is by the fossil record. For this purpose a paraconformity should be as useful as an unconformity, since a change in faunas can be noted without respect to the inclination of the bedding planes of the strata containing them. Jeletzky also notes this:

"It is indeed a well established fact that the (physical-stratigraphical) rock units and their boundaries often transgress geologic time planes in most irregular fashion even within the shortest distances."[2]

Since physical unconformities therefore do not necessarily indicate a significant time lapse, is it indeed possible that such breaks can be indicated by changes in fossil assemblages? This has often been assumed; in fact, the geological time-scale itself actually was originally worked out by the 19th-century geologists largely on this assumption. But even this venerable geologic belief is now being questioned:

"The boundaries between eras, periods and epochs on the geological time-scale generally denote sudden and significant changes in the character of fossil remains. For example, the boundary between the Triassic and Jurassic periods of the Mesozoic era (about 180 million years ago) was supposedly marked by spontaneous appearance of new species. . . . A reassessment of the data by Jost Wiedmann of the University of Tubingen in the Federal Republic of Germany gives a clearer picture of evolution at the boundaries of the Mesozoic (225 million to 70 million years ago). He concludes that there were no worldwide extinctions of species or spontaneous appearances of new species at the boundaries."[3]

[1] H.E. Wheeler and E.M. Beesley, "Critique of the Time-Stratigraphic Concept," *Bulletin, Geological Society of America*, Vol. 59 (1948), p. 84.

[2] J.A. Jeletzsky, "Paleontology, Basis of Practical Geochronology," *Bulletin, American Association of Petroleum Geologists*, April 1956, p. 685.

[3] "Fossil Changes: 'Normal Evolution,'" *Science News*, Vol. 102 (September 2, 1972) (Reporting International Geological Congress at Montreal), p. 152.

Now the two boundaries cited (Paleozoic to Mesozoic and Mesozoic to Cenozoic) are the most important and fundamental of all. If there is no observable time break between these, either in terms of physical unconformities or changes in faunas, then there is no such break anywhere! In other words, the stratigraphic record shows that each "age" merges gradually and imperceptibly into the next "age." One cannot really determine strictly where one age starts and another ends. In other words *there are no time-breaks; the record is continuous.*

Now recall again that each of the individual rock units shows evidence of rapid formation. The fossil deposits, which date the rock units, all show evidence of rapid formation. If there are no time breaks between the various ages (or, more precisely, between the various stratigraphic systems which supposedly denote the various ages), then it seems rigidly necessary to conclude that the entire assemblage of rock units constituting the geologic column shows evidence of rapid formation.

Let us summarize again this chain of reasoning:
1. Each stratum must have been formed rapidly, since it represents a constant set of hydraulic factors which cannot remain constant very long.
2. Each succeeding stratum in a formation must have followed rapidly after its preceding stratum, since its surface irregularities have not been truncated by erosion.
3. Therefore the entire formation must have been formed continuously and rapidly. This is further confirmed by the fact that its rock type required rapid formation and its fossil contents required rapid and permanent burial.
4. Although the formation may be capped by an unconformity, there is no worldwide unconformity, so that if it is traced out laterally far enough, it will eventually grade imperceptibly into another formation, which therefore succeeds it continuously and rapidly without a time break at that point.
5. The same reasoning will show that the strata of the second formation were also formed rapidly and continuously, and so on to a third formation somewhere succeeding that one.
6. Thus, stratum-by-stratum and formation-by-formation, one may proceed through the entire geologic column,

proving the whole column to have been formed rapidly and continuously.

7. The merging of one formation into the next is further indicated by the well-recognized fact that there is rarely ever a clear physical boundary between formations. More commonly the rock types tend to merge and mingle with each other over a zone of considerable thickness.

Our first question, therefore, as to whether the geologic column is continuous, rather than sporadic, seems clearly to have been answered in the affirmative. The rapid, even cataclysmic, character of most of its individual units thus plainly argue for the rapid formation of the entire system.

The other question is whether there is evidence that fossil organisms from different "ages" actually may have been living contemporaneously. Or, in other words, is the geologic column an objective reality, with distinctive fossils associated with each of its components, or is it partially an artificial system based on the evolution model?

In the preceding chapter, we pointed out much evidence that the plants and animals in the fossils were much the same as in the present world. The same classification system applies, with the same categories and the same gaps between the categories. Most modern plants and animals can be found in the fossils, and a great many fossil animals and plants are still living today, especially when we allow for variations within the kinds to adjust to changing environments.

All of which indicates that many organisms of the fossils, in all "ages," were indeed contemporaneous, since they have in fact survived into the present era.

Creationists do not question the general validity of the geologic column, however, at least as an indicator of the *usual* order of deposition of the fossils, since this same order fits perfectly the cataclysmic model. The *exceptions* to this usual order (of which there are many) are actually much easier to resolve in terms of the cataclysmic model (in fact, they are predicted by it) than in terms of the evolution model.

The exceptions to the standard order of the geologic column are primarily of two kinds: (1) localities where strata assigned to an "older" age in the column are found resting conformably on top of strata assigned to a "younger" age; (2)

strata in which fossils assigned uniquely to two or more different "ages" are found together.

Both types of situations are found fairly frequently, and evolutionists as well as creationists acknowledge this. Creationists as well as evolutionists acknowledge also that these situations are not normative, but exceptional. The question becomes one, then, of which model is least disturbed by these exceptions.

Before discussing these anomalies, however, we should first establish that the standard order of the geologic column is indeed the order predicted from the cataclysmic model. The order is not at all uniquely a prediction of evolution.

The creation model postulates that all the organisms of the fossil record were originally created contemporaneously by the Creator during the creation period. They thus lived together in the same world, just as the equivalent plants and animals all live together in the present world. However, they lived in ecologic communities, just as is true in the present world. Man would not live with dinosaurs and trilobites, for example, any more than he now lives with crocodiles and starfish.

Visualize, then, a great hydraulic cataclysm bursting upon the present world, with currents of waters pouring perpetually from the skies and erupting continuously from the earth's crust, all over the world, for weeks on end, until the entire globe was submerged, accompanied by outpourings of magma from the mantle, gigantic earth movements, landslides, tsunamis, and explosions. The uniformitarian will of course question how such a cataclysm could be caused, and this will be considered shortly, but for the moment simply take it as a model and visualize the expected results if it should happen today.

Sooner or later all land animals would perish. Many, but not all, marine animals would perish. Human beings would swim, run, climb, and attempt to escape the floods but, unless a few managed to ride out the cataclysm in unusually strong watertight sea-going vessels, they would eventually all drown or otherwise perish.

Soils would soon erode away and trees and plants be uprooted and carried down toward the sea in great mats on flooding streams. Eventually the hills and mountains themselves would disintegrate and flow downstream in great

117

landslides and turbidity currents. Slabs of rock would crack and bounce and gradually be rounded into boulders and gravel and sand. Vast seas of mud and rock would flow downriver, trapping many animals and rafting great masses of plants with them.

On the ocean bottom, upwelling sediments and subterranean waters and magmas would entomb hordes of invertebrates. The waters would undergo rapid changes in heat and salinity, great slurries would form, and immense amounts of chemicals would be dissolved and dispersed throughout the seaways.

Eventually, the land sediments and waters would commingle with those in the ocean. Finally the sediments would settle out as the waters slowed down, dissolved chemicals would precipitate out at times and places where the salinity and temperature permitted, and great beds of sediment, soon to be cemented into rock, would be formed all over the world.

The above of course is only the barest outline of the great variety of phenomena that would accompany such a cataclysm. The very complexity of the model makes it extremely versatile in its ability to explain a wide diversity of data (although, admittedly, this makes it difficult to test).

The immediate point under discussion, however, is what it would imply with respect to the order of the fossils in the geologic column. A little consideration will quickly yield the following obvious predictions.

1. As a rule, there would be many more marine invertebrate animals trapped and buried in the sediments than other types, since there are many more of them and, being relatively immobile, they would usually be unable to escape.

2. Animals caught and buried would normally be buried with others living in the same region. In other words, fossil assemblages would tend to represent ecological communities of the pre-cataclysmic world.

3. In general, animals living at the lowest elevations would tend to be buried at the lowest elevations, and so on, with elevations in the strata thus representing relative elevations of habitat or ecological zones.

4. Marine invertebrates would normally be found in the bottom rocks of any local geologic column, since they

live on the sea bottom.

5. Marine vertebrates (fishes) would be found in higher rocks than the bottom-dwelling invertebrates. They live at higher elevations and also could escape burial longer.

6. Amphibians and reptiles would tend to be found at still higher elevations, in the commingled sediments at the interface between land and water.

7. There would be few if any terrestrial sediments or land plants or animals in the lower strata of the column.

8. The first evidence of land plants in the column would be essentially the same as that for amphibians and reptiles, when the rafts of lowland vegetation were brought down to the seashore by the swollen rivers.

9. In the marine strata, where invertebrates were fossilized, these would tend locally to be sorted hydrodynamically into assemblages of similar size and shape. Furthermore, as the turbulently upwelling waters and sediments settled back down, the simpler animals, more nearly spherical or streamlined in shape, would tend to settle out first because of lower hydraulic drag. Thus each kind of marine invertebrate would tend to appear in its simplest form at the lowest elevation, and so on.

10. Mammals and birds would be found in general at higher elevations than reptiles and amphibians, both because of their habitat and because of their greater mobility. However, few birds would be found at all, only occasional exhausted birds being trapped and buried in sediments.

11. Because of the instinctive tendency of the higher animals to congregate in herds, particularly in times of danger, fossils of these animals would often be found in large numbers if found at all.

12. Similarly these higher animals (land vertebrates) would tend to be found segregated vertically in the column in order of size and complexity, because of the greater ability of the larger, more diversified animals to escape burial for longer periods of time.

13. Very few human fossils or artifacts would be found at all. Men would escape burial for the most part and, after the waters receded, their bodies would lie on the ground until decomposed. The same would apply to their lighter structures and implements, whereas heavier metallic objects would sink to the bottom and be buried so deeply

119

      in the sediments they would probably never be discovered.

14. All the above predictions would be expected statistically but, because of the cataclysmic nature of the phenomena, would also admit of many exceptions in every case. In other words, the cataclysmic model predicts the general order and character of the deposits but also allows for occasional exceptions.

Now there is no question that all of the above predictions from the cataclysmic model are explicitly confirmed in the geologic column. The general order from simple to complex in the fossil record in the geologic column, considered by evolutionists to be the main proof of evolution, is thus likewise predicted by the rival model, only with more precision and detail. But it is the exceptions that are inimical to the evolution model.

For example, consider the out-of-order strata. These have to be explained by the secondary assumptions of overthrusting or underthrusting, to provide for great earth movements to reverse the original order of deposition. Either great blocks of older rock have to be lifted up and then slid over the younger rocks, or else great thicknesses of younger sediments have to dip down and push under older sediments.

The forces involved in such behavior are obviously tremendous and geophysicists have found it difficult to account for them. Also the grinding and breaking action at the thrust plane would have to leave great amounts of debris and geologists have found it difficult to locate them. This subject, in so far as overthrusting is concerned, is discussed in some detail elsewhere[1] for those interested. The newer idea of underthrusting, associated with the "subduction" concept in current discussions of plate tectonics, seems even more imaginative.

> "Early studies of mountain geology revealed that mountains are sites of tremendous folding and thrusting of the earth's crust. In many places the oceanic sediments of which mountains are composed are inverted, with the older sediments lying on top of the younger. . . . At a

---

[1] J.C. Whitcomb and H.M. Morris, *The Genesis Flood* (Philadelphia, Presbyterian and Reformed Publ. Co., 1961) pp. 180-211.

trench in the eastern Mediterranean, one oceanic plate is sliding beneath another. . . . In one location, they found limestones 120 million years old directly above oozes only 5 million to 10 million years in age."[1]

The mechanics of how a young "ooze" would ooze under solid limestone at the bottom of the sea seems obscure at best.

The other exception to the usual order occurs when fossils from different zones are mixed together. The evolutionary explanation for this phenomenon has to be in terms either of "re-working" of originally separate strata or of "contamination" of ancient strata by some kind of intrusion of younger materials (or vice versa).

In the nature of the case, such explanations are difficult either to confirm or refute since we do not have at hand a "time-machine" to observe what actually happened. The cataclysmic model is not embarrassed in either case.

There are a few such instances which do seem exceedingly difficult to believe in terms of either re-working or contamination. The most spectacular cases are those in which fossils of the most "recent" evolutionary arrival, man, are found associated with much more "ancient" formations.

For example, consider the following:

"An ancient Mayan relief sculpture of a peculiar bird with reptilian characteristics has been discovered in Totonacapan, in the northeastern section of Veracruz, Mexico. Jose Diaz-Bolio, a Mexican archaeologist-journalist responsible for the discovery, says there is evidence that the serpent-bird sculpture, located in the ruins of Tajin, is not merely the product of Mayan flights of fancy, but a realistic representation of an animal that lived during the period of the ancient Mayan — 1000 to 5000 years ago.

"If indeed such serpent-birds *were* contemporary with the ancient Mayan culture, the relief sculpture represents a startling evolutionary oddity. Animals with such characteristics are believed to have disappeared 130 million years ago. The archaeornis and the archaeopteryx, to which the sculpture bears a vague resem-

---

[1] B.F. Ryan, "Mountain-Building in the Mediterranean," *Science News*, Vol. 98 (October 17, 1970), p. 316.

blance, were flying reptiles that became extinct during the Mesozoic age of dinosaurs."[1]

The evidence seems clear that archaeopteryx, or some equivalent ancient bird, was contemporaneous with man and only became extinct a few thousand years ago.

As a matter of fact, a great many such anomalous artifacts and fossils have been found. Unfortunately these have, for the most part, been reported in the popular press, then either ridiculed or passed over by the scientific authorities, and then forgotten. Human skeletons and implements have been reported deep in coal mines, even solidly embedded in coal, pictographs of dinosaurs found on cave and canyon walls, human footprints in ancient trilobite beds, fossil pollen from modern-type trees found in the most ancient marine strata, and so on.

One of the most spectacular examples of anomalous fossils is the now well-known case of the Paluxy River footprints, in the Cretaceous Glen Rose formation of central Texas. Here, in the limestone beds are found large numbers of both dinosaur and human footprints. The tracks occur in trails and in two or three locations, the dinosaur and human trials cross each other, with two known cases where human and dinosaur tracks actually overlap each other.

This particular case obviously cannot be dismissed as an example of "re-working" of two originally distinct fossil deposits. Neither can they be attributed to modern carvings, as many of the tracks, both of man and dinosaur, were freshly exposed by excavation of overlying strata within the past few years by a large team of workers and observers.

It seems that the only possible escape from the conclusion that man and dinosaurs were contemporary is to say that the human tracks were not really human but were made by some unknown two-legged animal with feet like human feet! Since no one has ever seen such an animal, living or fossil, such a suggestion (and it was made quite seriously in the presence of the writer, by a Ph.D. geologist while looking at the actual tracks!) is surely harder to believe than to believe that man and dinosaur lived at the same time.

---

[1] "Serpent-bird of the Mayans, *Science Digest*, Vol. 64 (November 1968), p. 1.

These tracks and their discovery have been conclusively documented by on-the-site, at-the-time, motion pictures. The skeptic is urged to arrange to see this film[1] before he dismisses the evidence out-of-hand, as too many evolutionists have done in the past. Also the book *Tracking Those Incredible Dinosaurs and the People Who Knew Them*[2] gives many photos and descriptions of these anomalous tracks.

Residual Catastrophism

Creationists are convinced there is more than adequate evidence confirming the general cataclysmic model of the fossiliferous strata. The greater part of the entire geologic column must have been formed rapidly and continuously, in one great complex of catastrophes in the not-too-distant past. Although volcanic and tectonic upheavals were involved, the strata were largely formed hydraulically, so that the cataclysm as a whole had the primary character of a worldwide flood.

Many of the uppermost formations, however, as well as most of the earth's present surface features, are no doubt attributable to the residual catastrophism of the post-Flood period, rather than to the Flood itself. There has been extensive tectonic, volcanic and glaciological activity, as well as storms and floods of regional (rather than global) extent essentially down to historic times.

To appreciate this continuing aspect of the cataclysmic model, we must consider further the nature and cause of the major cataclysm itself. What could cause a global flood, with attendant igneous and tectonic activity, such as we have postulated and such as the actual strata seem to reflect?

An important clue is found in the fact that rocks from all "ages," along with their fossil contents, all indicate a worldwide warm climate, with no distinct climatological zones such as we have today.

"It has long been felt that the average climate of the earth throughout time has been milder and more homo-

---

[1]*Footprints in Stone,* available on rental basis from Films-for Christ Association, R.R. 2, Eden Road, Elmwood, Illinois 61529.
[2]By Dr. John D. Morris (San Diego: Creation Life Publishers, 1980), 240 pp.

geneous than it is today. If so, the present certainly is *not* a very good key to the past in terms of climate."[1]

Some writers have suggested continental drift as an explanation of how fossils of sub-tropical fauna and flora are now found in polar regions. However, this explanation will not suffice.

"For example, there is little evidence that climatic belts existed in the earlier history of the earth, yet climatic zonation, both latitudinal and vertical, is clearly apparent in all parts of the earth today. This anomalous situation is difficult to explain. It is impossible to reconstruct a super-continent which could lie entirely within one climatic regime. Any rotating planet, orbiting the sun on an inclined axis of rotation, must have climatic zonation. It is obvious, therefore, that climatic conditions in the past were significantly different from those in evidence today."[2]

Even if the earth's axis were not inclined, there would still be a latitudinal climatic zonation. Consequently, the universal warm climate evidenced in the fossil record cannot be explained by any different arrangement of the earth's physical structure.

The most likely explanation is that something *outside* the earth's surface so controlled the incoming solar energy as to maintain a global greenhouse-type environment. There are three components of the atmosphere which, in lesser measure, have this function today; namely, ozone, carbon dioxide and water vapor.

If one or more of these were a much more abundant constituent of the atmosphere prior to the cataclysm, there would indeed have been a universal "greenhouse effect." The most important is water vapor. If there were, in the beginning, a vast thermal blanket of water vapor somewhere above the troposphere, then not only would the climate be affected, but there also would be an adequate source to explain the atmospheric waters necessary for the Flood.

---

[1] R.H. Dott and R.L. Batten, *Evolution of the Earth* (New York, McGraw-Hill Book Co., 1971) p. 298.

[2] Edgar B. Heylmun, "Should We Teach Uniformitarianism?," *Journal of Geological Education*, Vol. 19 (January 1971), p. 36.

However, the postulated cataclysm also involves tectonic and magmatic upheavals, as well as tremendous hydraulic and sedimentary disturbances, on the bottom of the ocean. Thus a secondary source of water is postulated as existing in vast subterranean heated and pressurized reservoirs, perhaps in the primeval crust or perhaps in the earth's mantle itself, a situation similar to that existing at present but greater in quantity. The explosive release of those waters, accompanied by magmas and followed by earth movements, provides another cause of the cataclysm.

The primeval creation of those two vast bodies of water, one above the troposphere and the other deep in the earth's crust, would thus serve the dual purpose of providing a perfect environment for terrestrial life and also for transmitting the energy for the universal cataclysm which later would destroy that life.

On the surface of the primeval world, it is postulated, there was probably an intricate network of narrow seas and waterways whose precise locations need yet to be determined. Though the uniform climate would inhibit air mass movements, as well as storms and heavy rains, a daily cycle of local evaporation and condensation would maintain an equable humidity everywhere. The favorable climate, aided by the highly effective radiation filter provided by the vapor canopy, would favor abundant plant and animal life, longevity of animal life, and growth of large-sized animal organisms.

The trigger to unleash the stored waters and initiate the cataclysm might have been any one of a number of things. The simplest explanation would be to assume that the pressurized waters below the crust suddenly erupted at a point of weakness. Collapse at one point would cause a chain reaction leading to similar eruptions at many other points around the world.

The turbulence in the atmosphere which would result, together with immense amounts of dust blown skyward, would then initiate the condensation and precipitation of the vapor canopy.

This concept, which seems quite realistic in terms of the basic cataclysmic model, suffices to explain a great many features of the geologic strata, and also a framework within which to research the origin of the other features.

Such a model of the cataclysm and its cause also indicates

that the after-effects would continue for centuries, perhaps in some measure even to the present time. A few of the more important of these after-effects so inferred are the following:

1. *Mountain-Building*

One of the most important unsolved problems in uniformitarian geology is the cause of mountain-building. As Dott and Batten admit:

"A uniquely satisfactory theory of mountain-building still eludes us."[1]

Furthermore, the major mountain systems of the present world are, geologically speaking, quite young, at least in so far as their most recent periods of uplift are concerned. Richard Foster Flint, the Yale glacial geologist, in fact attributed the onset of the glacial age in the Pleistocene Epoch largely to the worldwide orogenies just prior to that time. In a review of these phenomena, he said:

"The cumulative result of both gradual and successive uplifts throughout the entire second half of the Cenozoic era was an increase in the average height of the continents from an estimated value of less than 1000 feet to their present height of 2500 feet."[2]

The greatest mountain system of all, the Himalayas, was uplifted only after man's presence on the earth.

"Most of the vast uplift of the Himalayas is ascribed to the latest Tertiary and Pleistocene."[3]

The vast isostatic readjustments necessary after the Flood, perhaps augmented by drifting and colliding continents also triggered by the Flood, provides the best explanation of mountain-building now available.

2. *Glaciation*

Prior to the cataclysm, the greenhouse effect precluded the formation of glaciers and ice-caps. The dissipation of the canopy, however, quickly established latitudinal differentials in temperature. The tremendous release of energy at the Flood continued for a long time to supply moisture from the new ocean surfaces to the atmosphere, much of it to be re-

---

[1] R.H. Dott and R.L. Batten, *op cit*, p. 417.
[2] R.F. Flint, *Glacial Geology and the Pleistocene Epoch* (New York, John Wiley and Sons, 1947), p. 515.
[3] *Ibid*, p. 514.

precipitated as snow in the polar regions. These phenomena led to the development of the great continental ice-sheets of the Pleistocene Epoch.

It is significant that no satisfactory uniformitarian model exists for the cause of these great glaciers of the Pleistocene:

"Geologists and climatologists have tried for more than a century to explain the recurrence of glaciation on a continental scale. Theory after theory has been suggested, but all explain too little or too much. None can be considered satisfactory, at least in its present form."[1]

The cataclysmic theory, however, as outlined briefly above, does appear to provide a satisfactory explanation.

3. *Pluviation*

It is well known that, during and after the times of the continental glaciers in the higher latitudes, there was much more rainfall in the lower latitudes. The deserts, even the Sahara, had an abundance of water. All the lakes and interior basins had much higher water levels, and the rivers of the world all carried much greater volumes of water.

These rains often were in the form of violent storms and there is much evidence in the geological and archaeological records, as well as in the mythological traditions of man's early history, of devastating local and regional floods. All of this was a natural consequence of the great Flood itself, as the earth was gradually settling into a new hydrological balance.

4. *Volcanism*

In the subterranean eruptions accompanying the Flood, great quantities of molten rock were released from the earth's mantle, as evidenced in the abundance of igneous rocks and volcanic strata found throughout the geologic column. When the Flood subsided and isostatic readjustments had taken place, there must still have been many volcanic vents and fissures around the world which were not completely plugged. Consequently, volcanic action would continue intermittently long after the Flood itself.

That this has actually occurred is evident from the great volcanic terrains of Pleistocene and even post-Pleistocene

---

[1] J. Gilluly, A.C. Waters & A.O. Woodford, *Principles of Geology* (San Francisco, W.H. Freeman Co., 1952), p. 319.

date found at various places around the world. There are also a great number of volcanoes which are still active and an even greater number of volcanoes which have apparently become extinct only in very recent times.

5. *Continental Drift*

Until about 1960, the old idea of continental drift had been rejected and even ridiculed by practically all geologists, who were convinced they had worked out a complete explanation of earth history and the stratified rocks in terms of stable and permanent continents. Currently, however, the pendulum has swung and most geologists have become committed to the concepts of plate tectonics, sea-floor spreading and continental drift. All the older explanations, which they once dogmatically accepted as certainties, have now been discarded in favor of drift-centered concepts. There still remains a minority of outstanding earth scientists (Jeffries, Meyerhoff, the Russian geophysicists, *et al*) who oppose the idea of continental drift as geophysically impossible, and there are some signs that indicate the pendulum may be starting to swing back again.

The cataclysmic model makes no specific predictions regarding continental drift, so is not affected either way. However, one of the main difficulties with the concept as developed in a uniformitarian context has always been the absence of a source for the tremendous energy required to drive continents apart. The cataclysmic model, with its store of tremendous subterranean energy suddenly released at the time of the Flood, alone seems capable of accounting for the energy. It is plausible that it may have occurred, along with continued tectonic and volcanic activity, as another after-effect of the great Flood.

All of these phenomena of what we have called residual catastrophism — mountain-building, glaciation, pluviation, volcanism, and possibly continental drift, along with others that might be discussed if necessary — represent the dying phases of the great Flood. They must have occurred at high intensity during the closing phases of the Flood itself, as well as for perhaps centuries after the Flood. Their effects have asymptotically decreased in accordance with some sort of decay curve until they have reached a relative degree of quiescence at the present time.

This means that it is difficult to arrive at an exact chronology for the Flood itself. A goal of the Flood model would be to organize the geologic strata of the earth into a standard geologic column based on the cataclysmic chronology to substitute for the currently standard geologic column based on the evolutionary, uniformitarian chronology. In general, as we have noted, the general order of the strata is predicted from both models, so that to some extent it is possible to set up an "equation" converting uniformitarian stratigraphic nomenclature into corresponding chronologic units associated with the sequences of the cataclysm.

Such an equivalence, in preliminary form, might be roughly expressed in the following table.

Standard System	Corresponding Stage of the Flood
Recent	Period of post-Flood development of modern world
Pleistocene	Post-Flood effects of glaciation and pluviation, along with lessening volcanism and tectonism
Tertiary	Final phases of the Flood, along with initial phases of the post-Flood readjustments.
Mesozoic	Intermediate phases of the Flood, with mixtures of continental and marine deposits. Post-Flood possibly in some cases.
Paleozoic	Deep-sea and shelf deposits formed in the early phases of the Flood, mostly in the ocean.
Proterozoic	Initial sedimentary deposits of the early phases of the Flood.
Archaeozoic	Origin of crust dating from the Creation Period, though disturbed and metamorphosed by the thermal and tectonic changes during the Cataclysm.

A great deal of research needs yet to be done, of course, to work out the details of this proposed revised geologic column. It should be remembered that the work of thousands of geologists for 150 years has all been described and classified in terms of the standard evolutionary column, so that the work of re-classifying this mass of material represents a monumental task which cannot be done overnight by a relatively small number of creationist geologists.

The Resurgence of Catastrophism

Uniformitarianism has dominated orthodox historical geology for 150 years, despite the overwhelming evidences of catastrophism. However, beginning about 1970 (contemporaneously with the rapid growth of the creation movement), there has taken place an amazing revival of catastrophism among evolutionary geologists. A leading modern geologist and paleontologist says:

"A great deal has changed, however, and contemporary geologists and paleontologists now genrally accept catastrophe as a 'way of life' although they may avoid the word catastrophe. In fact, many geologists now see rare, short-lived events as being the principal contributors to geologic sequences. . . . The periods of relative quiet contribute only a small part of the record."[1]

Leading British geologist Derek Ager reaches the same conclusion:

"I am coming more and more to the view that the evolution of life, like the evolution of continents and of the stratigraphical column in general, has been a very episodic affair, with short 'happenings' interrupting long ages of nothing in particular."[2]

These "short happenings" are marked by the great beds of cataclysmically formed and deformed rocks found everywhere. The "long ages of nothing in particular" are evidenced almost solely by the necessity to provide time for evolution, not by the hydraulic or paleontological character of the fossil-bearing sedimentary rocks themselves.

Nevertheless, geologists continue to insist on long ages, refusing to acknowledge the possibility that all these catastrophic "episodes" in earth history could really be interconnected and essentially contemporaneous, comprising what would amount to a single worldwide hydraulic cataclysm. In view of the absence of any worldwide geological unconformities, however, as shown previously, the latter is a much more likely explanation of the geological column.

---

[1]David M. Raup, "Geology and Creation," *Bulletin of the Field Museum of Natural History* (Vol. 54, March 1983), p. 21.
[2]Derek Ager, *The Nature of the Stratigraphical Record* (New York: John Wiley and Sons, 1981), p. 99.

CHAPTER VI

OLD OR YOUNG?

How to Date a Rock

One of the main objections to creationism has always been its supposedly too-short time scale. It seems to be part of our modern culture somehow to believe that the earth is billions of years old. Prior to the acceptance of uniformitarianism in the early 19th century, however, a much shorter time scale had been held by the great majority of scientists.

The evolution model, of course, demands an immensity of time. As we have already noted, not even thirty billion years would suffice for the chance evolution of even the simplest living molecule, but somehow evolutionists continue to believe in evolution anyway. In any case, it is obvious that a vast amount of time is essential for the evolution model. For those who *believe* in evolution, therefore, physical processes which indicate a short time scale must be explained away; only those processes commensurate with a long time scale can be accepted for use in geochronology.

It should be remembered, however, that real *history* is available for only the past few thousand years. The beginning of written records, with anything approaching a verifiable chronology, dates from about the first dynasty in Egypt, (between 2200 and 3500 B.C.). To keep this problem in its right perspective, one should remember that no one can possibly *know* what happened before there were people to observe and record what happened. Science means "knowledge" and the essence of the scientific method is experimental observation.

No one was present to see when any of the rocks of the geologic column were laid down (except of course those volcanic rocks that have been formed by eruptions in historic times), so there can be no *direct* evidence as to their age. Any such determination must therefore be indirect, and will be uncertain at best.

One can study the physical aspects of the rock and its surroundings and then try, on the basis of uniformitarian extension of some present relevant process, to estimate the time

131

since its formation. However, as shown in the preceding chapter, there is stronger evidence for rapid, catastrophic formation of the rocks than for uniformitarian formation.

Before discussing the specific methoas now in use for supposed dating of rocks, it is well to remove certain popular misconceptions about how this is done. Note the following types of information which are *not* used to date rocks:

1. *Rocks are not dated by their appearance.*

"Old" rocks do not necessarily look old; neither do "young" rocks look young. That is, rocks which are dated as very old may actually be quite loose and unconsolidated, while rocks supposedly very young may be dense and indurated.

2. *Rocks are not dated by their petrologic character.*

Rocks of all types — shales, granites, limestones, conglomerates, sandstones, etc., — may be found in all "ages."

3. *Rocks are not dated by their mineralogic contents.*

There is no relation between the minerals or metallic ores that might be found in a rock and its "age." Even oil may be found in rocks of practically any "age."

4. *Rocks are not dated by their structural features.*

As noted in the preceding chapter, there is not necessarily any kind of physical break (unconformity) between any one age and its succeeding age. Faults and folds and other structural features bear no relationship to the chronology of the rocks.

> "It is, indeed, a well-established fact that the (physical-stratigraphical) rock units and their boundaries often transgress geologic time planes in most irregular fashion even within the shortest distances."[1]

5. *Rocks are not dated by their adjacent rocks.*

Rocks of any "age" may rest vertically on top of those of any other "age." The very "oldest" rocks may occur directly beneath those of any subsequent "age."

> "Further, how many geologists have pondered the fact that lying on the crystalline basement are found from

---

[1] J.A. Jeletzsky, "Paleontology, Basis of Practical Geochronology," *Bulletin, American Association of Petroleum Geologists*, Vol. 40 (April 1956), p. 685.

place to place not merely Cambrian, but rocks of all ages?"[1]

6. *Rocks are not dated by vertical superposition.*

As shown in the preceding chapter, "old" rocks are often found resting vertically, sometimes in perfect conformity, on top of "younger" rocks. Normally, sedimentary rocks are formed with the earliest sediments deposited on the bottom, and successively younger sediments deposited in ascending order, so that vertical position ought to provide at least a local relative chronology. The many cases of "inverted order," however, make this rule apparently an unreliable guide.

7. *Rocks are not dated radiometrically.*

Many people believe the age of rocks is determined by study of their radioactive minerals—uranium, thorium, potassium, rubidium, etc.—but this is not so. The obvious proof that this is not the way it is done is the fact that the geological column and approximate ages of all the fossil-bearing strata were all worked out long before anyone ever heard or thought about radioactive dating. Also, as we shall see in the next section, there are so many sources of possible error or misinterpretation in radiometric dating that most such dates are discarded and never used at all, notably whenever they disagree with the previously agreed-on dates.

8. *Rocks are not dated by any physical characteristics at all.*

There is nothing whatever in the physical appearance or contents of the rocks that is used to determine its "age."

"The more than amply proved and almost unanimously recognized impossibility of establishing any practically useful broadly regional or worldwide geologic time scale based on the physical-stratigraphical criteria alone for the vast expanse of pre-Cambrian time supplies conclusive proof that these phenomena are devoid of any generally recognizable geologic time significance."[2]

---

[1] E.M. Spieker, "Mountain-Building Chronology and the Nature of the Geologic Time-Scale," *Bulletin, American Association of Petroleum Geologists*, Vol. 40 (August 1956), p. 1805.

[2] J.A. Jeletzsky, *op. cit.*, p. 684.

9. *Rocks are not dated by their total fossil contents.*

We have seen previously that a great many fossils are remains of organisms that still live in the modern world. Consequently, such organisms are useless as geochronological indices. Sponges, for example, could presumably be found as fossils in rocks of any "age."

How, then, are rocks actually dated? What is it that determines the geologic "age" to which a given rock formation is assigned? The answer is *index fossils!*

"In each sedimentary stratum certain fossils seem to be characteristically abundant: these fossils are known as index fossils. If in a strange formation an index fossil is found, it is easy to date that particular layer of rock and to correlate it with other exposures in distant regions containing the same species."[1]

Index fossils are remains of organisms (usually marine invertebrates) that are assumed to have been of rather limited duration chronologically, but of essentially worldwide provenance geographically. Thus, their presence in a rock is believed to provide an unambiguous identification of its age.

But just how do geologists know which index fossils date which age? The answer to this question is *evolution!* That is, since evolution has taken place in the same direction all over the world, the stage of evolution attained by the organisms living in a given age should be an infallible criterion to identify sediments deposited in that age. Thus, rocks are dated by their fossil contents, especially their index fossils.

"That our present-day knowledge of the sequence of strata in the earth's crust is in major part due to the evidence supplied by fossils is a truism. Merely in their role as distinctive rock constituents, fossils have furnished, through their record of the evolution of life on this planet, an amazingly effective key to the relative positioning of strata in widely separated regions and from continent to continent."[2]

---

[1] J.E. Ransom, *Fossils in America* (New York: Harper and Row, 1964), p. 43.
[2] H.D. Hedberg, "The Stratigraphic Panorama," *Bulletin of the Geological Society of America*, Vol. 72 (April 1961), p. 499.

The author of the above statement was at the time president of the Geological Society of America, and so his statement may be considered authoritative. How is the sequence of strata determined? "Fossils have furnished . . . an amazingly effective key to the relative positioning of strata." And how do fossils do such an amazing thing? *"Through their record of the evolution of life."*

The ultimate key to geologic dating is evolution! All other methods are equivocal and subject to alteration and error. Only the sequence of evolution is sure.

"The only chronometric scale applicable in geologic history for the stratigraphic classification of rocks and for dating geologic events exactly is furnished by the fossils. Owing to the irreversibility of evolution, they offer an unambiguous time scale for relative age determinations and for worldwide correlations of rocks."[1]

In terms of the evolution model, of course, this would clearly be the best way to determine geologic age. If we really knew evolution were true — say by divine revelation or some other infallible means — then the stage-of-evolution of the fossils would definitely be the best way to date rocks.

"Vertebrate paleontologists have relied upon 'stage-of-evolution' as the criterion for determining the chronologic relationships of faunas. Before establishment of physical dates, evolutionary progression was the best method for dating fossiliferous strata."[2]

Paleontologists do not have divine revelation to justify their evolution model, however, so exactly what is the evidence that gives them such strong confidence in its validity? Let Dunbar answer again:

"Fossils provide the only historical, documentary evidence that life has evolved from simpler to more and more complex forms."[3]

---

[1]O.H. Schindewolf, "Comments on Some Stratigraphic Terms," *American Journal of Science*, Vol. 255 (June 1957), p. 394.

[2]J.F. Evernden, D.E. Savage, G.H. Curtis and G.T. James, "K/A Dates and the Cenozoic Mammalian Chronology of North America," *American Journal of Science*, Vol. 262 (February 1964), p. 166.

[3]Carl O. Dunbar, *Historical Geology* (New York: John Wiley & Sons, Inc., 1949), p. 52.

Here is obviously a powerful system of circular reasoning. Fossils are used as the only key for placing rocks in chronological order. The criterion for assigning fossils to specific places in that chronology is the assumed evolutionary progression of life; the assumed evolutionary progression is based on the fossil record so constructed. The main evidence for evolution is the assumption of evolution!

In the two preceding chapters it was demonstrated that the creation-cataclysm model provides a far more satisfactory framework for explaining the actual facts of the fossil record, with fewer problems and required secondary modifications, than the evolution-uniformitarian model.

Therefore, the fossils really do not provide a satisfactory means for dating rocks, and we have already seen that this method takes priority over all other methods. Consequently there is certainly no real proof that the vast evolutionary time scale is valid at all.

That being true, there is no compelling reason why we should not seriously consider once again the possibilities in the relatively short time scale of the creation model.

As a matter of fact, the creation model does not, in its basic form, *require* a short time scale. It merely assumes a period of special creation sometime in the past, without necessarily stating when that was. On the other hand, the evolution model does *require* a *long* time scale. The creation model is thus free to consider the evidence on its own merits, whereas the evolution model is forced to reject all evidence that favors a short time scale.

Although the creation model is not necessarily linked to a short time scale, as the evolution model is to a long scale, it is true that it does fit more naturally in a short chronology. Assuming the Creator had a purpose in His creation, and that purpose centered primarily in man, it does seem more appropriate that He would not waste aeons of time in essentially meaningless caretaking of an incomplete stage or stages of His intended creative work.

In any case, the creation model permits us to look seriously at those natural processes which seem to favor a young earth and a recent creation. We shall see later in this chapter that there exist many such processes. Unfortunately most people do not know this, since we were all indoctrinated as children in school, with one model of origins exclusively.

Only those processes which seem to favor an exceedingly old earth and old universe were included in our instruction. Teachers should now be careful to include a fair presentation of *both* types of processes — those which seem to support the evolution model by their consistency with a very old earth, and those which seem to favor the creation model by pointing to a recent origin of the earth and the universe.

Before considering these processes, however, we must first deal with the standard radiometric dating techniques, which have been heralded so widely and confidently as proving the great age of the earth and the geologic timescale. It will be found that each of them, rightly interpreted, is quite consistent with a short time scale.

Radiometric Dating

It may seem presumptuous to attempt a refutation of radioactive dating. Teachers have believed and taught their students for almost half a century now that uranium dating in particular has proved the earth to be billions of years old, with ample time, therefore, for evolution.

Actually, trillions or quadrillions of years would not suffice for evolution, as we have already shown. However, the concept of several billion years is sufficiently incomprehensible to make evolution at least *seem* possible in that length of time, and radioactive minerals decay so slowly and so constantly as to give at least an appearance of great age, if interpreted in a uniformitarian context.

In attempting to determine the real age of the earth, it should always be remembered, of course, that recorded history began only several thousand years ago. Not even uranium dating is capable of experimental verification, since no one could actually watch uranium decaying for millions of years to see what happens.

In order to obtain a prehistoric date, therefore, it is necessary to use some kind of physical process which operates slowly enough to measure and steadily enough to produce significant changes. If certain assumptions are made about it, then it can yield a date which could be called the *apparent age*. Whether or not the apparent age is really the *true age* depends completely on the validity of the assumptions. Since there is no way in which the assumptions can be tested, there is no *sure* way (except by divine revelation) of knowing the true age of any geologic formation. The processes which are most likely to yield dates, which approximate the true dates, are those for which the assumptions are least likely to be in error.

Theoretically, there should be any number of processes that could be used to measure time, since all involve changes with time. It is not surprising that the only processes which are considered acceptable to evolutionists are those whose assumptions and rates yield great ages.

As far as the age of geological formations and of the earth itself are concerned, only radioactive decay processes are considered useful today by evolutionists. There are a number of these, but the most important ones are: (1) the various uranium-thorium-lead methods; (2) the rubidium-strontium method, and (3) the potassium-argon method. In each of these systems, the parent (e.g., uranium) is gradually changed into the daughter (e.g., lead) component of the system, and the relative proportions of the two are considered to be an index of the time since initial formation of the system.

For these or other methods of geochronometry, one should note carefully that the following assumptions must be made:

1. *The system must have been a closed system.*
   That is, it cannot have been altered by factors extraneous to the dating process; nothing inside the system could have been removed, and nothing outside the system added to it.
2. *The system must initially have contained none of its daughter component.*
   If any of the daughter component were present initially, the initial amount must be corrected in order to get a meaningful calculation.
3. *The process rate must always have been the same.*
   Similarly, if the process rate has ever changed since the system was established, then this change must be known and corrected for if the age calculation is to be of any significance.

Other assumptions may be involved for particular methods, but the three listed above are always involved and are critically important. In view of this fact, the highly speculative nature of all methods of geochronometry becomes apparent when one realizes that *not one* of the above assumptions is valid! None are provable, or testable, or even reasonable.

1. *There is no such thing in nature as a closed system.*
   The concept of a closed system is an ideal concept, convenient for analysis but non-existent in the real world. The idea of a system remaining closed for millions of years becomes an absurdity.
2. *It is impossible to ever know the initial components of a system formed in prehistoric times.*
   Obviously no one was present when such a system was first formed. Since creation is at least a viable possibility, it is clearly possible that some of the "daughter" component may have been initially created along with the "parent" component. Even apart from this possibility, there are numerous other ways by which daughter products could be incorporated into the systems when first formed.
3. *No process rate is unchangeable.*
   Every process in nature operates at a rate which is influenced by a number of different factors. If any of these factors change, the process rate changes. Rates are at best only statistical averages, not deterministic constants.

Thus, at best, apparent ages determined by means of any physical process are educated guesses and may well be completely unrelated to the true ages. That is why the "stage-of-evolution," as discussed in the preceding section, is preferred over such methods by evolutionists, who consider it much more reliable than any physical process, even radioactive decay.

To show that the foregoing discussion is not merely academic, but very realistic, we shall now consider each of the three main radiometric dating methods in light of the above assumptions. Despite much textbook dogmatism on this subject, it is easy to document the fact that none of them is reliable.

The uranium, potassium and rubidium methods will be briefly considered in turn. The most important method is uranium dating, of course, since it not only is the first one used historically, but also the one against which others have been calibrated. The uranium method has been used to assign a so-called "absolute time" date to the earth's supposed oldest rocks, and thus is the main support for the

139

widely accepted idea that the earth is about 4.5 to 5 billion years old. Such radiometric ages are used especially for Precambrian rock, since there is no paleontologic control on the dating in these rocks.

1. *The Uranium Methods.*

Actually, the uranium method is a whole family of dating methods, all based on the decay of uranium and its sister element thorium through long decay chains into lead and helium. The process is called "alpha decay," in which the alpha particles (which are really positively charged atoms of helium gas) escape the nuclei of the parent atoms at rates which seem statistically to be constant.

Three decay chains are involved: (a) Uranium 238 decays into Lead 206 plus 8 helium atoms, with a half-life of 4.5 billion years; (b) Uranium 235 decays into Lead 207 plus 7 helium atoms, with a half-life of 0.7 billion years; (c) Thorium 232 decays into Lead 208 plus 7 helium atoms, with a half-life of 14.1 billion years. In a given deposit containing these elements, it is usual to find all of these isotopes together (this is not always true, but is typical), in conjunction with a fourth isotope of lead, Lead 204, which is believed to have no radioactive parent and is therefore called "common" lead. Furthermore, many or all of the intermediate products in the three decay chains will be present, ideally in equilibrium amounts. Some of these include radium, radon gas and another important lead isotope, Lead 210.

Without entering into the technical details of the use of various lead age methods from these data, it is immediately obvious that the three assumptions discussed are invalid for these methods. There are, therefore, serious difficulties, if not outright fallacies, in the lead age determinations, and some of these are discussed briefly below.

    (a) Uranium minerals always exist in open systems, not closed.

Uranium is easily leachable by groundwater, for example. The intermediate element, radon gas, can easily move in or out of a uranium system. There are, in fact, various ways by which the components of this type of system can enter or leave it. One of the chief authorities on radioactive dating, Henry Faul, said:

"Uranium and lead both migrate (in shales) in geologic time, and detailed analyses have shown that useful ages cannot be obtained with them. Similar difficulties prevail in attempts to date pitchblende veins. Here again much chemical activity is known to take place and widely diverging ages can be measured on samples from the same spot."[1]

Remember, that unless the system is known to have been a *closed* system through all the ages since its formation, its age readings are meaningless. A similar problem has been pointed out in connection with the dating of lunar rocks.

"If all of the age-dating methods (rubidium-strontium, uranium-lead and potassium-argon) had yielded the same ages, the picture would be neat. But they haven't. The lead ages, for example, have been consistently older. This led Leon T. Silver, of the California Institute of Technology, to study the temperatures at which lead volatilizes (vaporizes) and moves out of the lunar sample. Theoretically, this could happen on the moon and this volatized lead would become 'parentless'— separated from its uranium parent. More lead (parentless lead added to the material) would yield older ages."[2]

With so many factors pressing to upset the balance of components in such a system, it is no wonder that the several age-calculation methods available for each system much more often than not yield "discordant" ages.

An even more important phenomenon by which these balances can be upset is that of "free neutron capture," by which free neutrons in the mineral's environment may be captured by the lead in the system to change the isotopic value of the lead. That is, Lead 206 may be converted into Lead 207, and Lead 207 into Lead 208 by this process. It is perhaps significant that Lead 208 usually constitutes over half the lead present in any given lead deposit. Thus, the relative amounts of these "radiogenic" isotopes of lead in the system may not be a function of their decay from thorium

---

[1] Henry Faul, *Ages of Rocks, Planets and Stars* (New York: McGraw Hill Book Co., Inc., 1966), p. 61.
[2] Evelyn Driscoll, "Dating of Moon Samples: Pitfalls and Paradoxes" *Science News*, Vol. 101 (January 1, 1972), p. 12.

and uranium at all, but rather a function of the amount of free neutrons in the environment.

That this problem is quite serious has been shown conclusively by Dr. Melvin Cook,[1] who has analyzed two of the world's most important uranium bearing ores (e.g., in Katanga and Canada) with this in view. These ores contain no Lead 204, so presumably no common lead. They also contain little or no Thorium 232, but do contain significant amounts of Lead 208. The latter could therefore have come neither from common lead contamination, nor from thorium decay, and so must have been derived from Lead 207 by neutron capture. But then the calculations for such neutron reactions to make this correction, according to Dr. Cook, in effect will show that literally *all* of the so-called radiogenic isotopes of lead found in uranium-thorium systems anywhere can be accounted for by this process alone. Thus, none of them need have been formed by radioactive decay at all, and consequently the minerals may all be quite young, with essentially zero age!

(b) The uranium decay rates may well be variable.

Writers on this subject commonly stress the invariability of radioactive decay rates, but the fact is these rates, as well as all others, are subject to change. Since they are controlled by atomic structure, they are not as easily affected as other processes, but factors which can influence atomic structures and processes can also influence radioactive decay rates.

The most obvious example of such a factor is cosmic radiation and its production of neutrinos. Another would be the free neutrons discussed above. If anything happens to increase the incidence of these particles in the earth's crust, there is no doubt that radioactive decay rates would be accelerated.

Phenomena such as these would be generated by such events as the reversal of the earth's magnetic field or supernova explosions in nearby stars. Since such phenomena are commonly accepted now as having occurred in the past, even by uniformitarian astronomers and geol-

---

[1] M.A. Cook, *Prehistory and Earth Models* (London: Max Parrish and Co., Ltd., 1960), pp. 53-60.

ogists, there is a very real possibility that radioactive decay rates were much higher at various intervals in the past than they are at present. That this possibility is being considered seriously is evident from the following comment by Dr. Fred Jueneman, who is director of research for the Innovative Concepts Association.

"Being so close, the anisotropic neutrino flux of the super-explosion must have had the peculiar characteristic of resetting all our atomic clocks. This would knock our Carbon-14, Potassium-Argon, and Uranium-Lead dating measurements into a cocked hat! The age of prehistoric artifacts, the age of the earth, and that of the universe would be thrown into doubt."[1]

(c) The daughter products were probably present from the beginning.

There is no way of being sure that the radiogenic daughter products of uranium and thorium decay were not present in these minerals when they were first formed. This possibility is most evident in the case of modern volcanic rocks. Such rocks, formed by lava flows from the earth's interior mantle, commonly contain uranium minerals and these, more often than not, are found to have radiogenic, as well as common, leads with them when the lava first cools and the minerals crystallize.

Sidney P. Clementson, a British engineer, has recently made a detailed study[2] of such modern volcanic rocks and their uranium "ages," as published in Soviet geophysical journals and other papers, and has shown that in all such cases the uranium-lead ages were vastly older than the true ages of the rocks. Most of them gave ages of over a billion years, even though the lava rocks were known to have been formed in modern times. This is clear, unequivocal evidence that, as Clementson says:

"Calculated ages give no indication whatever of the age of the host rocks."[3]

---

[1] Frederick Jueneman, "Scientific Speculation," *Industrial Research* (September 1972), p. 15.
[2] S.P. Clementson, "A Critical Examination of Radioactive Dating of Rocks," *Creation Research Society Quarterly*, Vol. 7 (December 1970), pp. 137-141.
[3] *Ibid.*

Again, of course, the evolution model can be salvaged by a secondary assumption—namely, that the uranium and its accompanying lead isotopes were together in the mantle from which the lava flowed, that they stayed together during the flow and that they continued to stay together after the lava cooled. If this secondary assumption is correct, then uranium-lead ratios are a function of the mantle-forming process in the beginning (a different problem altogether), and not of the duration of radioactive decay after the rock was formed.

The creationist does not argue with this explanation. He merely points out the following inference: since, in those cases of igneous rocks whose age is actually *known*, the uranium method gives ages which are aeons too large, and since other uranium minerals are normally found in igneous rocks formed by the same kind of process, therefore it is very probable that their uranium "ages" also will be aeons too large, for the same reasons. Why should uranium ages be assumed correct when applied to rocks of unknown age when they are always tremendously in error when calculated on rocks of known age?

(d) Uranium dating gives discordant results which must be corrected by paleontology.

It is common to find that the several ages that are obtainable from a suite of uranium-thorium-lead isotopes are either discordant among themselves or "anomalous" with respect to the assumed age of the formation. Therefore, they must be either corrected to the assumed "true" age, or discarded as hopelessly discrepant. With so many sources of contamination and change, this is not surprising. The few that are actually concordant and consistent can be easily correlated with the creation-cataclysm model. The point to be stressed here is that, as noted earlier, the evolutionary interpretation of the fossil record is the factor that really determines the acceptable age of a rock (acceptable to evolutionists, that is).

"The most reasonable age can be selected only after careful consideration of independent geochronologic data as well as field, stratigraphic and paleontologic

144

evidence, and the petrographic and paragenetic relations."[1]

"And what essentially is this actual time-scale? On what criteria does it rest? When all is winnowed out and the grain reclaimed from the chaff, it is certain that the grain in the product is mainly the paleontologic record and highly likely that the physical evidence is the chaff."[2]

2. *The Potassium-Argon Method*

The method most widely used for dating rocks is the potassium-argon method. Potassium minerals are found in most igneous and some sedimentary rocks and are not as restricted in use as are uranium minerals. Potassium 40 decays by the "electron-capture" process (capture of an orbital electron by the nucleus) into Argon 40, with a half-life of 1.3 billion years. It also decays simultaneously by the "beta-decay" process (emission of an electron and a neutrino) into Calcium 40.

This process also involves a considerable number of serious problems, including the following:

(a) It must be calibrated by uranium-lead dating.

The so-called "branching ratio," which determines the amount of the decay product that becomes argon (instead of calcium) is unknown by a factor of up to 50 per cent. Since the decay rate is also unsettled, values of these constants are chosen which bring potassium dates into as close correlation with uranium dates as possible. Consequently, potassium dating can at best be only as accurate as uranium dating, which, as we have just seen, is not accurate at all.

(b) The potassium-argon system is an open system.

Since Argon 40 is a gas, it is obvious that it can easily migrate in and out of potassium minerals.

"Processes of rock alteration may render a volcanic rock useless for potassium-argon dating. . . . We have

---

[1] L.R. Stieff, T.W. Stern and R.N. Eichler, "Algebraic and Graphic Methods for Evaluating Discordant Lead-Isotope Ages," *U.S. Geological Survey Professional Papers*, No. 414-E (1963).

[2] E.M. Spieker, "Mountain-Building Chronology and the Nature of the Geologic Time-Scale," *Bulletin, American Association of Petroleum Geologists*, Vol. 40 (August 1956), p. 1806.

analyzed several devitrified glasses of known age, and all have yielded ages that are too young. Some gave virtually zero ages, although the geologic evidence suggested that devitrification took place shortly after the formation of a deposit."[1]

Not only is the argon content subject to alteration, however. Potassium also is quite mobile.

"The potassium-argon ages of the meteorites investigated ranged from 5×10^9 years to 15.6×10^9 years. . . . As much as 80 per cent of the potassium in a small sample of an iron meteorite can be removed by distilled water in 4.5 hours."[2]

(c) The decay rate of potassium is subject to change.

For the same reasons that uranium decay rates are subject to acceleration (e.g., increase in neutrino flux due to past intermittent increases in cosmic radiation at the earth's surface), so potassium decay could well have been much faster in the past than it is at present.

(d) Argon may be incorporated with potassium at time of formation.

Argon 40 is a very common component of both the atmosphere and the crustal rocks. In fact, Melvin Cook has calculated[3] that, even if the earth were 5 billion years old, as assumed by evolutionists, no more than one per cent of the Argon 40 now found in the earth could possibly have been formed by radioactive decay of potassium. Thus, there is an abundance of argon available and no doubt at least some of the Argon 40 in every potassium mineral has been derived from the environment rather than from the decay process.

That this possibility is very real is indicated by the following study made on submarine Hawaiian basaltic rocks of known age by the Hawaiian Institute of Geophysics.

---

[1] J.F. Evernden, D.E. Savage, G.H. Curtis and G.T. James, "K/A Dates and the Cenozoic Mammalian Chronology of North America," *American Journal of Science*, Vol. 262 (February 1964), p. 154.

[2] L.A. Rancitelli and D.E. Fisher, "Potassium-Argon Ages of Iron Meteorites," *Planetary Science Abstracts*, 48th Annual Meeting of the American Geophysical Union (1967), p. 167.

[3] M.A. Cook, *op. cit.*, pp. 66-68.

"The radiogenic argon and helium contents of three basalts erupted into the deep ocean from an active volcano (Kilauea) have been measured. Ages calculated from these measurements increase with sample depth up to 22 million years for lavas deduced to be recent. Caution is urged in applying dates from deep-ocean basalts in studies on ocean-floor spreading."[1]

Actually the dates of these basaltic rocks were known to be less than 200 years old! The comment about sea-floor spreading is most interesting, in view of the fact that the modern concept of continental drift, especially its very slow rate, is based mainly on similar potassium-argon dates in basalts at the bottom of the Atlantic.

Similar modern rocks formed in 1801 near Hualalei, Hawaii, were found to give potassium-argon ages ranging from 160 million years to 3 billion years. The reason given for these anomalously high ages was the incorporation of environmental argon at the time of lava flow. The authors of this study draw the following obvious (though understated) inference:

"It is possible that some of the abnormally high potassium-argon ages reported by other investigators for ultrabasic rocks may be caused by the presence of excess argon contained in fluid and gaseous inclusions."[2]

Still another study on Hawaiian basalts obtained seven "ages" of these basalts ranging all the way from zero years to 3.34 million years.[3] The authors, by an obviously unorthodox application of statistical reasoning, felt justified in recording the "age" of these basalts as 250,000 years.

The creationist does not question the fact that the anomalously high ages of the lava rocks noted above may well be due to incorporation of excess argon at the time of formation. Again, however, he points out that if this is known to have

[1]C.S. Noble and J.J. Naughton, "Deep-Ocean Basalts: Inert Gas Content and Uncertainties in Age Dating," *Science*, Vol. 162 (October 11, 1968), p. 265.

[2]J.G. Funkhouser and J.J. Naughton, *Journal of Geophysical Research*, Vol. 73 (July 15, 1968), p. 4606.

[3]J.F. Evernden *et al.*, *op. cit.*, Table 4, p. 157. See also A.W. Laughlin, "Excess Radiogenic Argon in Pegmatite Minerals," *Journal of Geophysical Research*, Vol. 74 (December 15, 1969), pp. 6684-6689.

happened so frequently in rocks of known age, it probably also happened frequently in rocks of unknown age. Since there is no way at all to distinguish Argon 40 as formed by unknown processes in primeval times and now dispersed around the world, from radiogenic Argon 40, it seems clear that potassium-argon ages are meaningless insofar as *true* ages are concerned.

(e) Potassium ages are extremely variable.

In view of all the sources of error in potassium dating, it is not surprising that it gives results that are so variable, even in a single rock.

"It is now well known that K-Ar ages obtained from different minerals in a single rock may be strikingly discordant."[1]

It would seem that the only remaining virtue of potassium ages is that they often yield ages of millions and billions of years, and are therefore generally compatible with the evolutionary model.

3. *Rubidium-Strontium Dating.*

The third most important rock dating method (other than evolution and the fossils) is the beta-decay of Rubidium 87 into Strontium 87, with an estimated half-life of 47 billion years (Some authorities estimate this half-life at 60 billion years, others up to 120 billion years.). Again, it must be calibrated against the uranium method and therefore can be no more reliable, at best, than uranium dating.

Other difficulties with rubidium dating are similar to those for uranium and potassium dating. Some of these are:

a. The decay rate would be accelerated by the same factors that would speed up uranium decay and potassium decay.

b. Extraneous Strontium 87 can easily be incorporated into Rubidium 87 minerals from the surrounding rocks. Cook says:

"Therefore, even if one were to agree for the sake of argument that the earth is five billion years old,

---

[1] Joan C. Engels, "Effects of Sample Purity on Discordant Mineral Ages Found in K-Ar Dating," *Journal of Geology*, Vol. 79 (September 1971), p. 609.

radiogenic Sr-87 would be only about 5 percent of all Sr-87 present in the rocks."[1]

c. Rubidium 87 can easily be partially leached out of a Rb-Sr system.

d. Strontium 87 can be formed by the same neutron capture process from Strontium 86 that can form Lead 208 from Lead 207.

There are other radiometric dating methods that have been proposed and used in a limited way. However, none are considered as reliable or as important as the three briefly discussed above, so there seems no need to discuss them here. The radiocarbon method, of course, is very important, but applies specifically only to very "recent" dates, geologically speaking. It will be discussed later in this chapter.

None of these processes gives any very good evidence, and certainly do not prove, that the earth is very old. All of the data fit equally well, or better, in a very short time-span model such as is favored in creationism.

Evidence for a Young Earth

We have shown in the preceding chapter sound physical evidence that the earth's varied geologic formations were formed continuously and rapidly, not intermittently and slowly over long ages. We have further shown, in the beginning sections of this chapter, that there is no sound physical evidence that the earth is very old. The few radioactive decay processes that have been interpreted in terms of durations of billions of years have been shown to be equally, if not more, consistent with a very short time-span. The only real evidence for a long history of the earth is its necessity to support the evolution model. We have seen that determinative dating of rocks is based ultimately on the fossil record, interpreted in the framework of evolution,

---

[1] Melvin A. Cook, "Do Radiological Clocks Need Repair?" *Creation Research Society Quarterly*, Vol. 5 (October 1968), p. 79.
Dr. Cook is a physical chemist (Ph.D., Yale), formerly Professor of Metallurgy at the University of Utah and now Chairman of the Board at IRECO Chemical Co. He holds numerous patents, especially in the fields of oil slurries and explosives, and has received several important scientific prizes.

which in turn finds its only real support from that same fossil record so interpreted.

The creation model, unlike the evolution model, is able to allow serious consideration to the many evidences that the earth is young. It must be remembered that, scientifically speaking, no one has proof for any dates prior to the beginning of written records, about 4000 to 6000 years ago, at most. Dates prior to the beginning of history must necessarily be based on the assumption of uniformitarianism, in three parts, as follows: (1) initial boundary conditions for the geochronometric system, with all components quantitatively known; (2) constant process rate for the system, converting one component into another uniformly; (3) continuously closed system, so that none of the internal components could be changed by external conditions.

These assumptions are always untestable and, therefore, uncertain scientifically. They are certainly not valid in the case of the standard radiometric dating methods which have been used to calculate great ages for the earth.

As a matter of fact, neither can these assumptions be strictly valid for those processes which indicate a young age for the earth. The point is, that exactly the same kinds of assumptions which are made in the case of uranium and potassium dating, will yield young ages in the case of certain other processes. In fact, there are many more processes which yield young ages than processes which give old ages. Furthermore, even though they do involve the uniformitarian assumption, they are often much less vulnerable to errors in this assumption. Several types of such processes are considered:

1. *Efflux of gases into the atmosphere.*

Certain radioactive elements produce gases as they decay, notably Helium 4 in the case of uranium decay and Argon 40 in the case of potassium decay. These products migrate upward through the rocks and eventually escape into the atmosphere. Most of the argon must have been present there, or in the crust, from the beginning, since there is far too much to have been produced even in five billion years by potassium decay, assuming Cook's calculations are right.

The small amount of helium in the atmosphere has, however, perplexed evolutionists for many years. Cook points out the problem as follows:

"At the estimated 2×10^{20} gm. uranium and 5×10^{20} gm. thorium in the lithosphere, helium should be generated radiogenically at a rate of about 3×10^9 gm/yr. Moreover, the (secondary) cosmic-ray source of helium has been estimated to be of comparable magnitude. Apparently nearly all the helium from sedimentary rocks and, according to Keevil and Hurley, about 0.8 of the radiogenic helium from igneous rocks, have been released into the atmosphere during geological times (currently taken to be about 5×10^9 yr). Hence more than 10^{20} gm of helium should have passed into the atmosphere since the 'beginning.' Because the atmosphere contains only 3.5×10^{15} gm Helium 4, the common assumption is therefore that about 10^{20} gm of Helium 4 must also have passed out through the exosphere, and that its present rate of loss through the exosphere balances the rate of exudation from the lithosphere."[1]

This "common assumption," however, is only an assumption. There is no evidence at all that Helium 4 either does, or can, escape from the exosphere in significant amounts. On the contrary, Cook has shown there is a strong probability that Helium 4 is actually *entering* the atmosphere from outer space, by means of the sun's corona.

Consequently the maximum age of the atmosphere, assuming no original helium in the atmosphere, would be

$$\frac{3.5 \times 10^{15}}{10^{20}} \times (5 \times 10^9) = 1.75 \times 10^5 \text{ years.}$$

As a matter of fact, Henry Faul has cited evidence that the rate of efflux of helium into the atmosphere is over 3×10^{11} gms/year,[2] which is about 100 times greater than the value used by Cook. This in turn would reduce the age of the atmosphere down to several thousand years!

2. *Influx of meteoric material from space.*

It is known that there is essentially a constant rate of cosmic dust particles entering the earth's atmosphere from

---

[1] Melvin A. Cook, "Where is the Earth's Radiogenic Helium?" *Nature*, Vol. 179 (January 26, 1957), p. 213.
[2] Henry Faul, *Nuclear Geology* (New York: John Wiley, 1954).

space and then gradually settling to the earth's surface. The best measurements of this influx have been made by Hans Pettersson, who obtained the figure of 14 million tons per year.[1] This amounts to 14×10^{19} pounds in 5 billion years. If we assume the density of compacted dust is, say, 140 pounds per cubic foot, this corresponds to a volume of 10^{18} cubic feet. Since the earth has a surface area of approximately 5.5×10^{15} square feet, this seems to mean that there should have accumulated during the 5-billion-year age of the earth, a layer of meteoritic dust approximately 182 feet thick all over the world!

There is not the slightest sign of such a dust layer anywhere of course. On the moon's surface it should be at least as thick, but the astronauts found no sign of it (before the moon landings, there had been considerable fear that the men would sink into the dust when they arrived on the moon.)

Lest anyone say that erosional and mixing processes account for the absence of the 182-foot meteoritic dust layer, it should be noted that the composition of such material is quite distinctive, especially in its content of nickel and iron. Nickel, for example, is a very rare element in the earth's crust and especially in the ocean. Pettersson estimated the average nickel content of meteoritic dust to be 2.5 per cent, approximately 300 times as great as in the earth's crust. Thus, if all the meteoritic dust layer had been dispersed by uniform mixing through the earth's crust, the thickness of crust involved (assuming no original nickel in the crust at all) would be 182×300 feet, or about 10 miles!

Since the earth's crust (down to the mantle) averages only about 12 miles thick, this tells us that practically all the nickel in the crust of the earth would have been derived from meteoritic dust influx in the supposed (5×10^9) year age of the earth!

---

[1] Hans Pettersson, "Cosmic Spherules and Meteoritic Dust," *Scientific American,* Vol. 202 (February 1960), p. 132. More recent measurements indicate a much great influx of dust than Pettersson calculated, and thus a still younger age for Earth and the moon (see G.S. Hawkins, Ed., *Meteor Orbits and Dust,* published by NASA, 1976). Figures obtained by actual measurements in space as listed in this publication, yield 200 million tons of dust coming to earth each year.

Another interesting calculation can be made by noting that river water carries about 0.75 billion pounds of nickel each year to the ocean and the ocean contains about 7000 billion pounds. Thus the nickel dissolved in the ocean's waters could have accumulated from river flows in slightly over 9000 years. Consequently the absence of the appropriate percentage of nickel arriving on the earth's surface from meteoric infall cannot be attributed to erosion and transportation to the ocean. The only possible way of accounting for the small amount of nickel found in the earth's crust and ocean seems to be in terms of an age for the earth of only a few thousand years.

3. *Influx of materials into the ocean.*

Entirely apart from the meteoritic nickel question, the mere fact that the ocean's nickel content could have accumulated from river inflow in about 9000 years seems to set an upper limit to the age of the ocean, unless it can be shown that this dissolved nickel either precipitates out on the ocean bottom, or is somewhere returned through the atmosphere to the continents. Neither has been shown. It apparently is not precipitating on the ocean bottom, for in 5 billion years 3.75 billion-billion pounds would accumulate. Since the ocean covers about 3.9×10^{15} square feet of surface area, this means about 960 pounds of nickel on every square foot of ocean bed!

The same kind of calculation can be made for other dissolved chemicals in the ocean. That is, the amount of any given chemical in the ocean, divided by the annual increment of that chemical through river inflow, will yield the time required to accumulate the chemical, assuming none was present in the ocean to begin with and the inflow rate has always been the same.

Since there are many chemicals in the ocean, a great many different calculations can be made. Many different answers will be obtained, for the reason that an unknown amount of each chemical was present in the ocean to start with, and also because in some cases mechanisms for recycling may exist to return portions back to the continents.

The significant thing to note, however, is that in every case the calculated apparent age of the ocean is vastly less than the supposed 5 billion year age of the earth. Cook has pointed out this fact in the case of uranium, stating that:

". . . the annual uranium flux in river water (is) (10^{10} to
10^{11} gm/yr) compared with the total uranium present
in the oceans (about 10^{15}gm)."[1]

In this case, the apparent age of the ocean based on this
particular form of "uranium dating" is obviously calculated
to be from 10,000 to 100,000 years.

This correlates approximately with the estimate made by
Riley and Skirrow who give the figure of 500,000 years.[2]
These authors have made similar calculations for many other
chemicals, with the following typical results.

Chemical Element	Years to Accumulate in Ocean from River Inflow
Sodium	260,000,000
Magnesium	45,000,000
Silicon	8,000
Potassium	11,000,000
Copper	50,000
Gold	560,000
Silver	2,100,000
Mercury	42,000
Lead	2,000
Tin	100,000
Nickel	18,000
Uranium	500,000

Many others are listed, practically all far under a billion
years, and many even less than 1000 years (aluminum, for
example, gives only 100 years!).

This situation is difficult to understand if the earth's lithosphere and hydrosphere are indeed billions of years old, and
if uniformitarianism is a valid assumption in geochronology.
The attempt to explain the small amounts of these elements
in terms of precipitation on the ocean bottom will not work.
One of the world's leading oceanographers, Ph. H. Kuenen,
said:

"Under normal conditions, sea water is not supersaturated with any product, and circulation is automatically

[1] M. A. Cook, "Where is the Earth's Radiogenic Helium?," *Nature*, Vol. 179
(January 26, 1957), p. 213.
[2] *Chemical Oceanography*, Ed. by J. P. Riley and G. Skirrow (London:
Academic Press, 1965), Vol. 1, p. 164.

set up in areas of excess evaporation, preventing excessive concentrations."[1]

Chemicals normally do not precipitate out of solution until the water is first supersaturated with them. Although not much is known as yet about the chemical composition of all the world's ocean bottom sediments, there is no evidence at all to indicate that the vast quantities of "missing" chemicals can be found there. Neither is there evidence that significant quantities of most of them could have been moved back to the continents by atmospheric transport of salt spray. The conclusion indicates that these quantities are missing because they were never there in the first place; which means, of course, that the ocean and the earth must be very young.

Not only do the dissolved chemicals indicate a young age for the ocean, but the same is true for the actual bottom sediments themselves. Geologist Stuart Nevins has apparently shown this fact conclusively in a recent study.[2] Approximately 27.5 billion tons of sediment are being transported to the ocean every year. The total mass of sediments already in the ocean is about 820 million billion tons. Dividing the total mass by the transport rate yields 30 million years as the maximum age of the ocean since sediments first started to flow into it (average rates of inflow have certainly been at least as high in the past as they are at present, even using the evolutionary model).

Nevins also has shown that the total mass of continental rocks above sea level is only about 383 million billion tons, which is slightly less than half the mass of sediments in the present ocean. Thus, in only 383/27.5, or 14, million years, the present continents, eroding at present rates, would have been eroded to sea level!

One cannot account for the small amount of sediments on the ocean bottom by assuming they have somehow been uplifted to form the sedimentary rocks on the continents, for the obvious reason that the total amount of sediments on

---

[1] Ph. H. Kuenen, "Geological Conditions of Sedimentation," *Chemical Oceanography*, ed. by Riley and Skirrow (London: Academic Press, 1965), Vol. 11, p. 5.

[2] Stuart E. Nevins, "Evolution: the Ocean Says No!," *Acts and Facts, Impact Series No. 8* (October, 1973).

both continents and ocean bottoms could have been formed at present rates in a period of time shorter than the Tertiary Period alone.

The only other escape from the conclusion that the earth is not old is to assume that somehow the ocean sediments are being "subducted" into deep ocean trenches and finally into the earth's mantle itself. However, modern theorists have only been able to account for a loss in this manner of less than 1/10 the sediments being brought into the ocean each year. All processes combined therefore can still account for an earth-age of only about 75 million years at the most.

Finally, it can be shown that even the *water* of the ocean has been brought to the earth's surface in far less time than the supposed evolutionary age of the ocean. It is probable that at least a cubic mile of water is added annually to the waters of the ocean through juvenile sources — that is, from the mantle through volcanoes, hot springs, and other vents to the surface.[1] There is a total amount of water on the earth's surface equal to 340 million cubic miles. Consequently, an upper limit to the age of the ocean (even under the unreasonable assumptions that there was no water in the ocean to start with and that volcanic activity in the past was no greater than it is at present) could be only about 340 million years. Such a date would only take us back about to the Silurian Period (i.e., the age of fishes!).

4. Efflux of Materials from the Mantle into the Crust.

Not only is water brought to the earth's surface from the mantle but so are rock materials which form igneous rocks. There are, at present, an average of at least a dozen volcanoes which erupt within a period of a year, emitting significant quantities of lava (there are probably many more than this, since the sea floor is relatively unexplored; also in the past, the average undoubtedly was much higher, in view of the great number of extinct volcanoes and vast amounts of igneous rocks).

If it is assumed that the Mexican volcano Paricutin was typical, its lava emissions were measured at 0.2 cubic kilo-

---

[1] H.M. Morris and J.C. Whitcomb, *The Genesis Flood* (Philadelphia: Presbyterian and Reformed Publishing Co., 1961), pp. 357-359.

meters per year.[1] The average igneous rock increment on the surface would then be about 2.4 cubic kilometers per year. The great masses of subterranean igneous rock throughout the earth's crust indicate that formation of *intrusive* rocks is much more common than *extrusive* igneous rocks (i.e. surface lava rocks) so that it seems reasonable to assume that at least 10 cubic kilometers of new igneous rocks are formed each year by flows from the earth's mantle.

The total volume of the earth's crust is about 5×10^9 cubic kilometers. Thus, the entire crust could have been formed by volcanic activity at present rates in only 500 million years, which would only take us back into the Cambrian period.

5. Decay of the Earth's Magnetic Field.

A somewhat different, but very important, geochronometer is based on the strength of the earth's magnetic field. This evidence is found in a remarkable study by Dr. Thomas G. Barnes, Professor of Physics at the University of Texas in El Paso.[2] Dr. Barnes is author of many papers in the fields of atmospheric physics and a widely used college textbook on electricity and magnetism. He has pointed out that the strength of the magnetic field (that is, its magnetic moment) has been measured carefully for 135 years, and also has shown, through analytical and statistical studies, that it has been decaying exponentially during that period with a most-probable half-life of 1400 years.

This would mean that the magnetic field was twice as strong 1400 years ago than it is now, four times as strong 2800 years ago, and so on. Only 7000 years ago it must have been 32 times as strong. It is almost inconceivable that it ever could have been much stronger than this. Thus, 10,000 years ago, the earth would have had a magnetic field as

---

[1]Carl Fries, Jr., "Volumes and Weights of Pyroclastic Material, Lava, and Water Erupted by Paricutin Volcano," *Transactions, American Geophysical Union,* Vol. 34 (August 1953). p. 611.

[2]Thomas G. Barnes, *Origin and Destiny of the Earth's Magnetic Field,* 2nd Edition, (San Diego: Institute for Creation Research, 1983), 132 pp. In this new edition, Barnes firmly refutes the various arguments (e.g., supposed magnetic field reversals) that have been offered by evolutionists against this strong evidence.

strong as that of a magnetic star! This is highly improbable, to say the least.

Magnetic stars have thermonuclear processes with which to establish and maintain magnetic fields of such strength, but the earth has no such source. Dr. Barnes shows beyond reasonable question that the only possible source for the earth's magnet must be free circulating electric currents in the earth's iron core. Electric currents, however, must flow against resistance, and such resistance generates heat, which is then dissipated through the surrounding medium and lost. Such currents must gradually decay because of this heat loss and this, in turn, accounts for the decay of its induced magnetic field.

Thus, 10,000 years seems to be an outside limit for the age of the earth, based on the present decay of its magnetic field. Any objections to this conclusion must be based on rejection of the same uniformitarian assumption which evolutionists wish to retain and employ on any process from which they can thereby derive a great age for the earth.

6. Other Methods.

We have discussed a number of physical processes (or families of processes) which indicate the earth is much younger than five billion years, and, indeed, much too young to accommodate the evolution model at all. Many others could be discussed[1], but we have restricted our discussion only to a few typical processes which are of worldwide effect (as distinct from radiometric dating, for example, which applies in each case only to a particular mineral in a particular geologic formation).

Furthermore, we have only discussed terrestrial processes. There are many astronomic processes which point to a recent origin of the solar system (e.g., the continued presence of short-period comets in the solar system, when available measurements indicate such comets dissipate and disappear in about 10,000 years).

---

[1]See Henry M. Morris, *The Biblical Basis for Modern Science* (Grand Rapids: Baker Book House, 1984, pp. 477-480), for a listing of 68 global processes indicating a recent creation.

The obvious way by which the evolution model can be accommodated to all these processes is to modify the uniformitarian assumption adequately for each case. It should be remembered, however, that this is done in order to accommodate the evolution model, not because any scientific evidence requires it!

As noted earlier, any estimated date prior to the beginning of written records must necessarily be based on uniformitarian assumptions applied to specific physical processes. Since there are many different physical processes which theoretically might be used to *measure* time (since all such systems *change* with time), criteria are needed to decide which processes are more likely to give accurate dates. In other words, when is the uniformitarian assumption more likely to be valid?

The following rules seem to be reasonable:
(a) Uniformitarian rates are more likely to hold up for short periods of time than for long periods; therefore, if other things are equal, a process yielding a young age is more likely to be correct than one giving an old age.
(b) Processes which apply on a worldwide basis are more likely to give a meaningful age for the earth than those which apply only locally, since errors in the uniformitarian assumption may be very great in a specific locality, but tend to average out when applied regionally or globally.
(c) Processes, for which the rates used are based on a long period of measurement, are more likely to give valid dates than those which have only a short period of measurement behind them.

Thus, a potassium-argon measurement is highly unreliable because it has a very slow rate of decay and requires very long periods of time to give measurable results; it applies only to a specific mineral in a particular rock, and its time-constants are still not adequately measured and known. The magnetic field method, on the other hand, is very likely to be accurate because it involves a short half-life and only has to remain uniform for a relatively short period of time, because it applies worldwide, being based on measurements made all over the world and statistically averaged, and finally because its decay rate constant is based on the

159

longest period of record available for any geochronometer now in use.

Finally, we mention again the fact that there are many more processes which give young ages than processes which give old ages. This fact ought also count for something. Even those few processes which do give old ages can be interpreted equally well, or better, in terms of young ages, as noted in the preceding section.

When one gets down to the real facts on the bottom of the pile, it becomes clear that the only genuine evidence for an age of billions of years is the fact that the evolution model demands such an age and that *most* scientists believe in evolution.

Teachers would do well to emphasize to their students, however, that scientific truth is never determined by taking a vote. Majorities can be, and often have been, wrong.

Contrary to popular opinion, the actual *facts* of science do correlate better and more directly with a young age for the earth than with the old evolutionary belief that the world must be many billions of years in age. Along with all the other evidence fitting the creation model, it now appears more than ever that the evolution model is on very weak ground.

The Antiquity of Man

Heretofore in this chapter, our primary concern has been evidence of the earth's age, and of the various geologic formations which supposedly antedate man's arrival. In this section, we wish to deal mainly with evidence related to the time of man's origin.

Although written records made by early man go back only several thousand years, evolutionists generally believe that man and the apes diverged from their unknown common ancestor about 30 to 70 million years ago, and that true modern man had arrived at least one million years ago, possibly more than three million years ago.

The fossil evidence associated with the hypothetical evolutionary history of man will be discussed in the next chapter. The dates attached to these fossils have been derived mostly by the potassium-argon and other similar methods. The fallacies in these methods have already been discussed. The creation model would tend to place them all within the chronologic framework suggested by, say, the decay of the earth's magnetic field; in other words, within the past six to ten thousand years.

In this case, however, we must also reckon with the radiocarbon method, which has been widely used in the past 25 years to date cultural artifacts of man back to about 50,000 years. We also shall find that a study of human population statistics gives significant chronologic data on man's origin. There are other methods which could be discussed if space warranted, but these two are the most important.

1. *Radiocarbon Dating*

Radiocarbon is the popular name for the unstable isotope Carbon-14, whereas so-called "natural" carbon is Carbon-12. Radiocarbon is formed in the earth's upper atmosphere by a complex set of reactions between the incoming cosmic radiation and atmospheric Nitrogen-14. As soon as it is formed, Carbon-14 begins to decay back to Nitrogen-14, by the beta-decay process, with a half-life of approximately 5730 years.

Carbon unites with oxygen to form carbon dioxide, an important component in the life-processes of all plants and animals. In terms of chemical reactions, there is very little difference between the two isotopes of carbon, so that radioactive carbon dioxide and non-radioactive carbon dioxide should presumably be found in a constant proportion everywhere, provided there has been adequate time for mixing the C-14 with the C-12 (say about 100 years). Consequently, the ratio C-14/C-12 should be a constant in the biosphere, including its presence in living organisms.

When a plant or animal dies, it ceases to exchange carbon with its environment. As the C-14 which it contains continues to decay, its ratio C-14/C-12 decreases. The magnitude of this ratio at any time after death, inserted in the radiocarbon decay equation, should then yield the length of time since death, or the "age" of the specimen.

Since the half-life of radiocarbon is 5730 years, five half-lives (about 29,000 years) would leave only 1/32 of the original radiocarbon content and it is doubtful that any smaller amount could be measured with any reliability (although some have claimed the method could date objects as old as 80,000 years). Thus, it would also take about the same amount of time (about 30,000 years) for the radiocarbon content of the world to build up to a steady-state condition, with the total amount in formation in the upper atmosphere equal to the total decay in the terrestrial reservoir.

The radiocarbon dating method seems very useful and won for its inventor, Willard Libby, a Nobel prize. It has been checked with fair accuracy against known historical dates back to about 3000 years ago, although with considerable scatter and uncertainty.

Despite its high popularity, it involves a number of doubtful assumptions, some of which are sufficiently serious to make its results for all ages exceeding about 2000 to 3000 years, in serious need of revision. A few of these are as follows:

1. Many living systems are not in equilibrium for C-14 exchange.

The C-14 method assumes the standard $C-14/C-12$ ratio applies to all living organisms at the time of death. That this is not correct has been shown in many instances. For example, it has been found that the shells of living mollusks may show radiocarbon ages of up to 2300 years.[1] This seems to mean that there must be some kind of carbon exchange between these organisms and carbonate deposits which contained little or no C-14. If any such possibilities exist—that is, for carbon exchange between the organism and any carbon source deficient in Carbon-14—then, of course, the radiocarbon "age" of such an organism will be too great by an unknown amount.

2. The radiocarbon decay rate may not have been constant.

The possibility of past increases of decay rates has already been pointed out in the case of uranium decay. The same applies to radiocarbon. In fact, John Anderson has recently performed experiments which have shown[2] that C-14 decay rates actually could have varied in the past to an extent which would render invalid most radiocarbon "ages."

3. The amount of natural carbon may have varied in the past.

---

[1] M.S. Kieth and G.M. Anderson, "Radiocarbon Dating: Fictitious Results with Mollusk Shells," *Science* (August 16, 1963), p. 634.

[2] J.L. Anderson, *Abstracts of Papers for the 161st National Meeting, Los Angeles* (March, 1971), American Chemical Society, 1971.

The radiocarbon dating ratio involves the natural carbon background as well as radiocarbon itself. If, in the past, the earth contained either a significantly larger (or smaller) amount of vegetation than at present, then the $C-14/C-12$ ratio would be, respectively, either smaller or larger and the apparent radiocarbon "age" for material from that period correspondingly greater or less than the true age. The same corrections would be necessitated if, in the past, the amount of atmospheric carbon dioxide produced by volcanic emissions were larger or smaller than at present.

Both of these are real possibilities in light of both the fossil record and the cataclysmic model. Prior to the cataclysm, there was a global subtropical climate and a much greater proportion of land surface to water surface than at present. Consequently, there were tremendous amounts of vegetation, as indicated also by the vast amounts of coal deposits now known all over the world. Consequently, organisms living at that time would be subjected to only a very small $C-14/C-12$ ratio, and their remains now would contain no radiocarbon at all, even if they only lived, say, about 6000 years ago.

On the other hand, for many centuries after the cataclysm, with the land denuded of most of the vegetation, with water surfaces now occupying a much greater proportion (70.8%) of the earth's surface, and with ice sheets covering up to a third of the remaining land surface, there would have been much less C-12 than in the pre-cataclysm world, or even in the present world. Consequently, radiocarbon dates from organisms living in that period might tend to be younger than the true ages (assuming, however, that the other assumptions in radiocarbon dating did not cause greater errors in the opposite direction), since they would have a larger $C-14/C-12$ ratio while alive than organisms living today would have. This factor could possibly account for the discrepancies noted by several recent writers,[1,2] between radiocarbon dating and tree-ring dating for post-glacial artifacts. The tree-ring counts have tended to give greater ages by several centuries than radiocarbon ages.

[1] C.W. Ferguson, "Bristlecone Pine: Science and Esthetics," *Science* (February 23, 1968), pp. 839-846.
[2] Colin Renfrew, "Carbon-14 and the Prehistory of Europe," *Scientific American*, Vol. 225 (October, 1971), pp. 63-72.

4. The radiocarbon ratio may not have reached a steady state.

Probably the most important invalid assumption in radiocarbon dating now employed is that the C-14/C-12 ratio is in a steady state with time on a global basis. That is, the formation of C-14 in the atmosphere is assumed equal in amount to the worldwide decay of C-14, so that the total inventory remains the same. As noted before, the attainment of such an equilibrium would require about 30,000 years after the process of radiocarbon formation began.

Dr. Libby himself noted the importance of this assumption when he first developed the radiocarbon method.

"If one were to imagine that the cosmic radiation had been turned off until a short while ago, the enormous amount of radiocarbon necessary to the equilibrium state would not have been manufactured and the specific radioactivity of living matter would be much less than the rate of production calculated from neutron intensity."[1]

Furthermore, he noted that the available measurements on the rate of formation of radiocarbon indicated it exceeded the annual worldwide decay rate by over 25 percent, but he attributed this discrepancy to inadequate measurements, since it was obvious that the required 30,000 years to attain equilibrium was more than satisfied by the long history of the earth and its atmosphere.

The fact is, however, that subsequent and better measurements have confirmed this discrepancy. Lingenfelter pointed this out in 1963:

"There is strong indication, despite the large errors, that the present natural production rate exceeds the natural decay rate by as much as 25%. . . . It appears that equilibrium in the production and decay of Carbon-14 may not be maintained in detail."[2]

Another very active researcher on radiocarbon confirmed this even more recently.

---

[1] W.F. Libby, *Radiocarbon Dating* (Chicago: University of Chicago Press, 1955), p. 7.

[2] Richard E. Lingenfelter, "Production of C-14 by Cosmic 8 Ray Neutrons," *Reviews of Geophysics*, Vol. 1 (February, 1963), p. 51.

"It seems probable that the present-day inventory of natural C-14 does not correspond to the equilibrium value, but is increasing."[1]

And still more recently, Switzer reported on the results of a radiocarbon symposium, and said:

"These results . . . indicate that the concentration increases at least during the past 10,000 years."[2]

Thus, we can conclude that the imbalance between formation and decay of radiocarbon is real, and not merely due to inadequate measurements, as Libby originally thought.

The most reasonable conclusion from this fact is that the $C-14/C-12$ ratio is still building up in the world environment, for the reason that the required 30,000 years have not yet passed. In fact, this phenomenon of an increasing radiocarbon assay provides another very powerful means for estimating the age of the earth itself!

Here we have another worldwide process for which the rates are reasonably well determined, and for which the uniformitarian assumption, though necessary, does not involve excessive extrapolation. Melvin Cook has reviewed the relevant data,[3] concluding that the present formation rate of radiocarbon is 18.4 atoms per gram per minute and the decay rate is 13.3 atoms per gram per minute. The ratio of decay to formation is thus $13.3/18.4$, or 0.72; in other words, the formation of radiocarbon exceeds its decay by the factor $(1/0.72 -1)$, or 38 percent, and so the radiocarbon assay is still increasing.

Cook derives a non-equilibrium equation for this process and then calculates back to the initial boundary conditions, when radiocarbon assay was zero. The initial time, T_0, turns out to be only 10,000 years ago. This is the radiocarbon date, therefore, for the *age of the present atmosphere*, and probably for the earth itself!

---

[1] Hans E. Suess, "Secular Variations in the Cosmic-Ray Produced Carbon-14 in the Atmosphere and Their Interpretations," *Journal of Geophysical Research*, Vol. 70 (December 1, 1965), p. 5947.

[2] V.R. Switzer, "Radioactive Dating and Low-Level Counting," *Science*, Vol. 157 (August 11, 1967), p. 726.

[3] Melvin A Cook, "Do Radiological Clocks Need Repair?," *Creation Research Society Quarterly*, Vol. 5 (October, 1968), p. 70.

Cook's calculations were based on data obtained by Lingenfelter and Suess. However, Robert Whitelaw has shown[1] there is reason to modify the formation rate to 27 atoms/gram/minute instead of 18.4. If so, the ratio becomes $13.3/27$, or 0.49, and the formation rate is over 100 percent greater than the decay rate! In turn, this would mean that T_0 would be reduced to about 5000 years.

There are uncertainties in these measurements, but it appears reasonable to conclude, from radiocarbon buildup around the world, that this process began somewhere between 5000 and 10,000 years ago, even neglecting the other problems in the method. In terms of the cataclysmic model, this would probably be interpreted as dating tne conclusion of the cataclysm and initiation of the present economy, since prior to the cataclysm the ratio $C\text{-}14/C\text{-}12$ is inferred to have been negligibly small.

It should be noted, that this analysis also assumes a constant amount of background natural carbon in the environment. This factor, however, is actually believed to have increased with time after the cataclysm as the devastated lands gradually acquired a new plant cover and the carbon dioxide reservoir increased correspondingly. Consequently, the amounts of C-14 and C-12 were both increasing concurrently, with C-12 probably attaining an essentially constant value at perhaps 3000 to 3500 years ago, since which time history indicates climatologic conditions became stabilized at more or less the same conditions prevailing at present.

For the period prior to C-12 stabilization, the ratio $C\text{-}14/C\text{-}12$, while less than its equilibrium value, would nevertheless be larger than if the same amount of vegetation existed then as now. Consequently, radiocarbon ages for that period would be: (a) much larger than true ages if calculated from the equilibrium model; (b) somewhat less than true ages if calculated from the simple non-equilibrium model. The non-equilibrium model can be modified to allow for a gradual increase in vegetation, and then should give true ages.

---

[1] Robert L. Whitelaw, "Radiocarbon Confirms Biblical Creation," *Creation Research Society Quarterly*, Vol. 5 (October, 1968), p. 80. (Whitelaw is Nuclear Consultant and Professor of Mechanical Engineering, Virginia Polytechnic Institute and State University.)

It is significant that it is within the past 3000 years or so that there is some correlation between radiocarbon ages and historical dates. All three models—the equilibrium model, the simple non-equilibrium model and the modified non-equilibrium model—will yield about the same ages, within a margin of error commensurate with other uncertainties in the measurements and data during this period. It is also significant that the modified non-equilibrium model will yield radiocarbon dates for earlier periods of time that are in essential agreement with all confirmed dates of Biblical and other similar historical records.

2. *Population Statistics*

Another process that bears interestingly on the subject of human antiquity is that of the growth of population. The "population explosion" is, of course, a topic of much current interest, both to professional ecologists and to children, and teachers should help place it in proper perspective. If man has indeed been dwelling on this planet for a million years or more, it is strange that only in recent years has population become a problem.

The average family size today, worldwide, is about 3.6 children, and the annual population growth rate is 2 percent. Environmentalists would like to see these figures reduced to 2.1 children and a corresponding growth rate of 0 percent, so that the world population would not increase any more than it already has.

Whatever problems population increase may or may not pose for the future, it does offer an interesting study in man's past. According to the evolution model, man has been on the earth for at least a million years, whereas the creation model postulates probably only a few thousand years, corresponding to the approximately 4000-5000 years of recorded history. The question is, whether the creation model or the evolution model most easily correlates with the data of population statistics.

To compare the two models, assume an initial population of two people, the first parents. Assume they produce a total of $2c$ offspring, c boys and c girls, who then unite to form c families. Each of these families also has $2c$ children, meaning there will be $2c^2$ children in the second generation. These form c^2 families, and then $2c^3$ children in the third generation, and so on. In the nth generation, there will be

$2c^n$ individuals. If we assume, for simplicity, that only one generation is alive at one time, then the world population at the nth generation will also be $2c^n$ people.

Now let us equate this figure to the actual present world population.

$$2c^n = 3.5 \times 10^9$$

If we assume there have been 100 generations since the first pair (corresponding to about 4000 years, with 40 years per generation), then the average family size must have been

$$2c = 2\left(\frac{3.5 \times 10^9}{2}\right)^{1/100} = 2.46$$

In other words, an average family size of less than 1-1/4 boys and 1-1/4 girls will produce a population of 3.5 billion people in only 4000 years.

On a percentage basis, if the average annual population growth rate is G percent, then the population after Y years becomes

$$P_y = 2\left(1 + \frac{G}{100}\right)^Y$$

The average annual percentage growth to produce the present world population in 4000 years can be calculated by

$$G = 100\left[\left(\frac{P_y}{2}\right)^{\frac{1}{Y}} - 1\right]$$

$$= 100\left[\left(\frac{3.5 \times 10^9}{2}\right)^{\frac{1}{4000}} - 1\right] = 1/2$$

In other words, an average population growth of 1/2 per cent per year would give the present population in just 4000 years. This is only one-fourth the present rate.

In any case, it is obvious from the above analyses that the creation model of human chronology fits the facts very well and is, in fact, quite conservative. There is more than enough room in the model to allow long periods of time when, because of war or pestilence, the population growth rates were far below the required averages.

The evolution model, on the other hand, with its million-year history of man, has to be strained to the breaking point. It is essentially incredible that there could have been 25,000 generations of men with a resulting population of only 3.5 billion. If the population increased at only 1/2 per cent per year for a million years, or if the average family size were only 2.5 children per family for 25,000 generations, the number of people in the present generation would exceed 10^{2100}, a number which is, of course, utterly impossible (as noted in an earlier chapter, only 10^{130} electrons could be crammed into the entire known universe).

Although it is true that the evolution model can be modified by various secondary assumptions to fit the known data of population statistics, it is also true that the creation model fits the data directly, without such modifications. Even if the population were assumed to grow so slowly that it would only reach 3.5 billion in a million years, it is still true that at least a total of 3000 billion people would have lived and died on the earth in the past million years. Therefore, it is incredible that today there would be so little fossil or cultural evidence of ancient man preserved as is actually the case.

Age of the Sun

Evidence now exists that even the sun must be quite young, obtained both from direct measurement of its diameter and indirectly through the now well-documented absence of the expected flux of solar neutrinos that shoud have been generated in its interior.

"Astronomers were startled, and laymen amazed, when in 1979 Jack Eddy, of the High Altitude Observatory in Boulder, Colorado, claimed that the sun was shrinking, at such rate that, if the decline did not reverse, our local star would disappear within a hundred thousand years."[1]

"(Ronald Gilliland's) first conclusion, from a battery of statistical tests, was that the over-all decline in solar diameter of about 0.1 seconds of arc per century since the early 1700's is real."[2]

---

[1]John Gribbin, "The Curious Case of the Shrinking Sun," *New Scientist* (Vol. 97, March 3, 1983), p. 592.
[2]*Ibid.*, p. 594.

This means that the sun's output of radiant energy is generated, not by thermonuclear fusion processes in its own deep interior (a fact independently confirmed by the missing neutrinos[1]), but from the gravitational energy released by its inward collapsing process. This also means that, even if it were only decreasing at one-fifth this rate, it would have been "twice it present size a million years ago."[2] But this, by the standard geological chronology, would have been near the peak of the Ice Age! What it all really means, of course, is that the sun is bound to be very young.

Fiat Creation

An even more amazing development is the massive evidence accumulated by physicist Robert Gentry, from granite rocks all over the world, of "parentless" polonium, indicated by "radiohalos" of polonium without the corresponding halos of the uranium from which polonium is normally derived by radioactive decay.[3] Since polonium has an extremely short half-life, it should not be found in nature except with its uranium parent. Nevertheless, its halos *are* so found, in the earth's primordial granitic rocks everywhere. There seems no possible explanation for this phenomenon except essentially instantaneous creation of these primordial rocks together with the short-lived polonium atoms enclosed within them, leaving their decay halos as a permanent silent witness to the fact of the intitial fiat creation of the primordial rocks. However this "minor mystery", as one evolutionary geologist called it, has been largely ignored by the scientific establishment.

---

[1]Neutrinos are very powerful particles generated by nuclear reactions associated with cosmic radiation and processes in the interior of stars. Since they have no electric charge, they are difficult to detect.

[2]*Ibid.,* p. 593.

[3]For a summary of Gentry's many technical papers (which had been published in numerous referred journals before their creationist implications were realized), see Stephen L. Talbot, "Mystery of the Radiohalos," *Research Communication Network* (Newsletter No. 2: February 10, 1977), pp. 3-6.

CHAPTER VII

APES OR MEN?

The Origin of Man

The question of origins becomes most critical of all as it deals with the problem of the origin of man. Is man merely the product of a naturalistic evolutionary process or is he a special creation, prepared by the Creator to exercise dominion over the entire creation? The evolutionary model pictures man as slowly evolving from a nonhuman ancestor, whereas the creation model requires man to be created directly as man, with a fully human body and brain from the beginning.

The evolutionary history currently taught in the schools suggests that man and the apes were both derived from an unknown common ancestor that existed somewhere between five and twenty million years ago. The line leading to man proceeded through various evolutionary stages culminating in true man somewhere between one and three million years ago. Since that time, man's physical evolution has given way to a cultural and social evolution.

In support of this idea, evolutionists point to a number of fossil hominoids (a term which includes both apes and men) and hominids (a term applying to individuals in the line leading to men but still subhuman) which purportedly show various evolutionary stages of prehuman evolution. Creationists, on the other hand, insist that these are fossils either of apes or men, not of animals intermediate between apes and men.

Teachers find that this is the most sensitive area in the study of origins. "Cavemen" are, to most people, synonymous with the whole idea of evolution. Children almost from the first grade have been told about the very ancient men who lived in caves and how finally, long ago, some unknown primitive individuals among them discovered fire or invented the wheel. Even though such ideas may not have been labeled "evolution," as they were taught, the net effect on the child is to condition him even at that earliest stage to be ready to accept the full story of human evolution later on.

Truly conscientious teachers, however, will want to give their students both sides of the evidence, especially on this most vital of all issues—the origin of man and his purpose.

171

In orde: to give the creationist interpretation of these findings, we shall discuss briefly each of the more important types of fossils in the order of their assumed evolutionary advance.

1. *Common ancestor of man and ape.*

No name is indicated for this animal, since none of them has ever been found, and it is strictly an evolutionary inference that it ever existed. Creationists predict that this particular "missing link" is permanently missing.

2. *Ramapithecus.*

The suffix "pithecus" means "ape," and a considerable number of fossils have been publicized of extinct "pithecine" animals, some of which have been considered as possible ancestors of man. These include *Dryopithecus, Oreopithecus, Limnopithecus, Kenyapithecus* and others, all dated roughly 14 million years ago.

Most evolutionary anthropologists consider *Ramapithecus* to be the most important of this group. This fossil was found in India in 1932 and consisted of several teeth and jaw fragments. Because the incisors and canine teeth of this creature, although apelike, are smaller than those of modern apes, some evolutionists consider this form to be a hominid. However, Dr. Robert Eckhardt of Pennsylvania State University, in a thorough study of this entire group of fossils, said:

> "On the basis of these tooth-size calculations, at least, there would appear to be little evidence to suggest that several different hominoid species are represented among the Old World dryopithecine fossils of late Miocene and early Pliocene times. Neither is there compelling evidence for the existence of any distinct hominid species during this interval, unless the designation 'hominid' means simply any individual ape that happens to have small teeth and a correspondingly small face. Fossil hominoids such as *Ramapithecus* may well be ancestral to the hominid line in the sense that they were individual members of an evolving phyletic line from which the hominids later diverged. They themselves nevertheless seem to have been apes— morphologically, ecologically and behaviourally."[1]

[1] Robert B. Eckhardt, "Population Genetics and Human Origins," *Scientific American*, Vol. 226 (January, 1972), p. 101.

All of these different fossils are probably, therefore, merely different individuals in the same basic kind of extinct apes. They certainly cannot be considered as ancestral to man. Their peculiar teeth probably are related to their particular diet, not to any kinship with man.

3. *Australopithecus*

This name (meaning "southern ape") has been assigned to a considerable number of different fossils, found mostly in East Africa by Louis Leakey and others. In addition to those with the Australopithecine name, others assigned to this group include *Zinjanthropus, Paranthropus, Plesianthropus, Telanthropus*, and *Homo habilis*.

Australopithecus is considered to have lived from about two to three million years ago, to have walked erect and to have used crude tools. However, he had a brain size of only about 500 c.c., the same as that of some apes. The teeth were similar to those of *Ramapithecus*.

For many years, anthropologists have been confused and divided over *Australopithecus,* some convinced he was ancestral to man and others convinced he was an evolutionary dead end. For awhile, the issue appeared to have been settled by the latest finds of Richard Leakey, son of Louis Leakey, who has continued his father's work. Several new, and more nearly complete, sets of remains of *Australopithecus* had required several signficant changes in interpretation.

"*Australopithecus* limb bone fossils have been rare finds, but Leakey now has a large sample. They portray *Australopithecus* as long-armed and short-legged. He was probably a knuckle-walker, not an erect walker, as many archaeologists presently believe."[1]

Leakey later changed his mind again, deciding along with D.C. Johanson (discoverer of "Lucy") that the *Australopithecines* may have walked erect. Other specialists (Oxnard, Zuckerman, etc.) continue to argue otherwise.

The reason for his peculiar teeth, the same as in the case of *Ramapithecus*, was probably because of his habitat and resulting diet. In that connection, there is living today in Ethiopia a species of high-altitude baboon, *Theropithecus*

---

[1] "Australopithecus a Long-Armed, Short-Legged Knuckle-Walker," *Science News,* Vol. 100 (November 27, 1971), p. 357.

galada, which has teeth and jaw characteristics very much like those of both *Ramapithecus* and *Australopithecus*. The "human-like" characteristics of the teeth and jaws of this baboon are apparently related to his habitat and diet and are clearly *not* indicative of a near approach to humanhood!

4. *Homo erectus*

A number of fossil men are now grouped under the generic name *Homo erectus*, including the somewhat notorious Java Man, Peking Man, Heidelberg Man, and Meganthropus. These are believed to have lived about 500,000 years ago, to have walked upright, to have had brains of about 1000 c.c., and to have developed a crude culture involving simple implements and weapons.

The evidence for all this is equivocal, to say the least. Java Man was later repudiated by his discoverer, and the bones of Peking Man disappeared during World War II and are unavailable for examination. Heidelberg Man consisted solely of a large jaw and Meganthropus consisted of two lower jaw bones and four teeth and has been assigned by many to the Australopithecines.

However, other fossils of this general type have apparently been found at various locations around the world. It may well be that *Homo erectus* was a true man, but somewhat degenerate in size and culture, possibly because of inbreeding, poor diet and a hostile environment.

In 1984, a 12-year old boy of the *Homo erectus* species, dated at 1.6 million years old, was dug up in Kenya. His body skeleton was virtually indistinguishable from our own, and his skull and mandible looked much like Neanderthal man, except that the cranial capacity was only about 800 cc. This skeleton, identified by Alan Walker and Richard Leakey, is believed to be the most complete skeleton of an early human "ancestor" ever found.[1]

Some may question the true humanness of *Homo erectus* on the basis of his small brain size (900-1100 cc). However, that is definitely within the range of brain size of modern man, though on the low end of the scale.

---

[1] Boyce Rensberger, "Human Fossil is Unearthed," *Washington Post*, October 19, 1984, pp. AI, AII.

Furthermore, there is no necessary correlation of brain size with intelligence.

"In fact, increasing brain volume of itself tells us little, since it merely reflects changes in internal brain organization at a variety of levels."[1]

5. *Neanderthal Man*

The most famous of all the so-called "missing links" is *Homo neanderthalensis*, pictured for more than a hundred years as a stooped, brutish character with heavy brow ridges and the crudest of habits. Many skeletal remains of these people are available now, however, and there is no longer any doubt that Neanderthal Man was truly human, *Homo sapiens*, no more different from modern men than the various tribes of modern men are from each other. His brain capacity was certainly human, as Dobzhansky has noted:

"The cranial capacity of the Neanderthal race of *Homo sapiens* was, on the average, equal to or even greater than that in modern man. Cranial capacity and brain size are, however, not reliable criteria of 'intelligence' or intellectual abilities of any kind."[2]

As far as the stooped skeletal structure of Neanderthal is concerned, most anthropologists now believe this was due to disease, possibly arthritis or rickets.

"Neanderthal man may have looked like he did, not because he was closely related to the great apes, but because he had rickets, an article in the British publication NATURE suggests. The diet of Neanderthal man was definitely lacking in Vitamin D during the 35,000 years he spent on earth."[3]

It is known that Neanderthal man raised flowers, fashioned elegant tools, painted pictures, and practiced some kind of religion, burying his dead. There is now even some

---

[1] D.R. Pilbeam, "Review of *The Brain in Hominid Evolution*" (New York: Columbia University Press, 1971), pp. 170; *Science* (March 10, 1972), p. 1101.
[2] Theodosius Dobzhansky, "Changing Man," *Science*, Vol. 155 (January 27, 1967), p. 410.
[3] "Neanderthals Had Rickets," *Science Digest*, Vol. 69 (February, 1971), p. 35. (This reference is to an article by Francis Ivanhoe in the August 8, 1970 issue of *Nature*.)

evidence that Neanderthal man or some of his predecessors had a form of writing.

"Communication with inscribed symbols may go back as far as 135,000 years in man's history, antedating the 50,000-year-old Neanderthal man. Alexander Marshack of Harvard's Peabody Museum made this pronouncement recently after extensive microscopic analysis of a 135,000-year-old ox rib covered with symbolic engravings. The results of his findings are that it is a sample of 'pre-writing,' that there is a distinct similarity in cognitive style between it and those 75,000 years later, and . . . it establishes a tradition of carving that stretches over thousands of years."[1]

6. Modern Man

Contrary to common opinion, there is much evidence that modern man existed contemporaneously with all these hypothetical and very doubtful apelike ancestors.

"Last year Leakey and his co-workers found three jaw bones, leg bones and more than 400 man-made stone tools. The specimens were attributed to the genus *Homo* and were dated at 2.6 million years.

"Leakey further described the whole shape of the brain case as remarkably reminiscent of modern man, lacking the heavy and protruding eyebrow ridges and thick bones characteristic of *Homo erectus*.

"In addition to the as yet unnamed skull, the expedition turned up parts of the leg bones of two other individuals. These fossils surprisingly show that man's unique bipedal locomotion was developed at least 2.5 million years ago."[2]

Here is apparently good evidence that modern man—modern anatomically at least—was living prior to *Neanderthal,* prior to *Homo erectus,* and even prior to *Australopithecus!* This would place man well back within the Pliocene Epoch and, for all practical purposes, completely eliminate his imagined evolutionary ancestry.

---

[1] "Use of Symbols Antedates Neanderthal Man," *Science Digest,* Vol. 73 (March, 1973), p. 22.
[2] "Leakey's New Skull Changes our Pedigree and Lengthens our Past," *Science News,* Vol. 102 (November 18, 1972), p. 324.

In a recent popular review article, Ronald Schiller has called attention to the current confusion among anthropologists:

"The descent of man is no longer regarded as a chain with some links missing, but rather as a tangled vine whose tendrils loop back and forth as species interbred to create new varieties, most of which died out. . . . It may be that we did not evolve from any of the previously known human types, but descended in a direct line of our own."[1]

Now that man's origin is beginning to be recognized as being much earlier (geologically speaking, in terms of the orthodox geologic time system) than previously thought, perhaps anthropologists will take a serious look at the many other fossils of modern man that had been previously reported in earlier strata, but which had been ignored or explained away.

For example, there were the Castenedolo and Olmo skulls, found in Italy in 1860 and 1863, respectively. Both were identified as modern skulls and yet were found in undisturbed Pliocene strata. The Calaveras skull was found in California in 1886, also in Pliocene deposits, and it too was a fully developed modern skull. These were well-documented at the time, but later became more or less forgotten. Many others have been reported, but it has proved difficult to obtain convincing documentation. In any case, it seems the whole subject now needs to be reopened.

The above discussion has taken at face value the various dates assigned to the different hominid and human fossils. These have been obtained largely by the potassium-argon and other uniformitarian methods, placed in the standard geologic time framework.

From the critique of these methods in previous chapters, it is evident that the creation model would interpret all of them in a post-cataclysm context, within a period of the past 10,000 years or so. Be that as it may, our purpose here is to show there is no evidence supporting the assumed evolutionary descent of man from an apelike ancestor.

---

[1] Ronald Schiller, "New Findings on the Origin of Man," *Reader's Digest* (August, 1973), pp. 89-90.

Even in terms of the standard chronology, and accepting the fossil evidence at face value, we have shown that there is no objective evidence that man evolved from an ape or any other kind of animal ancestry. As far as the actual fossil evidence is concerned, man has always been man, and the ape has always been an ape. There are no intermediate or transitional forms leading up to man, any more than there were transitional forms between any of the other basic kinds of animals in the fossil records.

That, of course, was the explicit prediction of the creation model with respect to man's origin.

Languages and Races

Evolutionists apply evolutionary theory not only to man's origin but also to his later history, interpreting his societies and cultures, and even his economic and political systems, in terms of naturalistic development from one form into another. As a matter of fact, it is in the realm of the social sciences that the difference between evolutionist and creationist philosophy is most important, since these impinge most directly on man's personal commitments and daily activities.

That is, if man is merely a product of random natural processes, and is essentially an animal with no particular purpose or meaning in his life, then his commitments and actions will surely be significantly different from those of a man who considers himself as a being specially created by a personal Creator who had a specific purpose in his creation. The social sciences, which attempt to deal with man and his behavior (both as an individual and in societal organizations), tend to take radically different approaches to human problems, depending upon their philosophy with respect to human origins.

Consequently, it is especially important in these subjects that the teacher gives a balanced presentation of both points of view to students. Otherwise, the process of education for living becomes a process of indoctrination and channelization, and the school degenerates into a hatchery of parrots. In the remaining sections of this book, we shall compare the evolution and creation models in terms of concepts of origin and aspects of man's nature which distinguish him most sharply from all other creatures; namely, attributes of language, culture, and religion.

In dealing with man strictly as a biological organism in a "great chain of being" with all other organisms, the human "species" (*Homo sapiens*) has been divided by evolutionary biologists into various "subspecies," or *races*, in the same way that other species are subdivided. In evolutionary terminology, a race is an incipient species; if racial development is progressive and beneficial in the "struggle for existence," then that race will be preserved and others may die out, so it eventually becomes a new and better species. *Homo erectus* may have evolved into *Homo sapiens*, and, someday, it is theorized, a particularly virile race among the latter may evolve into, say, *Homo supremus* (superman!).

This concept was particularly dominant among the 19th century evolutionists, and it produced a number of aberrant philosophies such as the so-called social Darwinism, militaristic imperialism, and Nietzschean racism. It is significant that Charles Darwin gave his book, *The Origin of Species by Natural Selection*, the provocative subtitle "The Preservation of Favored Races in the Struggle for Life." Though in his book the discussion centered on races of plants and animals, it was clear that he also included the various races of men in the same concept.

As a matter of fact, he made his convictions on the subject quite clear in a well-known excerpt from one of his published letters, in which he wrote:

"The more civilized so-called Caucasian races have beaten the Turkish hollow in the struggle for existence. Looking to the world at no very distant date, what an endless number of the lower races will have been eliminated by the higher civilized races throughout the world."[1]

Similarly, Thomas Huxley, the leading evolutionary protagonist of the last century, said:

"No rational man, cognizant of the facts, believes that

---

[1] Letter from Charles Darwin to W. Graham, July 3, 1881, *Life and Letters*, *I*, p. 316, cited by G. Himmelfarb, *Darwin and the Darwinian Revolution* (London: Chatto & Windus, 1959), p. 343.

the average negro is the equal, still less the superior, of the white man."[1]

The same sentiment was shared by practically all the evolutionary scientists of that day:

"*Ab initio*, Afro-Americans, were viewed by these intellectuals as being in certain ways unredeemably, unchangeably, irrevocably inferior."[2]

Modern-day evolutionists, for the most part, do not regard any one race of men as intrinsically superior or inferior to any other. Nevertheless, the very concept of "race" is fundamentally a category of evolutionary biology, and leading modern evolutionists recognize this. George Gaylord Simpson says:

"Races of man have, or perhaps one should say 'had,' exactly the same biological significance as the subspecies of other species of mammals."[3]

The creation model, on the other hand, recognizes only the *kind* as the basic created unit, specifically, in this case, mankind. Many varieties of dogs have been developed from one ancestral dog "kind," yet they are still interfertile and capable of reverting back to the ancestral form. Similarly, all the different tribal groups among men have developed from the originally created man and woman and are still basically one biological unit.

One of the most vexing questions today among evolutionary biologists and anthropologists is the question of the origin of the races. If, indeed, all mankind has the same ancestors, and no one race is better than another, as most modern evolutionists affirm, then how did they ever get to be so different in appearance? It would seem that each distinct race must have its own peculiar history of segregation, mutation, selection and adaptation, or it could not have developed so differently from other races. But, if that is so,

[1] Thomas Huxley, *Lay Sermons, Addresses and Reviews* (New York: Appleton, 1871), p. 20.

[2] Sidney W. Mintz, "Review of *Outcasts of Evolution: Scientific Attitudes of Racial Inferiority, 1859-1900* (Urbana: University of Illinois Press, 1971, 228 pp.)," *American Scientist*, Vol. 60 (May-June, 1972), p. 387.

[3] George Gaylord Simpson, "The Biological Nature of Man," *Science*, Vol. 152 (April 22, 1966), p. 474.

why shouldn't differences in intellect and physical capacities also have developed by the same processes? These would surely have greater "survival value" in natural selection than such relatively innocuous differences as skin coloration. Such thoughts as these, however, lead to racism, and evolutionists today quite rightly repudiate racism on ethical grounds, even though this leaves them with an unsolved scientific puzzle.

Creationists also have the same problem of explaining the origin of the different tribal physical characteristics from one common ancestral population. Obviously, segregation into small groups is necessary in either model if distinctive characteristics are to emerge and become stabilized in each group. One of the top anthropologists of modern times, Ralph Linton of Yale, put it in the following words:

> "Observation of many different species has shown that the situation of small, highly inbred groups is ideal for the fixation of mutations and consequent speeding up of the evolutionary process. In general, the smaller the inbreeding group, the more significant any mutation becomes for the formation of a new variety."[1]

The problem, however, is that mutations are harmful, not helpful! Mutations spreading through a small, inbreeding population would most likely destroy the population long before the imaginary beneficial mutations would ever occur.

On the other hand, creationists would agree completely with Linton's statement (and, of course, the basic phenomenon of rapid physiological changes in small inbreeding populations *has* been well established by observation) provided the term "recessive Mendelian characteristics" were substituted for "mutations." As long as there is a large population, with free gene flow, the population will tend to exhibit only a fairly constant set of dominant characteristics. The variational potential for each kind of organism implicit in its DNA molecular structure, is tremendously diverse but for any of the "recessive" genetic characters ever to become typical, a small sub-population would somehow have to be isolated from the main population and forced to propagate by inbreeding.

---

[1] Ralph Linton, *The Tree of Culture* (New York: Alfred A. Knopf, 1955), p. 23.

It would be difficult, if not impossible, to prove that a new characteristic expressed in a population was a true mutation rather than a mere recessive characteristic. The difference is that a recessive characteristic is already implicitly present in the structured genetic program for the organism, but hitherto hidden. A mutation, on the other hand, represents a mistake, or an accidental disarrangement, in the implementation of that structured program.

Mutations are almost always harmful; therefore the development of a new subspecies by the mutation route would take an exceedingly long time—if indeed it could ever be done. A designed genetic structure, however, even though previously recessive, might very well have immediate benefits in a given environment.

Therefore, the concept of rapidly developing physical distinctives in small, inbreeding populations fits perfectly into the creation model. In fact, it can be regarded as an actual prediction of the creation model, involving creative forethought on the part of the Creator, who equipped each kind of organism with a wide variety of potential structures to enable it to adapt rapidly to a wide variety of potential environments in order to conserve and preserve its basic kind.

To achieve such results by mutation would require a tremendously long period of segregation of each race, and as noted before, leads naturally and almost inevitably to racism —the concept that each race has a long evolutionary history of its own.

Now, the question is, how would it be possible to force the ancestral human population to split up into small, inbreeding groups in order to permit the process of change, whatever it was, to take effect? Since they originated together, it would seem advantageous to the group as a whole to have remained together, or at least in communication and commerce with each other, as such would have discouraged and minimized inbreeding.

It seems plausible that effective segregation only could have been achieved if communication were somehow made *impossible*.

The mention of communication immediately brings up the subject of *language*. The real fundamental difference between one group of men and another is, not that of racial distinctives, but rather, language. If two groups cannot talk to each other, there is no way they can work effectively together, or intermarry. Different languages will effectively enforce segregation, where nothing else (except pure force) could.

The basic cause of racial or tribal differences, therefore, must be differences in language. But, then, how can we explain the origin of different languages? If all tribes and races came from a common ancestral population, they must all have had, at one time, the same language. As long as they had the same language, they would never separate sufficiently to develop distinct racial characteristics. The fact is, however, that by some means such characteristics have developed; which means that tribes were somehow segregated; which means that languages somehow became different. Which came first, the segregation or the language, the chicken or the egg?

As far as the evolution model is concerned, this language question presents an impasse. The creation model, however, presupposes a Creator and a creative purpose for man, and the problem can be resolved in this context.

First, however, we should consider the origin of language itself. The capacity for abstract, personalized thought and the ability to articulate and communicate that thought in symbolic sounds to other individuals is, no doubt, the most obvious difference between man and the animals. The differences between animal instincts and human reason, and between the grunts and barks of animals and the intelligent speech of man, are practically infinite. Even such a doctrinaire evolutionist as Simpson says:

"Human language is absolutely distinct from any system of communication in other animals. That is made most clear by comparison with other animal utterances, which most nearly resemble human speech and are most often called 'speech.' Non-human vocables are, in effect, interjections. They reflect the individual's physical or, more frequently, emotional state. They do not, as true language does, name, discuss, abstract, or symbolize."[1]

---

[1] George Gaylord Simpson, "The Biological Nature of Man," *Science*, Vol. 152 (April 22, 1966), p. 476.

How could animal noises ever have evolved into human language? This is certainly one of the major evolutionary mysteries. Many scientists have studied the chatterings of apes and monkeys, with attendant publicity and the usual overestimation of the linguistic potential in this sort of thing. However, one of the leading workers in this field has concluded:

"The more that is known about it, the less these systems seem to help in the understanding of human language."[1]

The evolutionary model seems completely incapable of explaining the origin of human language. Yet this is probably the most important evolutionary gap of all of them, marking the unbridgeable gulf between man and the animals. The anthropologist, Ralph Linton, has said, for example:

"The use of language is very closely associated with the superior thinking ability of humans. In his ability to communicate man differs even more from other animals than he does in his learning or thinking. . . . However, man is the only species which has developed communication to the point where he can transmit abstract ideas. . . . It is a curious fact that there is no mammalian species other than man which imitates sounds. . . . In this respect, humans are truly unique.

"We know absolutely nothing about the early stages in the development of language. . . ."[2]

The creation model, of course, states explicitly that man is absolutely distinct from animals, and this would be especially true with respect to the all-important sphere of thought and speech.

Assuming the existence of language as a general entity, however, the question is how did the original language ever proliferate into all the different languages in order to allow the development of distinct tribal physical characteristics? It was definitely not a slow evolutionary development, for the obvious reason that the most "primitive" tribes have the most complex languages.

---

[1] J.B. Lancaster, *The Origin of Man*, Symposium ed. P.L. DeVore (New York: Wenner-Gren Foundation, 1965).
[2] Ralph Linton, *op. cit.*, pp. 8, 9.

"The so-called primitive languages can throw no light on language origins since most of them are actually more complicated in grammar than the tongues spoken by civilized people."[1]

As far as ancient languages are concerned, Simpson states:

"The oldest language that can reasonably be reconstructed is already modern, sophisticated, complete from an evolutionary point of view."[2]

There seems to be no clue whatever in evolutionary theory to the origin of different languages, since vastly different and highly complex languages have been in existence as far back as historical evidence goes.

There are thousands of different languages and it is quite difficult for a person to learn another language than his own. Nevertheless, it is a fact that all languages can be analyzed in terms of the science of linguistics and all *can* be learned by men of other languages. This fact demonstrates that all languages are somehow related, as are all the different tribes of men.

There really seems no way to explain the different languages except in terms of the special creative purpose of the Creator. Evolution has no explanation either for language in general or for languages in particular. Exactly when or how the Creator transformed the primeval language of the original human population into distinctive languages of different tribes and nations (not "races"!), and impelled them to separate into different groups, perhaps can be determined by a close study of the records of pre-history. But this is not a problem susceptible to scientific evaluation.

Ancient Civilizations

The typical evolutionary approach to the study of early man is to picture him first as brutish and ignorant, existing by hunting animals and gathering wild fruits and nuts, often living in caves. He then is seen slowly developing a crude form of agriculture and animal domestication, then living in

---

[1] *Ibid.*
[2] George Simpson, *op. cit.*, p. 477.

villages with some kind of social organization, finally discovering how to use metals and ultimately developing into "civilized" man. Thus, it is believed that biological evolution leading up to man has, in some respects, given way to social and cultural evolution in man's societies. There are many who would build on this supposed foundation by advocating further uncontrolled evolution (*laissez-faire* capitalism, economic or militaristic imperialism, or even anarchism). Others would advocate some form of controlled evolution (socialism, communism, etc., probably involving even genetic engineering and deterministic control of the social structure).

The creationist approach, on the other hand, suggests that man was created as a fully developed man, equipped with high intelligence and capabilities right from the beginning. He was not furnished with ready-made cities and technological equipment, of course, but he was entrusted by the Creator with the ability and responsibility to develop and utilize the earth and its resources in ways that would be consistent with His creative purposes.

The obvious progress in man's technological developments over the centuries may seem, superficially, to represent a form of evolutionary progress, but it really is an evidence against evolution instead. That is, such progress is attributable to a capacity in man which sets him completely apart from the animals; namely, the ability to acquire knowledge and skills in one generation and then pass those on to the next generation. Thus, the advances in civilization over the period of human history do not represent evolution at all, but rather man's unique ability to transmit new knowledge.

Some animals (e.g., ants, bees, prairie dogs) may seem to have quite intricate social systems, but these are all instinctive and remain the same, generation after generation. Some animals may seem quite intelligent and may be taught to do marvelous things, but this acquired knowledge is not transmitted in any degree to their progeny. Only man has this ability and his developing civilizations give testimony to that fact. The only model adequate to account for such a remarkable power seems to be that of special creation in the beginning.

The currently accepted implications of the evolutionary

model of man's early history can be expressed roughly by the following table.

Evolutionary Age	Culture	Practices	Implements	Time B.P.
Eolithic (Dawn Stone Age)	Animalistic	Hand-to-Mouth	Natural Stone	3,000,000
Paleolithic (Old Stone Age)	Savagery	Food Collecting	Chipped Stone	1,000,000
Mesolithic (Middle Stone Age)	Barbarism	Incipient Agriculture	Wood-Stone Composites	15,000
Neolithic (New Stone Age)	Civilization	Village Economy	Polished Stone	9,000
Copper Age	Urbanization	Organized State	Polished Stone	7,500
Bronze Age	Urbanization	Organized State	Metal	7,000
Iron Age	Urbanization	Organized State	Metal	5,000

The dates shown are those generally accepted by evolutionists until very recently. As we shall see, these may now be in need of drastic revision.

Creationists, of course, recognize that there have been people who lived in caves, who used stone tools, and who lived by hunting and gathering. They deny, however, that these phenomena represent stages of evolution.

There are, for example, many people who have a "stone age" culture,[1] in today's age of science and technology. If such people are living today, it is obvious that there must have been similar people living in the world during every age. Nevertheless, they are all typical men; with the proper incentives and opportunities, these people have the same range of potential skills as those who were born in more civilized societies.

The creation model explains these same data in a completely different context, of course, but the data fit the creation model at least as well as the evolution model. In the creation model, the various tribes and languages all stemmed from one ancestral population that had developed from a remnant that survived the worldwide flood, which is an integral part of the creation-cataclysm model of earth history. They had been forced to break into a number of

---

[1]The writer's daughter and son-in-law, Leslie and Kathleen Bruce, for 15 years were missionary linguists with one such tribe, the Alamblaks, in northwestern Papua-New Guinea. These people live entirely by hunting and gathering, with wooden implements. Nevertheless, they live in organized villages, have an exceedingly complex language, an intricate social structure, and are very intelligent and friendly people.

small sub-populations by the Creator's direct creative restructuring of their common language into many languages.

Each of the tribes was then obliged to migrate away from the center of dispersion until it could settle in a suitable locality and develop its own social system. Moving into a new and unknown region, they would necessarily have to survive for a time by hunting and gathering, perhaps living in (or at least using) caves if any were available. Even though they may have been familiar with metals and ceramics, they could not use them until they could discover new ore bodies, and then set up smelters, furnaces and other manufacturing works, and gradually, build a new civilization.

It is not an evidence of evolution, therefore, but of migration and establishment of new settlements, when the "oldest" cultures at a given site seem to be stone-age type, followed by increasingly civilized communities and practices. Furthermore, the more capable and industrious tribes would tend to settle in the more desirable regions, presumably nearest the original center of dispersion. Others would be pushed out toward the periphery to become the real pioneers, opening up new regions. As the population grew in the more civilized centers, new waves of migration would take place, displacing the pioneer settlers and forcing them still further out into the unknown until, finally, they would be scattered all over the world.

This rather simple and straightforward concept of human history is a natural prediction from the basic creation-cataclysm model. It seems abundantly supported by archaeological investigation. Note, for example, some of the specific predictions based on this model:

1. The origin of civilization would be located somewhere in the Middle East, near the site of Mount Ararat (where historical tradition indicates the survivors of the antediluvian population emerged from the great cataclysm) or near Babylon (where tradition indicates the confusion of languages took place). This region is located near the geographical center of the post-cataclysm land areas[1] and so would be the natural location for the Creator of man-

---

[1] Andrew J. Woods and Henry M. Morris, *The Center of the Earth* (San Diego: Institute for Creation Research, 1973), 18 pp.

kind, who had providentially preserved a remnant through the Flood, to arrange for the post-diluvian dispersion to begin.

2. Wherever a new settlement was located, it would be evidenced first by a brief "stone-age" interval.

3. The stone-age would be followed rather quickly by evidences of urbanization and other marks of civilization.

4. A state of high technological ability would be evidenced very early in the history of each region, often followed by invasion from outside or by internal decline.

5. Evidences of civilization would appear more or less contemporaneously all over the world, with a slight priority in time noted at closer distances to the center of dispersion.

All of the above predictions are supported by the actual data of archaeology, and each new discovery seems to lend more support. As has been shown in previous chapters, all commonly cited dates of civilizations can justifiably be revised downward to within the past several thousand years, also in accordance with the creation model. With this reservation, a brief documentation and confirmation of several of the foregoing predictions will be given, considering several factors that are considered indicative of real human civilization.

1. *Pottery*

The invention of the ceramic arts for pottery, buildings and sculptures, occurred quite early, and pottery has become essentially the stock-in-trade of the archaeologist. "Figurines were certainly being fired by 9000 B.C. in the Middle East."[1]

2. *Agriculture*

The domestication of plants and animals was of first importance if man was ever to produce more food than he needed for bare survival, and thus free others to develop other needed skills and vocations.

"Thus we may conclude from present distribution studies that the cradle of Old World plant husbandry

Cyril S. Smith, "Materials and the Development of Civilization and Science," *Science*, Vol. 148 (May 14, 1965), p. 908.

stood within the general area of the arc constituted by the western foothills of the Zagros Mountains (Iraq-Iran), the Taurus (southern Turkey), and the Galilean uplands (northern Palestine)."[1]

3. *Animal Husbandry*

It is significant that domestication of both plants and animals is believed to have occurred about the same time and place.

"In very rough outline, the available evidence now suggests that both the level of incipient cultivation and animal domestication and the level of intensive food-collecting were reached in the Near East about 9000 B.C."[2]

Note the close juxtaposition in time of food collecting and food cultivation. It is interesting that probably the first animal used for domestication was the sheep—used not only for food and clothing but also for religious sacrifices.

"The sheep, on the basis of statistics found at Shanidar Cave and at the nearby site of Zawi Chemi Shanidar, now appears to have been domesticated by around 9000 B.C., well before the earliest evidence for either the dog or the goat."[3]

4. *Metallurgy*

The use of metals, occurred quite early, though it is hardly possible that its use developed as early as that of wood, stone, ivory, antler, or clay.

"The oldest known artificially shaped metal objects are some copper beads found in northern Iraq and dating from the beginning of the 9th millennium B.C."

Metals such as copper were originally worked cold, but it was not long before the arts of smelting and alloying were developed.

---

[1] Hans Helbaek, "Domestication of Food Plants in the Old World," *Science*, Vol. 130 (August 14, 1959), p. 365.

[2] Halet Cambel and Robert J. Braidwood, "An Early Farming Village in Turkey," *Scientific American*, Vol. 222 (March, 1970), p. 52.

[3] Robert H. Dyson, Jr., "On the Origin of the Neolithic Revolution," *Science*, Vol. 144 (May 8, 1964), p. 674.

[4] Cyril S. Smith, *op. cit.*, p. 910.

"At some point in time—not well established but probably shortly after 5000 B.C., and in the mountains that form the northern boundary of the Fertile Crescent—it was found that heating certain greenish or bluish minerals in the proper kind of fire would produce metal —in other words, smelting had been discovered."[1]

Evolutionists imagine these all to have been accidental discoveries. It is quite possible, however, that knowledge of metallurgy had been possessed by the antediluvians. Use of such knowledge by post-diluvian men, however, had to await the discovery of suitable metallic ores and the construction of mines and smelting works.

5. *Cities and Towns*

The practice of living in permanent organized communities no doubt closely accompanied the development of the other civilized practices enumerated above.

"In most civilizations urbanization began early. There is little doubt that this was the case for the oldest civilization and the earliest cities: those of ancient Mesopotamia."[2]

The great cities of the Sumerians are usually considered to be the oldest urban culture. However, even before these, there were towns of considerable complexity.

"We now know that somewhat earlier than 7500 B.C. people in some parts of the Near East had reached a level of cultural development marked by the production, as opposed to the mere collection, of plant and animal foodstuffs and by a pattern of residence in farming villages."[3]

These simple "farming villages," as archaeological excavation has revealed them, contained imposing stone buildings, cobbled streets, plows and wheeled vehicles, and a variety of clay and stone ornaments and implements.

6. *Writing*

Most evidence, until very recently, placed the origin of writing somewhat later than the other attributes of civiliza-

---

[1] *Ibid.*
[2] Robert M. Adams, "The Origin of Cities," *Scientific American*, Vol. 203 (September, 1960), p. 154.
[3] Cambel and Braidwood, *op. cit.*, p. 51.

tion mentioned above, but once again the origin was in the same region of the world.

"Writing was also a Near Eastern invention and one whose contribution to civilization has been even greater than that of metal. . . . Writing appears almost simultaneously some 5000-6000 years ago in Egypt, Mesopotamia, and the Indus Valley."[1]

The gap in dates between the beginnings of civilization and the first evidence of writing, is narrowed or even eliminated when it is realized that writing was evidently practiced from the beginning of the urbanization stage in Egypt and Sumeria. Dr. William F. Albright, probably the greatest authority on Near Eastern archaeology, said:

"The Sumerians . . . created the oldest urban society with an advanced higher culture during the fourth millennium B.C."[2]

Now, it should be noted that the historical dates assigned to the beginnings of Egyptian and Sumerian history are based primarily on actual written records in the form of king-lists. These all go back to somewhere around 3000-3500 B.C., although a number of unresolved questions make these dates uncertain, and they may well be too high.

In any case, the other dates noted earlier (all centering around 8000-9000 B.C.) for the beginning of civilization are based primarily on radiocarbon dating, which gave considerably earlier dates.

"Instead of yielding the expected dates of around 4000 or 4500 B.C., the earliest villages in the Near East proved to date back to as early as 8000 B.C."[3]

Such radiocarbon datings are based on the equilibrium model of radiocarbon, which, as shown in the last chapter, is an invalid model that gives dates much too large.

When corrected to the non-equilibrium model, as it should be, a radiocarbon date of 8000-9000 B.C. would be reduced

[1] Ralph Linton, *The Tree of Culture* (New York: Alfred A Knopf, 1955), p. 110.

[2] William F. Albright, "Sumerian Civilization," *Science*, Vol. 141 (August 16, 1963), p. 623.

[3] Colin Renfrew, "Archaeology and the Prehistory of Europe," *Scientific American*, Vol. 225 (October, 1971), p. 67.

to somewhat less than 5000 B.C. When corrected further by virtue of the earth's decaying magnetic field, the radiocarbon age of the beginning of food production, metallurgy and urbanization would coincide very closely with the historical age for the beginning of writing.

Recently, studies in dendrochronology (tree-ring dating) have tended to support, or even to stretch, radiocarbon chronologies. The bristlecone pine, of California and Nevada, is the basis for this type of dating. However, the oldest living tree of this sort is supposedly 4900 years old (assuming that every ring represents one year, an assumption which almost certainly will give an age at least 20 percent too large, since two or more growth periods frequently occur in a single year). The tree ring chronology has been extended by superimposing what are interpreted as equivalent patterns of growth cycles from a number of dead trees, starting from a living tree 1200 years old, and going back to 8200 years ago.

The wood so dated has also been dated by radiocarbon, to develop a conversion table between radiocarbon and tree ring dates. However, the whole procedure is highly subjective and is still very much open to question. Until it can be much more soundly established and accepted than it is at present, it need not be considered further in this connection. It is much more significant to note that the oldest living thing on earth is somewhat younger than 4900 years old and probably less than 4000. Here again is good support for a recent date for the postulated worldwide cataclysm.

In general, creationists see no good reason not to believe that all the evidences of ancient man and his cultures, as preserved in archaeological sites, support a date of man's new start after the global cataclysm as around 4000 to 6000 years B.C.

As far as parts of the world other than the Near East are concerned, the dates all seem commensurate with this model (after correcting the radiocarbon dates for the non-equilibrium condition).

In Africa, for example, evidence of migrations of talented people are found almost everywhere.

"Africa uniquely contains tens of thousands of paintings and engravings on the surfaces of rocks. . . . The sites

193

of these pictures range from the northern fringe of the Sahara, to the Cape of Good Hope. . . . They date from a possible 8000 B.C. until recent times, and exhibit a continuity of art styles from one end of the continent to the other."[1]

The 8000 B.C. date, is based on radiocarbon and could probably be revised downward to about 2000-5000 B.C. in terms of true age, as discussed above. It is the *continuity* of prehistoric civilized man throughout Africa which is significant.

In Asia, both India and China have very old civilizations. As far as China is concerned, Linton says:

"The earliest Chinese date which can be assigned with any probability is 2250 B.C., based on an astronomical reference in the *Book of History*."[2]

There were neolithic cultures in China before this, so the original settlement of China (as well as Siberia, where extensive cave and rock art is found) and other parts of eastern Asia dates from not long after the original civilization in the Near East.

The last lands to be settled, as would be anticipated, were the islands of the Pacific.

"A date of 122 B.C. has been established for human occupation in the Marquesas at the eastern edge of Polynesia, while a date of A.D. 9 has been obtained for Samoa, at the western extremity."[3]

New Zealand was not settled until about 1000 A.D., and Antarctica not until modern times by scientific research teams.

One more recent discovery must be mentioned, one that either completely negates the standard methods for dating ancient man, or that completely revolutionizes current anthropological orthodoxy regarding the origin of civilization.

"In the last couple of years, two phenomenal discoveries have been made in Africa that . . . challenge the validity

---

[1]Carleton S. Coon, "The Rock Art of Africa," *Science*, Vol. 142 (December 27, 1963), p. 1642.
[2]Ralph Linton, *op. cit.*, p. 520.
[3]Edwin N. Ferdon, Jr., "Polynesian Origins," *Science*, Vol. 141 (August 9, 1963), p. 500.

of long-cherished theories concerning the origin and evolution of the human race. One was the finding in Kenya of a human skull and bones below a layer dated about 2.8 million years. The second was the discovery that a cave in southern Africa on the border between Swaziland and Natal was inhabited by men of modern type quite possibly as long as 100,000 years ago.

". . . The Border Cave dwellers had already learned the art of mining. They manufactured a variety of sophisticated tools, including agate knives with edges still sharp enough to slice paper. They could count and kept primitive records on fragments of bone. They also held religious convictions and believed in the after life."[1]

If this interpretation is taken at face value, real civilization began not only 9000 years ago, but 100,000 years ago, in Africa! Remember, also, the discoveries of Alexander Marshack of Harvard, who found evidence that men 135,000 years ago were able to carve symbolic engravings which essentially were a form of writing.[2]

Obviously, in terms of the creation model, these dates should be revised drastically downward. The *relative* dates are no doubt significant, however, and these tell us that ancient man (even antedating Neanderthal Man) was not only a true man, but a civilized and technologically skilled man. Furthermore, he had penetrated with his skills and civilization essentially all over the world, not too many centuries after the original dispersion.

The creation model of early human history is thus seen to fit all the actual facts of ethnology, archaeology, linguistics, and related sciences at least as well—actually much better— than the evolution model. Therefore, once again, we urge schools in general and teachers in particular to see that their students have full instruction on both sides of this vital issue.

There is one other important attribute of man which marks him off as completely unique among living things. This is his religious nature, a quality not shared in any degree by even the highest animals. As just noted, even the

---

[1] Ronald Schiller, "New Findings on the Origin of Man," *Reader's Digest* (August, 1973), pp. 86, 87.

[2] "Use of Symbols Antedates Neanderthal Man," *Science Digest*, Vol. 73 (March, 1973), p. 22.

100,000-year-old Border Cave dwellers had religious convictions. The origin and significance of this aspect of man will be discussed in the concluding section of this book.

The Origin of Religion

We do not wish in this section to discuss religion in a religious context, but rather in a scientific context. No Biblical quotations or religious doctrines will be discussed, nor any specific religion. However, in order to deal adequately with the subject of human origins, the whole scope of man's nature must be considered in terms of what it really is.

And the fact is that, whether it has come about by evolution or creation, man really is a moral, esthetic, idealistic, religious being, and animals are not. This is an objective fact with which science must deal. And certainly it is essential that the educational process should deal with it. Teachers hope to inculcate values of some kind in their pupils (something trainers can never hope to do with animals), and this very fact presupposes their pupils to possess moral natures. How can a teacher meaningfully convey value systems without dealing with the fact that their listeners possess natures capable of comprehending and appropriating values?

We are using the term "religion" in a very broad sense, as including any concepts of ethics, values, or ultimate meanings. Evolution is, in fact, a religious belief in this sense, and so is atheism. In fact, this is one very cogent reason why creationists object to the exclusive teaching of evolution in the schools, since in effect this amounts to indoctrinating young people in a particular religion, with its own system of ethics and values and ultimate meanings.

That evolution is fundamentally religious, is recognized officially by the American Humanist Association.

"Humanism is the belief that man shapes his own destiny. It is a constructive philosophy, a non-theistic religion, a way of life. . . . The American Humanist Association is a non-profit, tax-exempt organization, incorporated in the early 1940's in Illinois for educational and religious purposes."[1]

---

[1] Membership Brochure (San Jose, California) "What is Humanism?," Humanist Community of San Jose.

Many prominent evolutionists, such as Julian Huxley, H. J. Muller, Hudson Hoagland, and others are listed as leading members of the association. One of the founders is listed as John Dewey, the man more responsible than any other single individual for our modern philosophy of public education. The A.H.A. promotional brochure quotes Julian Huxley as follows:

> "I use the word 'humanist' to mean someone who believes that man is just as much a natural phenomenon as an animal or plant; that his body, mind and soul were not supernaturally created but are products of evolution, and that he is not under the control or guidance of any supernatural being or beings, but has to rely on himself and his own powers."[1]

No one questions the right of Julian Huxley, John Dewey or anyone else to *believe* such things if he wishes, but that does not give them the right to indoctrinate students in such beliefs, especially under the name of "science." Creationism also must be "believed," of course, but the creation model provides at least as effective a framework for the scientific data as does the evolution model.

Many teachers have the mistaken impression that the United States Supreme Court has outlawed the teaching of creation in the public schools. What it actually has done is to ban the *exclusive* teaching of creation, and creationists heartily support this ruling. As a matter of fact, the ruling applies equally to evolution as well as creation. In his judicial comment, Justice Abe Fortas said:

> "Government in our democracy . . . state and federal, must be neutral in matters of religious theory. . . . It may not aid, foster, or promote one religious theory as against another."[2]

Thus if evolution is to be taught, then creation should be taught and vice versa. Furthermore, they must be taught equally. One may not be promoted as against another. We suggest that the best and fairest way to do this is simply to

---

[1] *Ibid.*
[2] Abe Fortas, comment in connection with U.S. Supreme Court ruling striking down Arkansas anti-evolution law.

define and present the two models, with the scientific evidence evaluated in light of both on a comparative basis. The material in this book has been prepared primarily to enable teachers to give the evidence supporting the creation model. They have already been instructed, no doubt, in the evolutionary model and all the regular textbooks in use in the public schools likewise favor the evolution model. It is this situation which the present book attempts to help balance.

Recognizing, however, that some kind of religious commitment is intrinsic in the very nature of man (and children, in particular), even if he calls it a non-supernatural religion, the question immediately before us is the meaning of this fact. How did man's religious nature originate?

Once again, we can compare the evolutionist and creationist explanations of this phenomenon. Consider first the evolution model. How does evolution explain man's moral nature? Let John Dewey himself expound this subject:

"There are no doubt sufficiently profound distinctives between the ethical process and the cosmic process as it existed prior to man and to the formation of human society. So far as I know, however, all of these differences are summed up in the fact that the process and the forces bound up with the cosmic have come to consciousness in man. That which was 'tendency to vary' in the animal is conscious foresight in man. That which was unconscious adaptation and survival in the animal, taking place by the 'cut and try' method until it worked itself out, is with man conscious deliberation and experimentation. That this transfer from unconsciousness to consciousness has immense importance, need hardly be argued. It is enough to say that it means the whole distinction of the moral from the unmoral."[1]

One reads the above words, and is impressed with their eloquence, but somehow the conclusions do not seem to follow from the premises. The question unsolved is *how* does animal instinct evolve into human conscious impulse? *How* does the 'cut and try' method transmute unconscious adaptation into conscious deliberation?

---

[1] John Dewey, "Evolution and Ethics," *The Monist*, Vol. VIII (1897-1901), as reprinted in *The Scientific Monthly*, Vol. 78 (February, 1954), p. 66.

There is a tremendous gap here, and the postulated causes seem utterly inadequate to produce the effects. Nevertheless, this seems to be the basis of John Dewey's thinking and his philosophy has had profound effect on public education for more than half a century. His entire approach seems to have been a sort of esoteric extension of Darwinian theory into the realm of human moral behavior. "Dewey was the first philosopher of education to make systematic use of Darwin's ideas."[1]

Another common theme among evolutionists is that since evolution has now "come to consciousness in man," and generated moral and ethical values, as well as an intellectual capacity for understanding the evolutionary process, we are now able to plan and direct all future evolution. One of America's leading evolutionary geneticists, H.J. Muller, said:

"Through the unprecedented faculty of long-range foresight, jointly serviced and exercised by us, we can, in securing and advancing our position, increasingly avoid the missteps of blind nature, circumvent its cruelties, reform our own natures, and enhance our own values."[2]

Similarly Hudson Hoagland, at the time president of the American Academy of Arts and Sciences, said:

"Man's unique characteristic among animals is his ability to direct and control his own evolution, and science is his most powerful tool for doing this. We are a product of two kinds of evolution, biological and cultural. We are here as a result of the same processes of natural selection that have produced all the other plants and animals. A second kind of evolution is psychosocial or cultural evolution. This is unique to man. Its history is very recent; it started roughly a million years ago with our hominid tool-making ancestors."[3]

---

[1] Christian O. Weber, *Basic Philosophies of Education* (New York: Rinehart Publ., 1960), p. 252.
[2] H.J. Muller, "Human Values in Relation to Evolution," *Science*, Vol. 127, (March 21, 1958), p. 629.
[3] Hudson Hoagland, "Science and the New Humanism," *Science*, Vol. 143 (January 10, 1964), p. 111.

This belief that man can control future evolution is simply another evidence that evolution is itself a religion. Even assuming that geneticists and biochemists ever acquire enough understanding of genetic mechanisms to do such things, a tremendous number of value judgments will have to be made by someone when they are carried out. Every decision, as to the desirable traits of a future individual or the future course of evolution in general, will involve a vast system of ethical-values philosophy, and this is obviously religious in essence.

But again, the question is how can a random, impersonal, nonmoral process like evolution produce a complex animal possessing personal consciousness and moral principles with which to make such plans and judgments? Hoagland, who is a social scientist rather than a natural scientist, simply says:

> "But man himself and his behavior are an emergent product of purely fortuitous mutations and evolution by natural selection acting upon them. Non-purposive natural selection has produced purposive human behavior, which in turn has produced purposive behavior of the computers."[1]

One may believe this, but does saying it make it so? Is this science, where effects must have adequate causes, or is it a belief in magic? If a person wants to *believe* that wishes make horses, and randomly rushing particles in time will produce conscious, emotional, volitional, moral, religious behavior, then such a belief may be adopted as an article of faith. But, one has no right to call fantasies science and to indoctrinate them in the minds of young people in the name of science!

The evolution model is in trouble if it must explain man's moral and religious nature by meaningless cliches such as those of Hoagland and Dewey. Yet, these men are acknowledged leaders in the field of psychosocial evolution and a search of the literature reveals nothing any better.

But what about the creation model? The creation model postulates an omnipotent, omniscient, personal, purposive, moral Creator who created all things, including man. Unlike the evolution model, the creation model recognizes the

---

[1] *Ibid.*, p. 113.

scientific law of cause-and-effect. The Creator, the First Cause, is obviously capable of creating man as a religious being, with intelligence, purpose and ethical motivation. The creation model fits all the observed facts, directly and without embarrassment or equivocation.

It has been now shown, in fact, that the creation model, supplemented by the cataclysmic model, fits all of the real facts of every field of science and every aspect of experience with a far better degree of correlation than does the evolution model. Neither can be ultimately proved or disproved, since ancient history is non-observable and non-repeatable, but creationism fits the facts of the real world more naturally and directly than does evolutionism, as this book has attempted to prove.

The Pitfalls of Paleoanthropology

As a footnote to the scientific discussions in this book, just before looking at the Biblical teachings regarding origins, it is worth noting that the interpretations of evolutionary anthropologists have proved highly variable and unreliable in the past. Since new "hominid" fossils continue to be discovered from time to time, and such finds will undoubtedly continue to receive an inordinate amount of news media promotion by the liberal humanists who control these media, it is well to regard them all with careful skepticism. The mistakes of the past by expert anthropologists should not be forgotten.

"But we have merely to remember cases like Piltdown Man, which turned out to be a fraudulent composite of a genuine fossil skull cap and a modern ape jaw, or *Hesperopithecus*, the ape of the west, which was eventually discovered to be a peccary, ..."[1]

"Ancient humans are going through changes that no theory of evolution could predict. The oldest known hominid (ancestor of apes and man) from northern Africa was recently transformed into an ancient species of dolphin, while in East Africa one of the earliest bipedal hominids, or primitive humans, has changed into something like a dancing bear. While the changes do not fundamentally alter views of early humanity, they have

---

[1]Charles E. Oxnard, "Human Fossils: New View of Old Bones," *American Biology Teacher* (Vol. 41: May 5, 1979), p. 264.

sparked much discussion about anthropologists' over-zealous pursuit of human ancestry."[1]

Anthropologist Tim White thereupon named the "hominoid" *Flipperpithecus!*

"There is a long tradition of misinterpreting various bones as human clavicles. . . . skilled anthropologists have erroneously described an alligator femur and the toe of a three-toed horse as clavicles."[2]

One problem, of course, is the extreme rarity of humanoid fossils (strange, in view of the billions upon billions that must once have lived, if evolution is true!)

"I know that, at least in paleoanthropology, data are still so sparse that theory heavily influences interpretations."[3]

In fact, there are more paleoanthropologists than there are specimens to study!

"The remarkable fact is that all the physical evidence we have for human evolution can still be placed, with room to spare, inside a single coffin."[4]

Because of the scarcity of data, some are now seriously proposing that, instead of man evolving from an ape-like ancestor, the apes evolved from a man-like ancestor.

"We think that the chimp is descended from man, that the common ancestor of the two was much more man-like than ape-like."[5]

These are mere samples of the disagreements that reign in the realm of paleoanthropology today. Yet the evolution of man should be the clearest and best-documented record of all, if it ever really happened!

So much for humanistic speculation about origins. The real factual record is in the Bible, and that is the subject of our final chapter.

[1]W. Herbert, "Hominids Bear Up, Become Porpoiseful," *Science News* (Vol. 123: April 16, 1983), p. 246.

[2]*Ibid.*

[3]David Pilbeam, "Rearranging Our Family Tree," *Human Nature* (June 1978, p. 45.

[4]Lyall Watson, "The Water People," *Science Digest* (Vol. 90: May 1982), p. 44.

[5]John Gribbin and Jeremy Cherfas, "Descent of Man — Or Ascent of Ape?" *New Scientist* (Vol. 91; September 3, 1981), p. 594).

CHAPTER VIII

CREATION ACCORDING TO SCRIPTURE

The Historicity of the Genesis Record

In the preceding chapters it has been shown that the basic facts of science today fit the special creation model much better than they do the evolution model. Although there are certain problems that still need solutions, none are of sufficient gravity to disturb the basic creation framework, whereas the many problems in the evolution model are serious. Strictly from scientific considerations, the validity of special creationism and catastrophism can be considered as established to an exceedingly high level of probability.

However, the details of the creation period—duration, order, methods, purposes, etc.—cannot be determined from science. The scientific method is limited to the study of processes as they occur at present, and these processes cannot create anything, as demonstrated conclusively by the laws of thermodynamics.

If creation is really a fact, this means there is a Creator, and the universe is His creation. He had a purpose in creation and man is apparently at the center of that purpose, since only man is able to understand even the concept of creation. It is reasonable, therefore, that God, the Creator, would somehow reveal to His creature man the necessary information concerning the creation which could never be discovered by himself.

This is exactly what He *has* done in His book of "beginnings," the book of Genesis. Rather than outmoded folklore, as most critics allege, the creation chapters of Genesis are marvelous and accurate accounts of the actual events of the primeval history of the universe. They give data and information far beyond those that science can determine, and at the same time provide an intellectually satisfying framework within which to interpret the facts which science *can* determine.

203

The old arguments against the historicity of Genesis no longer carry weight. It once was maintained that neither Moses nor any of his predecessors could have written Genesis since they could not have known even how to write. No one dares suggest such a notion any more. Archaeologists have long since established that writing was practiced even by the common people long before Moses and even before the time of Abraham. New discoveries in all parts of the world are still revealing that early man was a highly skilled technologist in many fields at dates far earlier than imagined possible by evolutionists only a few years ago. Actually there is no reason at all, other than evolutionary preconceptions, why it shouldn't be believed that man has been able to read and write since he was first created.

Similarly, there has been a great deal of archaeological confirmation that the general setting of Genesis, from Chapter 12 onward (culture, customs, etymology, geography, political units, etc.), is very realistic—so much so that its narratives must have come originally from contemporaries of the people described. There seems no good reason, except for evolutionary preconceptions, to reject the probable historicity of Genesis 11, which merges naturally into Genesis 12.

Finally, all the writers of the New Testament, and Jesus Christ Himself, accepted the historical accuracy and divine inspiration of all the early chapters of Genesis, as will be shown in this chapter. To believe these records as being altogether true and reliable is the only position consistent with accepting Christ as true and reliable.

Divisions of Genesis

There are several helpful ways of subdividing the Genesis record for effective understanding. The most obvious division is that of the six days of creation. Another important distinction has to do with God's works of creation and His works of formation.

Still another involves the structural divisions of the entire book of Genesis itself. These divisions are indicated wherever the phrase "These are the generations of . . ." occurs. Each such occurrence marks the termination of one narrative and the beginning of another. This fact strongly implies that each of these divisions had a different original author.

1. *The Original Writers of Genesis*

The liberal myth that Moses could not have written Genesis because men did not know how to write in his time was dispelled a long time ago. Nevertheless, certain differences in style and vocabulary still have seemed to many to justify some kind of "documentary" theory of Genesis pointing to more than one author of the original documents.

It is significant that, although the book of Genesis is frequently quoted in the New Testament, nowhere are any of these quotations attributed to Moses. Quotations from the other four books of the Pentateuch, however, frequently *are* ascribed to him. There is no doubt, on the other hand, that the Jews regarded all five books as the books of Moses. This paradox is easily resolved when it is realized that Moses was the editor, rather than the author, of Genesis. The original writers of the various divisions were the patriarchs themselves, the ones whose names appear in the formula "These are the generations of . . . ."

In accord with the common practice of ancient times, records and narratives were written down on tables of stone and then handed down from family to family, perhaps, finally, to be placed in a library or public storehouse of some sort. It seems most reasonable to believe that the original records of Genesis were written down by eyewitnesses and handed down through the line of patriarchs, from Adam through Noah and Abraham and finally to Moses.

All of these ancient records were then compiled and edited by Moses, with the necessary transitional and explanatory comments, into their final form. He later followed this with his own narratives, which we now have in the books of Exodus, Leviticus, Numbers and Deuteronomy. Realization of this fact makes these primeval histories *live* in an exciting way. They are not simply old traditions, handed down by word-of-mouth transmission for many generations, but are actual firsthand accounts written by eyewitnesses—men who knew and observed and reported things as they really happened.

The word "generations" in Hebrew became "Genesis," when translated into the Greek language for the Septuagint version. Genesis was adopted for the title of the entire book—a book of the collected "generations" of the ancient patriarchs. The word "genesis" conveys the idea both of origin and chronological records. It was common in antiquity, when a chronicler completed a tablet, to affix his signature at its end. "These are," he would write, "the historical records of Nahor" (or whatever his name was). Then, if some other writer later were to continue the same chronicle on another tablet, he would key it in to the previous one by some identifying word or phrase which corresponded to the closing portion of the previous tablet.[1]

Although there is some uncertainty about whether the "generations" formula applies to the verses preceding it or following it, the weight of evidence seems to favor the former. In every case the events described in each section could have been known by the man whose name followed it, but not by the man whose name preceded it. For example, the so-called "second creation account," from Genesis 2:3 to 5:1 is identified as "the book of the generations of Adam," but Adam could not have known of all the events described from 5:1 through 6:8. The latter was identified as "the generations of Noah" in Genesis 6:9.

Therefore, there really are two creation accounts, the second written by Adam, from his viewpoint. The first (Genesis 1:1 - 2:3) could not have been observed by any man at all, and must have been written directly by God Himself, either with His own "finger," as He also did the Ten Commandments (Exodus 31:18), or else by direct supernatural revelation. This is the only one of the "generations" not identified with the name of a particular man. "These are the generations of the heavens and of the earth when they were created . . ." (Genesis 2:4). In a very direct and peculiar way, this constitutes the Creator's personal narrative of heaven and earth. It would be well not to try to explain away its historicity by calling it merely a literary device of some kind. Rather, man should bow before its Author in believing obedience, acknowledging that He has clearly spoken, in words that are easy to be understood, concerning those things which man could never discover for himself.

---

[1] P. J. Wiseman, *New Discoveries in Babylonia about Genesis* (London: Marshall, Morgan & Scott, 1946). The "patriarchal documentary" theory of the writing of Genesis is developed fully and convincingly in this book.

2. God's Works of "Creating" and "Making"

The first creation account is concluded with the statement ". . .He had rested from all His work which God created and made" (Genesis 2:3). There are evidently two types of "work" accomplished by God in the creation week and reported in His record. In some cases, His work was to *create* (Hebrew *bara*); in others, it was to *make* (Hebrew *asah*) or *form* (Hebrew *yatsar*). This statement provides another important direction for classifying God's works as recorded in this chapter.

God's work of creation, in other words, was that of calling into existence out of nothing (except God's own power, of course) that which had no existence in any form before. Only God can create in this sense, and in all the Bible no other subject appears for the verb "create" than God. It is possible for man with his God-created intelligence and abilities to "make" things, assembling complex systems out of simpler components, but he cannot "create" anything.[1] God also can "make" things, and can do so far more effectively than man. He was, in fact, doing just this during the creation week, along with His work of creating, and both types of works—creating and making—were terminated at the end of that week. ". . . the works were finished from the foundation of the world" (Hebrews 4:3).

It is significant that only three works of real creation (that is, as specified by the verb *bara*) are recorded in Genesis 1. These are: (1) the creation of the basic elements of the physical cosmos—space, mass and time (i.e., heavens, earth, beginning) recorded in Genesis 1:1; (2) the creation of consciousness (Hebrew *nephesh*, the "soul"), which is also associated with the "breath of life" (Hebrew *ruach*, the "spirit" or "mind" or "breath")—recorded in Genesis 1:21, where "creature" is *nephesh*, which in the Hebrew is usually translated as "soul" or "life"; and (3) the creation of the "image of God" in man, as recorded in Genesis 1:27.

Thus, there are three basic created entities: the physical elements of the cosmos, of which all inorganic and uncon-

---

[1] Sometimes a literary work, an artistic design, or even a new dress, is called a "creation," but this is not really correct. A new combination of matter or ideas is a formation, not a true creation.

scious organic systems [1] (e.g., plants) are "made"; the animal world, whose physical systems consist of the same physical elements, but which also has the created capacity of consciousness; and the human realm, which shares the physical matter of the cosmos and the consciousness of the animal world, but which also has the uniquely created capacity for God-likeness—the "image of God."

3. *The Work of the Six Days*

Between these great acts of *creation* were placed innumerable acts of *formation*, climaxed finally by the formation of man's body out of the physical elements, the "dust of the ground," and his soul and breath from God's own spirit (Genesis 2:7). These acts of formation were spaced out in an effective and logical manner during the six days of creation, as follows:

Day	Formation
One	Energizing of the physical elements of the cosmos.
Two	Formation of the atmosphere and hydrosphere.
Three	Formation of the lithosphere and biosphere.
Four	Formation of the astrosphere.
Five	Formation of life in the atmosphere and hydrosphere.
Six	Formation of life for the lithosphere and biosphere.
Seven	Rest from the completed work of creating and making.

The logic and symmetry of the formative works of the six days are evident from the above outline. It is not the purpose here to give a full Biblical exposition of these

---

[1] The exact boundary line between unconscious replicating chemical systems and creatures that have life in the Biblical sense (that is, creatures possessing *nephesh*) is not yet clear from either science or Scripture. It may be possible that some of the simpler invertebrate animals are in the former category. In the case of plants, at least, the fact that they were designed by God to be used as food by men and animals means that they did not really possess life and therefore they could not "die." Death came into the world only as a result of man's sin (Romans 5:12).

verses,[1] but only to point out certain basic principles involved in their application.

(a) *Purposive Progress in Creation*

Note, for example, that each stage was an appropriate preparation for the succeeding stage and all of them for the ultimate purpose of providing a suitable home for man. Note also that each created entity had a specific purpose—none was the mere outworking of natural random forces. This implies that God directly fitted each for its own purpose—no "trial and error" system of evolutionary meandering was involved.

The theological objections to the notion of theistic evolution will be listed shortly, along with similar objections to its semantic substitute, progressive creation. Each system and each organism were created specifically the way God designed them to be, and He intended each to retain its own character. Similarly, the creation week was continuous, with no "gaps" and was a true week; in fact, the very prototype of all subsequent weeks—consisting of seven literal days, no more and no less. The "gap theory" and "day-age theory" will be considered in detail shortly, and it will become evident that neither one is based on legitimate Biblical exegesis nor is either harmonious with science.

(b) *Appearance of Age*

Another point important to recognize is that the creation was "mature" from its birth. It did not have to grow or develop from simple beginnings. God formed it full-grown in every respect, including even Adam and Eve as mature individuals when they were first formed. The whole

---

[1] From our present viewpoint, there is little difference between entities that were "created" by God and those that were "made" by Him. For practical purposes, it seems likely that He made things (e.g., land, water, stars, animal bodies) essentially instantaneously, so that in effect they had been specially created. Nevertheless, only one specific act of physical creation is recorded as such, since at that time (Genesis 1:1) God created the basic space-mass-time continuum out of whose elemental structure all other physical systems must be formed. Similarly, only one act of biological creation is recorded (Genesis 1:21), though the *nephesh* principle then created would likewise be implanted thereafter in every subsequent animal (or man) either formed directly by God or indirectly through reproduction.

universe had an "appearance of age" right from the start. It could not have been otherwise for true creation to have taken place. "Thus the heavens and the earth were finished, and all the host of them" (Genesis 2:1).

This fact means that the light from the sun, moon and stars was shining upon the earth as soon as they were created, since their very purpose was ". . . to give light on the earth" (Genesis 1:17). As a matter of fact, it is possible that these light-waves traversing space from the heavenly bodies to the earth were energized even *before* the heavenly bodies themselves in order to provide the light for the first three days.[1] It was certainly no more difficult for God to form the light-waves than the "light-bearers" which would be established to serve as future generators of those waves.

Note that this concept does not in any way suggest that fossils were created in the rocks, nor were any other evidences of death or decay so created. This would be the creation, not of an appearance of age, but of an appearance of evil, and would be contrary to Gods nature.

(c) *The World That Then Was* (*II Peter 3:6*)

It must also be recognized that this primordial-created world was different from the present world in many significant ways. There were, in that world, ". . . waters which were above the firmament" (Genesis 1:7), and this corresponds to nothing in the present world. The word "firmament" (Hebrew *raqia*, meaning "stretched-out thinness") is essentially synonymous with "heaven" (note Genesis 1:8), and thus means simply "space," referring either to space in general or to a specific space, as the context requires. In this case, the firmament was essentially the atmosphere, where birds fly (Genesis 1:20). The waters above it must

---

[1]The light for the first three days obviously did not come from the sun, moon and stars, since God did not make them and place them in the heavens until the fourth day (Genesis 1:16-19). Nevertheless, the light source for the first three days had the same function ("to divide the light from the darkness") as did the heavenly bodies from the fourth day onward (Genesis 1:4,18). This "division" now results from the sun and moon and the earth's axial rotation. For practical purposes, therefore, the primeval light must essentially have come from the same directions as it would later when the permanent light-sources were set in place.

have been in the form of a vast blanket of invisible water vapor, translucent to the light from the stars but productive of a marvelous greenhouse effect which maintained mild temperatures from pole to pole, thus preventing air-mass circulations and the resultant rainfall (Genesis 2:5). It would certainly have had the further effect of efficiently filtering harmful radiations from space, markedly reducing the rate of somatic mutations in living cells, and, as a consequence, drastically decreasing the rate of aging and death.

Another great difference was in the antediluvian geography. The Edenic river system (Genesis 2:10-14) obviously does not exist in the present earth. The artesian nature of the source of the four rivers, plus the later references to the breaking-up of the fountains of the great deep (Genesis 7:11), indicate there were great reservoirs of water under pressure below the earth's crust. These waters, and the waters above the firmament, must now be in the present oceanic systems and this, in turn, implies that the antediluvian oceans were much less extensive than now. Therefore, the lands were *more* extensive, and the mild climates and fertile soils would have supported far greater numbers of plants and animals all over the world than is now the case.

In addition to all this, there was in the beginning no death! Death only came into the world when sin came into the world (Romans 5:12; 8:22). Man would have lived forever had he not sinned, and so, apparently, would have the animals (at least all those possessing the *nephesh*, the "soul"). Plant life, of course, is not conscious life, but only very complex replicating chemicals. The eating of fruits and herbs was not to be considered "death" of the plant materials since they had no created "life" (in the sense of consciousness) anyhow.

All this has changed now. Decay and death came with the Curse, and the antediluvian environment changed to the present environmental economy at the time of the great Flood.

The Fall, the Curse and the Laws of Thermodynamics

The entire world was designed for man and he was appointed by God to exercise dominion over it, as God's steward. It was a perfect environment and man was perfectly

211

equipped to manage it. He should, by all reason, have been content and supremely happy, responding in loving thanksgiving to His Creator who had thus endowed him.

God, however, did not create man as a mere machine. God's love was voluntary and for there to be real fellowship, man's love also must be voluntary; in fact, an "involuntary love" is a contradiction in terms. Man was endowed with freedom to love or not love, to obey or not obey, as well as with the responsibility to choose. The history of over six thousand years of strife and suffering, crime and war, decay and death, is proof enough that he chose wrongly.

Sin came into the world when man first doubted, then rejected, the Word of God, in the garden of Eden. And death came into the world when sin came into the world. God was forced to tell Adam ". . . cursed is the ground for thy sake . . . for dust thou art, and unto dust shalt thou return" (Genesis 3:17-19). The basic physical elements ("dust" of the "ground") were thus placed under the Curse, and all flesh constructed from those elements was also cursed.

The classic passage of the New Testament on this subject is Romans 8:20-22:

"For the creation was made subject to vanity, not willingly, but by reason of him who hath subjected the same in hope. Because the creation itself also shall be delivered from the bondage of corruption (or, more literally, 'decay') into the glorious liberty of the children of God. For we know that the whole creation groaneth and travaileth in pain together until now."

This universal "bondage of decay" can be nothing less than the universal principle which scientists have finally formalized as their Second Law of Thermodynamics. By the same token, God's "rest" at the end of His work of creating and making all things (Genesis 2:1-3), together with the providential sustenance of His creation ever since (Nehemiah 9:6), must constitute the universal principle now known as the First Law of Thermodynamics, the Law of Conservation of Mass-Energy.

Scientists have demonstrated the universality of the two Laws, but they are unable to discover *why* they work. The answer to the question—Why should energy always be conserved and entropy always increase?—can only be found in these Biblical records. There are numerous other Biblical allusions to the First Law (Colossians 1:16,17; Hebrews 1:2,3; II Peter 3:5,7; Psalm 148:5,6; Isaiah 40:26; Ecclesiastes 1:9,10; 2:14,15, etc.) and to the Second Law (Psalm 102:25-27; Isaiah 51:6; I Peter 1:24,25; Hebrews 12:27; Romans 7:21-25; Revelation 21:4; 22:3, etc.). It is significant that these two universal (and all-important) principles, discovered and formally recognized little more than a century ago, have been implicit in the Biblical revelation for thousands of years.

Overflowed With Water

The Noahic Flood marks the great hiatus between the original world and the present world. ". . . by the word of God the heavens were of old, and the earth standing out of the water and in the water . . . the world that then was, being overflowed with water, perished" (II Peter 3:5,6).

There were thus two great worldwide changes imposed by God on His original creation. The first was when He cursed the ground for man's sake (Genesis 3:17). The second was when He was forced to say, ". . . behold, I will destroy them with the earth" (Genesis 6:13). The first changed the basic nature of all processes by imposing a universal *internal* principle of decay on them; the second changed the structure of the earth's atmosphere, hydrosphere, lithosphere and biosphere, as formed in creation week, by a cataclysmic change in the rates and *external* behavior of those processes. The Curse introduced the universal tendency toward death; the Flood was the greatest visitation of *actual* death the world has experienced since time began.

These two worldwide judgments on sin constitute God's final efforts to speak to man through natural phenomena on a universal scale. At the termination of the Flood, He said (Genesis 8:21):

1. ". . .I will not again curse the ground any more for man's sake; for the imagination of man's heart is evil from his youth;

2. ". . . neither will I again smite any more every thing living, as I have done."

The Curse and the Flood should constitute a permanent witness to man concerning God's hatred of sin and His desire to call men to repentance. Every process that man experiences in his daily life should continually remind him of the judgment of the Curse, and every feature that man sees as he looks at the world around him should remind him of the judgment of the Flood. All that he sees and all that he experiences should constantly be telling him that he is out of fellowship with his Creator and urgently needs the Saviour.

But man is perverse and his imaginations are evil. Instead of responding to the remedial purposes of the Curse, he tried to circumvent it and soon became so irretrievably evil that God had to destroy the world with the Flood. Then, instead of gratitude for deliverance from the antediluvian morass of wickedness by the Flood, the survivors soon manifested their own perversity by a new rebellion at Babel. Man has now somehow, in his warped thinking, converted the universal decay principle into an imagined universal evolutionary process and the worldwide testimony in stone concerning the Flood into a contrived record of the history of evolution. The Flood itself he explains away altogether, either as a local flood or a tranquil flood or an allegorical flood (these theories, incidentally, will shortly be evaluated and eliminated as possible options).

Accordingly, God ceased to concern Himself directly with mankind as a whole, after routing the conspirators at Babel, choosing rather to work through an elect nation, Israel, and then an elect assemblage, the Church, to accomplish His redemptive work in the world. Not again would He impose another remedial curse of some kind on the ground, nor would He again send another world-purging cataclysm, as long as He continued to offer salvation and redemption to man.

"While the earth remaineth," He said, "seedtime and harvest, and cold and heat, and summer and winter, and day and night shall not cease" (Genesis 8:22). That is, the earth's axial rotation and orbital revolution, which processes largely control all other terrestrial processes in the present economy, would remain unchanged and so would all other processes until man's probation and God's reconciliation were accomplished.

Summary of the Biblical Model

In summary, the Biblical model of earth history centers

around three great worldwide events: (1) a period of six days of special creation and formation of all things, the completion and permanence of which are now manifest in the Law of Conservation of Energy; (2) the rebellion of man and the resultant Curse of God on all man's dominion, formalized now in the Law of Increasing Entropy; and (3) the world-destroying Flood in the days of Noah, leaving the new world largely under the domain of natural uniformity.

This framework does not, of course, preclude the occurrence of later events of worldwide implications, such as the confusion of tongues at Babel, the long day of Joshua and the midday darkness at the crucifixion of Christ. The Flood itself occupied only a year, but the after-effects were felt all over the world for many centuries.

The main key, however, to the true interpretation of the physical data relating to earth history, must lie in full recognition of the effects of creation, the Curse and the Flood. The evolutionary system, on the other hand, has tried to correlate all these data in a completely naturalistic framework which either rejects or ignores the significance of these events. It implicitly, if not explicitly, denies God as Creator, Redeemer and Judge.

There are many Christians who seek, by one means or another, to compromise Scripture with the assumed evolutionary history of the earth and man. These theories must be examined critically. As it is done, there is no intent to criticize or judge individual advocates of such theories. Good Christian men have at one time or another, no doubt with excellent motives, promoted these various ideas. It is not the proponents, but the theories, that are criticized. The Word of God must take first priority, and secondly, the observed facts of science, rather than the reputations of men. Each of these various compromising theories will be shown as unacceptable on Biblical, theological and scientific grounds. The only truly satisfactory model is the simple, literal, historical view of Genesis and science that is supported in this book.

Theistic Evolution

According to Scripture, all things were specially created by God in six days. Is it possible that God's method of "creation" might really have been what the modern evolutionist means by "evolution"? (The question as to the exact length or nature of these days of creation will be discussed later.) A popular cliche of neo-orthodox and liberal writers is to the effect that God has revealed in Scripture the *fact* of creation but has left the *method* of creation to be worked out by scientists. This is merely a circuitous way of saying the fact of evolution should be accepted in the hope that the scientists will allow the belief that God is the one controlling the process.

There are various forms of theistic evolution, and different terms that have been used. These include "orthogenesis" (goal-directed evolution), "nomogenesis" (evolution according to fixed law), "emergent evolution," "creative evolution," and others. None of these concepts are accepted among modern *leaders* of evolutionary thought. The evolutionary scheme which is least objectionable to Christians is, of course, simply the idea that Jehovah used the method of evolution to accomplish His purpose in creation, as described in Genesis. This theory might be called "Biblical evolution."[1] Any sound approach to Bible exegesis, however, precludes this interpretation.

1. *Creation of Distinct Kinds Precludes Transmutations between Kinds.*

The Scriptures are very clear in their teaching that God created all things as He wanted them to be, each with its own particular structure, according to His own sovereign purposes. The account of creation in Genesis 1, for example, indicates that at least ten major categories of organic life were specially created "after his kind." These categories are, in the plant kingdom: (1) grass; (2) herbs; (3) fruit trees. In the animal kingdom the specific categories mentioned are: (1) sea monsters; (2) other marine animals; (3) birds; (4) beasts of the earth; (5) cattle; (6) crawling animals. Finally,

---

[1] Richard Bube, *The Encounter Between Science and Christianity* (Grand Rapids: Eerdmans Publ. Co., 1968). One of the many books by evangelical Christians advocating theistic evolution. Dr. Bube is a Stanford professor and a former president and the current Journal Editor of the American Scientific Affiliation. Though it takes no official position on evolution, most of the leaders of A.S.A., nominally an organization of Bible-believing scientists, have been either theistic evolutionists or progressive creationists.

man "kind" was created as another completely separate category. The phrase "after his kind" occurs ten times in this first chapter of Genesis.

Even though there may be uncertainty as to what is meant by "kind" (Hebrew *min*), it is obvious that the word does have a definite and fixed meaning. One "kind" could not transform itself into another "kind." There is certainly no thought here of an evolutionary continuity of all forms of life, but rather one of definite and distinct categories. Furthermore, the sense of the passage is that a great many different kinds were created in each of the nine major groups (excluding man) that are specifically listed. There is certainly room for variations within each kind, as is obvious from the fact that all the different races and nations of men, with all their wide variety of physical characteristics, are descended from the first man and are therefore all included within the human "kind." The same must be true for the other kinds. Many different varieties can emerge within the basic framework of each kind, but at the same time such variations can never extend beyond that framework.

This clear teaching of the creation chapter is accepted and confirmed in other parts of the Bible. For example, consider I Corinthians 15:38,39: ". . .God giveth . . . to every seed his own body. All flesh is not the same flesh: but there is one kind of flesh of men, another flesh of beasts, another of fishes, and another of birds."

Not only is such distinctiveness true in the organic realm of plants and animals, but also in the inorganic realm. "There are also celestial bodies and bodies terrestrial: but the glory of the celestial is one and the glory of the terrestrial is another" (I Corinthians 15:40). That is, the earth is quite different from the stars and planets (as has been abundantly confirmed in this age of space exploration), and thus must have been the object of a distinct creative act by God. It was, in fact, created by God, on the first day (Genesis 1:1-5), whereas the heavenly bodies were not made until the fourth day (Genesis 1:14-19).

Furthermore, even the stars (and this term in the Bible includes all celestial objects except the sun and moon), were each created with its own particular structure. "There is one glory of the sun, and another glory of the moon, and another glory of the stars: for one star differeth from another star in glory" (I Corinthians 15:41). The tremendous variety of heavenly bodies revealed by modern astronomy—planets, comets, meteors, white dwarfs, red giants, variable stars, star clusters, binary stars, dark nebulae, interstellar dust, radio stars, quasars, neutron stars, black holes, etc.—also confirms this statement. No two stars, out of the innumerable host of Heaven, are exactly alike. Each was created with its own structure and purpose (though these matters now are beyond our present knowledge, perhaps awaiting exploration and utilization in the eternal ages to come). Although there are various theories to explain how the various "species" of stars and galaxies may have evolved from one into another, there is no observational evidence of such imagined evolution.

Perhaps the most striking Biblical statement of the absolute uniqueness of each of the foregoing created entities is found in I Corinthians 15:42-44: "So also is the resurrection of the dead. . . . There is a natural body, and there is a spiritual body."

That is, the radical difference in kind between man's natural body and his glorified resurrection body (and obviously the one does not by natural processes evolve into the other!) is taken as analogous to the unbridgeable gaps between the created kinds of things in the present universe.

There are numerous other passages in the Bible which clearly prove special creation, but those discussed above should be adequate to demonstrate that so-called "Biblical evolution" is a semantic confusion, about like "inorganic metabolism" or "Christian atheism." The Bible simply does not permit evolution in its hermeneutical system.

2. *The Theological Contradictions of Theistic Evolution*

There are many people who believe in God without any strong commitment to the Bible as His Word. Therefore, the fact that the teachings of the Bible cannot be harmonized with evolution is of no particular concern to them since they only accept the inspiration of Scripture in a very loose and generalized way, if at all. To them the Bible is considered a valuable book in terms of religious insights and ethical values, but not in matters of science and history.

However, even apart from Scripture, there are still a number of serious contradictions in theistic evolution (assuming that the God who supposedly created things by this process is really a personal, eternal, omnipotent, omniscient, gracious, loving, purposive God). Most theistic evolutionists (not considering pantheistic evolution) would probably agree with such a concept of God, and, of course, this is the type of God revealed in the Bible.

But if God is like this, it seems completely incongruous that He would use evolution as His method of creation, for the following reasons:

(a) Evolution is inconsistent with God's omnipotence; since He has all power, He is capable of creating the universe in an instant, rather than having to stretch it out over aeons of time.

(b) Evolution is inconsistent with God's personality. If man in His own image was the goal of the evolutionary process, surely God should not have waited until the very tail-end of geologic time before creating personalities. No personal fellowship was possible with the rocks and seas, or even with the dinosaurs and gliptodons.

(c) Evolution is inconsistent with God's omniscience. The history of evolution, as interpreted by evolutionary geologists from the fossil record, is filled with extinctions, misfits, evolutionary cul-de-sacs, and other like evidences of very poor planning. The very essence of evolution, in fact, is random mutation, not scientific progress.

(d) Evolution is inconsistent with God's nature of love. The supposed fact of evolution is best evidenced by the fossils, which eloquently speak of a harsh world, filled with storm and upheaval, disease and famine, struggle for existence and violent death. The accepted mechanism for inducing evolution is overpopulation and a natural selection through extermination of the weak and unfit. A loving God would surely have been more considerate of His creatures than this.

(e) Evolution is inconsistent with God's purposiveness. If God's purpose was the creation and redemption of man, as theistic evolutionists presumably believe, it seems incomprehensible that He would waste billions of years in aimless evolutionary meandering before getting to the point. What semblance of purpose could there have been in the hundred-million-year reign and eventual extinction of the dinosaurs, for example?

(f) Evolution is inconsistent with the grace of God. Evolution, with its theology of struggle for survival in the physical world, fits perfectly with the humanistic theory of works for salvation in the spiritual world. The Christian concept of the grace of God, providing life and salvation in response to faith alone on the basis of the willing sacrifice of Himself for the unfit and unworthy, is diametrically opposite to the evolutionary concept.

Progressive Creation

A large group of evangelicals, sensitive to the traditional opposition to evolution in their own constituencies, have tried to circumvent this opposition while at the same time embracing the essential framework of the evolutionary system through what they have called "progressive creation."[1] A similar concept is called "threshold evolution." Other labels have been suggested for these general concepts, but all of them are nothing but semantic variants of the fundamental system of theistic evolution.

The idea in the progressive creation approach is to suppose that, while life was developing over the vast span of geologic time the way evolutionists have imagined it, God intervened at various occasions to create something new, which the evolutionary process could not accomplish unaided.

For example, early in the Tertiary period, God presumably stepped in to create *Eohippus*, the small three-toed "dawn horse." He then withdrew to let subsequent horse evolution continue through the stages of *Mesohippus*, *Parahippus*, etc., until finally they developed into the modern *Equus*. Similarly, a long succession of humanoid forms developed from their unknown apelike ancestor until, at the right moment, God intervened and placed an eternal soul in one of them by special creative power.

Details vary considerably in the exposition of the progressive creation concept by various writers, with greater or

---

[1] The best known advocate of progressive creation is Dr. Bernard Ramm in his influential book, *The Christian View of Science and Scripture* (Grand Rapids: Eerdmans Publ. Co., 1954). Also, the writers in the American Scientific Affiliation symposium, *Evolution and Christian Thought Today* (Grand Rapids: Eerdmans Publ. Co., 1959) propose either theistic evolution or progressive creation.

lesser numbers of creative acts interspersed in the evolutionary process according to the taste of the writer. All, however, accept the basic framework of the evolutionary geologic ages and visualize progressive creation as taking place over five billion years instead of six days.

It is difficult to see any Biblical or theological advantage which the progressive creation idea has over a straightforward system of theistic evolution. Exactly the same theological problems as outlined in the preceding section still apply, whether the process is called theistic evolution or progressive creation.

In fact, if one were forced to choose between the two, theistic evolution seems less unreasonable and inconsistent with God than progressive creation. It involves one consistent process, always the same, established by God at the beginning and maintained continually thereafter. Progressive creation, on the other hand, implies that God's creative forethought was not adequate for the entire evolutionary process at the beginning. He, therefore, frequently interfered in the process, setting it back in the right direction and providing enough creative energy to keep it going a while longer until He could get back later for another shot-in-the-evolutionary-arm. Theistic evolution is creation by continuous evolutionary processes initiated by God. Progressive creation is creation by discontinuous evolutionary processes initiated by God, but having to be shored up by sporadic injections of non-evolutionary processes. Of the two, theistic evolution is less inconsistent with God's character. However, progressive creation may seem less offensive to college boards of trustees, contributing alumni, and supporting churches. It permits Christian academics to say they believe in "creation," for the sake of their constituents, without incurring opposition from their non-Christian evolutionist colleagues.

The Day-Age Theory

Many Bible expositors have felt that the geological ages were so firmly established by science that it would be folly to question them and, therefore, that some means of accommodating Genesis to geology must be devised. The most obvious way of attempting this is to interpret the Genesis account of creation in such a way that the ages of geology correspond to the history of creation. Since the latter is given in terms of six "days" of creative work by God, the creation week must somehow be expanded to incorporate all of earth history from its primeval beginning up to and including man's arrival. Hence, the "days" must correspond more or less to the geological "ages."[1]

In fact, some writers have even built what they feel is a strong case for the divine origin of the Genesis account on the basis of an assumed "concordance" between the order of creation in Genesis 1 and the order of the development of the earth and its various forms of life as represented by the geological ages. That is, in both Genesis and geology, first comes the inorganic universe, then simple forms of life, then more complex forms of life, and finally man.

However, such a proposed concordance cannot be pressed successfully for more details than that. Theories about the early history of the earth and the universe are still quite varied and indefinite. The general order noted above is only what must be postulated for *either* creation or evolution and therefore proves nothing at all. That is, if the evolutionary ages really occurred, the necessary order must be from simple to complex. Similarly, if God employed a six-literal-day week of special creation, as the Bible indicates, again the order must logically be from simple to complex, with the inorganic world first prepared for plant growth, which was then created for animal life, which was then created to serve man, who was finally created in God's image. Since the same order is clearly to be expected in both cases, the fact that it thus occurs in both cases has no apologetic value either way.

The day-age theory is normally accompanied by either the theory of theistic evolution or the theory of progressive creation. In the previous section it was seen that neither theistic evolution nor progressive creation is tenable Biblically or theologically. Thus, the day-age theory must likewise be rejected. Nevertheless, in this chapter the day-age

---

[1] There are many books and articles which expound the day-age theory. Two of the most thorough studies are, from the scientific standpoint, *Science Speaks*, by Peter Stoner (Chicago: Moody Press, 1952) and, from the Biblical standpoint, "The Length of the Creative Days," by J. Oliver Buswell, Jr., *Christian Faith and Life*, Vol. 41 (April 1935), pp. 123ff.

theory specifically will be considered, showing that it is quite unacceptable on both exegetical and scientific grounds.

1. *The Proper Meaning of "Day" and "Days"*

The main argument for the day-age theory, other than the desire to obtain a framework corresponding to geologic theory, is the fact that the Hebrew word *yom* does not have to mean a literal day, but could be interpreted as "a very long time." Specific Biblical warrant for such an interpretation is presumably found in II Peter 3:8, ". . . one day is with the Lord as a thousand years."

There is no doubt that *yom* can be used to express time in a general sense. In fact, it is actually translated as "time" in the King James translation 65 times. On the other hand, it is translated as "day" almost 1200 times. In addition, its plural form *yamim*, is translated as "days" approximately 700 times.

It is obvious, therefore, that the normal meanings of *yom* and *yamim* are "day" and "days," respectively. If a parabolic or metaphorical meaning is intended, it is made obvious in the context. In approximately 95% of its occurrences, the literal meaning is clearly indicated.

Even in those cases where a general meaning is permitted in the context, it is always indefinite as to duration, such as the "time of adversity" or the "day of prosperity." In fact, it would be very difficult to find even a single occurrence of *yom* which could not be interpreted to mean a literal solar day, and would have to mean a long period of time. Whenever the writer really intended to convey the idea of a very long duration of time, he normally used some such word as *olam* (meaning "age" or "long time") or else attached to *yom* an adjective such as *rab* (meaning "long"), so that the two words together, *yom rab*, then meant "a long time." But *yom* by itself can apparently never be proved, in one single case, to *require* the meaning of a long period of time, and certainly no usage which would suggest a geologic age.

It might still be contended that, even though *yom* never *requires* the meaning of a long age, it might possibly *permit* it. However, the writer of the first chapter of Genesis has very carefully guarded against such a notion, both by modifying the noun by a numerical adjective ("first day," "second day," etc.), and also by indicating the boundaries of the time period in each case as "evening and morning." Either one of these devices would suffice to limit the meaning of *yom* to that of a solar day, and when both are used, there could be no better or surer way possible for the writer to convey the intended meaning of a literal solar day.

To prove this, it is noted that whenever a limiting numeral or ordinal is attached to "day" in the Old Testament (and there are over 200 such instances), the meaning is always that of a literal day. Similarly, the words "evening" and "morning," each occurring more than a hundred times in the Hebrew, never are used to mean anything but a literal evening and a literal morning, ending and beginning a literal day.

As added proof, the word is clearly defined the first time it is used. God defines His terms! "And God called the light Day, and the darkness He called Night. And the evening and the morning were the first day" (Genesis 1:5). *Yom* is defined here as the light period in the regular succession of light and darkness, which, as the earth rotates on its axis, has continued ever since. This definition obviously precludes any possible interpretation as a geologic age.

The objection is sometimes raised that the first three days were not days as they are today since the sun was not created until day four. One could of course turn this objection against those who raise it. The longer the first three days, the more catastrophic it would be for the sun not to be on hand during those days, if indeed the sun is the only possible source of light for the earth. The vegetation created on the third day might endure for a few hours without sunlight but hardly for a geologic age!

Regardless of the precise length of the first three days, there must have been some source of light available to separate light and darkness, evening and morning. It was apparently not the sun as it is now known, but of course God is not limited to the sun as a source of light.[1] Whatever it may have been, the earth was evidently rotating on its axis, since evenings and mornings were occurring regularly for those three days. The placing of the two great "light-bearers" in the heavens need have no great effect on the

---

[1] In fact, as noted before, it may well be that the light source for the first three days was the stream of light waves formed directly by God as if already in transit from the light source which would be formed to generate them beginning on the fourth day.

rate of this rotation, so that the duration of day four and those following was most probably the same as that of days one through three.

It is interesting to note also that Genesis 1:14-19 further clarifies the meaning of "day" and "days": "Let there be lights in the firmament of the heaven to divide the *day* from the night; and let them be for signs, and for seasons, and for *days*, and years . . . the greater light to rule the *day*, and the lesser light to rule the night: . . . and the evening and the morning were the fourth *day*." It would certainly seem that there could be no possible doubt as to the meaning of *day* after at least this fourth day.

In view of all the above considerations, it seems quite impossible to accept the day-age theory, regardless of the number of eminent scientists and theologians who have advocated it. The writer of Genesis 1 clearly intended to describe a creation accomplished in six literal days. He could not possibly have expressed such a meaning any more clearly and emphatically than in the words and sentences which are actually used.

Not only is a six-literal-day creation taught in Genesis, but also in Exodus in the Ten Commandments. The Fourth Commandment says: "Remember the sabbath day, to keep it holy. Six *days* shalt thou labor, and do all thy work: But the seventh *day* is the sabbath of the Lord thy God. . . . For in six *days* the Lord made heaven and earth, the sea and all that in them is, and rested the seventh *day:* . . . and hallowed it" (Exodus 20:8-11).

It is quite clear that the six work days of God are identical in duration with the six days of man's work week. The basis for this very precise commandment is trivial and vacuous otherwise.

Furthermore, the plural *yamim* is used here for the six work "days" of God. As mentioned, this word is used over 700 times in the Old Testament. In none of these occurrences can it be proved to have any meaning except that of literal days.

Two or three secondary arguments relating to the word "day" need to be mentioned. It is frequently urged that since it is not used in a strict literal sense in Genesis 2:4 which says, "These are the generations of the heavens and of the earth when they were created, in the *day* that the

Lord God made the earth and the heavens," it is proper also to interpret it that way in Genesis 1.

At the most, of course, the interpretation could be rendered "in the time that the Lord God . . . ," and this has been already recognized as a proper use of *yom* when the context so justifies. The context does *not* so justify in Genesis 1, as has been seen. On the other hand, this verse may primarily refer to the first day of creation when, as stated in Genesis 1:1, "God created the heavens and the earth."

Another argument has been that since God is still "resting" from His work of creation, the seventh day is still continuing. Then, if the seventh day has a duration of at least six thousand years, the other six days also may have been long periods. The Jehovah's Witnesses denomination, in fact, teaches this, stating that since the seventh day is 7000 years in length (including the coming millennium), each of the days is 7000 years, so that God's work week is 42,000 years long! Theistic evolutionists or progressive creationists would, on the same basis, have to say that God's rest day has been at least a million years long since the appearance of man on earth.

Such exegesis is strained, to say the least. The verse does not say "God *is resting* on the seventh day" but rather "God *rested* on the seventh day." In Exodus 31:17, it even says ". . . in six days the Lord made heaven and earth, and on the seventh day He rested, and was refreshed." It is recorded that God "blessed" and "sanctified" the seventh day (Genesis 2:3), but such a beatitude can hardly apply to this present evil age. God's rest was soon to be interrupted by the "entrance of sin into the world, and death by sin" (Romans 5:12), so that He must set about the work of redeeming and restoring His groaning creation. As Jesus said, "My Father worketh hitherto, and I work" (John 5:17). Were it not for the weekly rest-day, recalling God's all-too-brief rest after creation, and now also commemorating His victory over death and the grave, ". . . all the works that are done under the sun; . . . are vanity and vexation of spirit" (Ecclesiastes 1:14).

Similarly, the familiar verse in II Peter 3:8, ". . . one day is with the Lord as a thousand years," has been badly misapplied when used to teach the day-age theory. In the context, it teaches exactly the opposite, and one should remember that "a text without a context is a pretext." Peter is dealing with the conflict between uniformitarianism and creationism prophesied in the last days. Thus, he is saying that, despite man's naturalistic scoffings, God can do in one day what, on uniformitarian premises, might seem to require a thousand years. God does not require aeons of time to accomplish His work of creating and redeeming all things. It is even interesting that on the above equation—one day for a thousand years or 365,000 days—the actual duration of God's work with the earth and man—say about 7000 years—becomes about two and a half billion years, which is at least of the order of magnitude of the "apparent age" of the world as calculated by uniformitarianism!

2. *Contradictions between Genesis and the Geological Ages*
    Even if it were possible to understand "day" in Genesis as referring to something like a geological age (and it is not hermeneutically possible, as just seen), it still would not help any in regard to the concordist motivation. The vague general concordance between the order of creation in Genesis and the order of evolutionary development in geology (and as noted earlier such a vague concordance is to be expected in the nature of the case and thus proves nothing) becomes a veritable morass of contradictions when we descend to an examination of details.

At least 25 such contradictions exist. Note just a few of them.

Uniformitarianism	Bible
Matter existed in the beginning	Matter created by God in the beginning
Sun and stars before the earth	Earth before the sun and stars
Land before the oceans	Oceans before the land
Sun, earth's first light	Light before the sun
Contiguous atmosphere and hydrosphere	Atmosphere between two hydrospheres
Marine organisms, first forms of life	Land plants, first life forms created
Fishes before fruit trees	Fruit trees before fishes
Insects before birds	Birds before insects ("creeping things")

227

Uniformitarianism	Bible
Sun before land plants	Land vegetation before the sun
Reptiles before birds	Birds before reptiles ("creeping things")
Woman before man (by genetics)	Man before woman (by creation)
Rain before man	Man before rain
"Creative" processes still continuing	Creation completed
Struggle and death necessary antecedents of man	Man, the cause of struggle and death

The above very sketchy tabulation shows conclusively that it is impossible to speak convincingly of a concordance between the geological ages and Genesis. Apart from the question of evolution or creation, the Genesis record is stubbornly intransigent and will not accommodate the standard system of geological ages. A decision must be made for one or the other—one cannot logically accept both.

3. Identification of the Geological Ages with Evolutionary Suffering

The most serious fallacy in the day-age theory is that it impugns the character of God. It, of course, provides the basic exegetical framework for either so-called Biblical evolutionism or progressive creationism. These concepts have been discussed and rejected in the previous section on this very basis. The God described in the Bible (personal, omnipotent, omniscient, purposeful, gracious, orderly, loving) simply could not use such a process of creation as envisaged by our leading evolutionists, with all its randomness, wastefulness, and cruelty.

But Christians need to realize that the geological ages are to all intents and purposes *synonymous with evolution!* When they accept the geological ages they are implicitly (though many do not realize it, and would even deny it) accepting the evolutionary system.

The geological ages obviously provide the necessary framework of time for evolution. If the universe began only several thousand years ago, then evolution is impossible. It requires billions of years to have even a semblance of plausibility.

Conversely, the only real assurance men have of the geological ages is the assumption of evolution. That is, since evolution "must" be true (the only alternative is creation!), therefore it is "known" that life, the earth and the universe must be extremely old. The various geologic systems and epochs are identified, and even *named* (e.g., Paleozoic, Mesozoic, Eocene, etc.) on the basis of the fossils found in the rocks, interpreted and dated on the basis of the supposed "stage-of-evolution" of the corresponding faunas. Whenever any other identification or dating technique (lithology, radiometry, etc.) conflicts with this approach (as is quite often the case), these paleontologic criteria always govern.

Thus, evolution is the basis for interpreting the fossil record and the fossil record is the basis for establishing and identifying the geologic ages. The geologic ages with their fossil sequences provide the basic framework and the only evidence of any consequence for evolution. Here is one of the most classic and subtle examples of circular reasoning in all the complex history of metaphysical opposition to Biblical creationism. The Bible-honoring Christian needs to realize that the geologic ages are merely one component in the whole evolutionary package. If one wants to have the framework (geologic time), the glue which keeps it together (evolution) must also be accepted.

Again, however, even if one deliberately rejects or ignores the evolutionary implications of the geological ages, one must still face the massive problem of why God chose to use five billion years of chance variations, natural selection, geologic upheavals, storm, disease, extinctions, struggle, suffering and death as an inscrutable prelude to His creation of man right at the very tail-end of geologic time. "God is not the author of confusion." Yet, He is said to have surveyed the whole monstrous spectacle and pronounced it all "very good" (Genesis 1:31). The Bible is quite explicit in teaching that there was no suffering and no death of sentient life in the world before man brought sin into the world (Genesis 3:14-19; Romans 5:12; 8:20-23; I Corinthians 15:21,22; Revelation 21:4,5; etc.). But if the rocks of the earth's crust were already filled with fossilized remains of billions of animals, and even of hominid forms that looked like men, then God Himself is directly responsible for creating suffering and death, not in judgment upon rebellion but as an integral factor of His work of creation and sovereign rule. And this is theological chaos!

4. *Variants of the Day-Age Theory*

Some expositors, acknowledging that exegetical honesty compels recognition of the "days" of Genesis as literal days, have tried two other devices for harmonizing the geological ages with literal days. One method is to suggest that the literal creative days were each separated by vast spans of geological time. The other is that the six days were six days of *revelation*, rather than *creation*.

As to the first theory, it should be noted that the six widely separated days of creation included creation of the earth, heaven, the stars, sun and moon, oceans, lands, plants, fishes, birds, reptiles, mammals (all of them), and man. Nothing much is left for the vast spans of time between the days, so why are they needed? (This theory is essentially the same as the "progressive creation theory," which has already been discussed.)

As for the revelatory-day theory,[1] there is not a single word in the entire record that suggests such a thing. Visions and revelations of the Lord are frequently encountered in Scripture, but the writer always *says* so, when it is so. In refuting such an extraneous idea, God Himself said (Exodus 20:11) ". . . in six days, the Lord made heaven and earth, the sea, and all that in them is, and rested the seventh day." (Why should He wish to rest on the seventh day, if all His actual work on each of the previous days consisted of about one minute of speaking to some unidentified vision-recipient?)

In addition, all the previously mentioned scientific contradictions and theological fallacies apply in exactly the same way to the isolated-day and revelatory-day theories as they do to the standard day-age theory. The conclusion is, therefore, that the day-age theory in any form is unacceptable Biblically, scientifically and theologically.

---

[1] P. J. Wiseman, *Creation Revealed in Six Days* (London: Marshall, Morgan & Scott, 1949). (One of the best expositions of this theory.)

The Gap Theory

The Christian who desires to accommodate the geologic-age system in his theology must somehow fit them into the creation record of Genesis 1. Since the first chapter of Genesis covers the creation of all forms of life, including man, it is obvious that the geologic ages could not have occurred *after* the creation week. In the preceding section, dealing with the day-age theory, it was shown conclusively that the ages of geology did not occur *during* the creation week. The only other possibility, if they occurred at all is that they took place *before* the creation week. This latter theory is popularly known as the "gap theory," since it places the geologic ages in a supposed gap between Genesis 1:1 and Genesis 1:2.[1]

The gap theory, in its usual form, assumes primeval creation as stated in Genesis 1:1. "In the beginning God created the heavens and the earth." This creation, coming direct from the creative hand of God, is supposed to have been complete and beautiful in every respect. Genesis 1:2 is then said to describe a different condition of the earth, many aeons after the primeval creation. It is pointed out that the connective word, *waw*, at the beginning of Verse 2 can be translated either as "and" or "but," and that the verb, *hayetha*, can be translated as "became" instead of "was." Furthermore, the phrase "without form and void" (*tohu va bohu*) is rendered by some as "ruined and empty." Putting all this together, Genesis 1:1-2 becomes "In the beginning God created the heavens and the earth; but the earth became ruined and empty and darkness was upon the face of the deep."

The geological ages are then placed in the interval after the primeval creation and before the ruined condition of the earth described in verse 2. It is usually held that some gigantic cataclysm terminated the geologic ages, leaving the earth shattered and uninhabited and surrounded by darkness.

---

[1] Two books expounding and defending the gap theory in much detail are: L. A. Higley, *Science and Truth* (New York: Fleming H. Revell Co., 1940). Arthur C. Custance, *Without Form and Void* (Brockville, Canada: Doorway Publishers, 1970).

Then, according to the theory, God proceeded to "re-create" or "re-make" the earth in the six literal days described in Genesis 1:3-31. Those who advocate the gap theory are of course anti-evolutionists and believe that God created all things in the present world by special creation in the six-day creation week. However, they do not hold to a recent creation of the earth itself, since it dates from Genesis 1:1, the date of which presumably could be any number of billions of years in the past. A rather common cliche among fundamentalists has been to the effect: "Let the geologists have all the time they want; the Bible does not give the date of the earth's creation. All the vast expanses of geologic time are irrelevant to the Biblical record, since they occurred before Genesis 1:2."

Many holding this theory, though not all, have found it convenient to place the fossils of dinosaurs and ape-men and other extinct forms of life in this great gap, hoping thereby to avoid having to explain them in the context of God's present creation. Others have tended to postulate only a partial pre-Adamic cataclysm, allowing plant seeds from the pre-world to survive and even certain pre-Adamite hominids to survive in order to provide a wife for Cain (Genesis 4:17) and mothers for the "giants" (Genesis 6:4). For the most part, however, expositors advocating the gap theory believe the cataclysm to have devastated the whole world, leaving it completely waste and empty.

1. *Death Before Sin*

This interpretation does seem superficially to provide an easy solution to the problem of the geological ages. The problem is that it is much *too* superficial. It solves the problem by ignoring it.

The geological age problem is more complex than merely accounting for five billion years of time. Much more important is what took place *during* those years. Five billion years of geologic ages mean three billion years of organic evolution, accompanied by universal suffering, struggle and death. As already pointed out, the very existence of the geologic ages is based on evolution, and the identification of their various subdivisions depends on the supposed stage-of-evolution of the fossils found in the corresponding sedimentary rocks. Furthermore, whatever the fossils really say about evolution, one thing is sure, they speak of death—and violent, sudden death at that.

If the geological ages are real, then the evolutionary succession of life on earth which identifies those ages is also real. The gap theory does not settle the evolution problem for the fundamentalist; it merely inserts it in the gap before Genesis 1:2, and indeed makes it even worse. Not only is the entire evolutionary system still intact, but the added problem exists as to why God suddenly terminated the evolutionary process and then began again with six days of special creation—especially since the plants and animals and men whom He created all had their counterparts in the world He had just destroyed.

There seems no way of avoiding the conclusion—if the geological ages really occurred before Genesis 1:2, that is—that God was using the same processes which exist in the present world to develop the pre-Adamic world. Sedimentation, volcanism, and the other present geologic processes are clearly evident throughout the geologic column. So are disease, decay and death! And yet, this was supposedly ages before man brought sin into the world, and death by sin. Is God actually the author of evil and death, as the gap theory suggests?

2. *The Fall of Satan after the Geological Ages*

The great pre-Adamic cataclysm, which is basic to the gap theory also needs explanation. It needs a scientific explanation, for one thing, but more importantly it needs a theological explanation. Why would the Creator spend billions of years developing a world and then suddenly reduce it to chaos in a shattering cataclysm?

The explanation commonly offered is that the cataclysm was caused by Satan's rebellion and fall as described in Isaiah 14:12-15 and Ezekiel 28:11-17. Lucifer—the highest of all God's angelic hierarchy, the anointed cherub who covered the very throne of God—is presumed to have rebelled against God and tried to usurp His dominion. As a result, God expelled him from heaven, and he became Satan, the great adversary.

Satan's sin and fall, however, was in heaven on the "holy mountain of God," not on earth. There is, in fact, not a word in Scripture to connect Satan with the earth prior to his rebellion. On the other hand, when he sinned, he was expelled from heaven *to* the earth. The account in Ezekiel says: "Thou wast perfect in thy ways from the day that thou wast created, till iniquity was found in thee . . . therefore I will cast thee as profane out of the mountain of God: and I will destroy thee, O covering cherub, from the midst of the stones of fire. Thine heart was lifted up because of thy beauty, thou hast corrupted thy wisdom by reason of thy brightness: I will cast thee to the ground (or 'earth,' the same word in Hebrew)" (Ezekiel 28:15-17).

There is, therefore, no scriptural reason to connect Satan's fall in heaven with a cataclysm on earth. It seems much more probable that his expulsion to the earth was directly connected with man's presence on earth. It seems plausible that Satan first became resentful and envious because of God's great plan for man and that this was a major factor leading to his rebellion. God cast him to the earth, where he was permitted to test man's faithfulness to his Creator, to see whether he, too, would desire to "be as gods."

That Satan was not on earth, at least not as a wicked rebel against God, prior to Adam's creation is quite definite from Genesis 1:31. "And God saw *every thing* that He had made, and . . . it was very good." As a matter of fact, the next verse indicates that this observation included "the heavens and the earth, and all the host of them," so that everything was good in heaven! Therefore, Satan's sin must have occurred after man's creation.

It has occasionally been suggested that man's creation was God's response to Satan's rebellion. The idea is that God is teaching a great object-lesson to Satan and his angels; since they had not kept their first estate, God created man in Satan's place. Then, when Satan brought about man's fall also, God decided to redeem man, in order to demonstrate His power and grace before the watching angels.

There is no doubt that the angels are intensely interested in God's great work of salvation (I Corinthians 4:9, 6:3; Ephesians 3:10; I Peter 1:12), but this is not because it was an afterthought on God's part. Rather, it is because their very purpose in being created was to participate in God's plan for man. "Are they not all ministering spirits, sent forth to minister for them who shall be heirs of salvation?" (Hebrews 1:14). Throughout all the Scriptures, they are always thus seen as ministering in some way to man, particularly in relation to man's salvation and growth in grace.

Since the angels were created specifically for service to man, there is no reason to suppose they were created much earlier than man. They were present to "shout for joy" when God "laid the foundations of the earth" (Job 38:4; Psalm 104:4,5). However, this erection of the lands upon foundations, when they had previously been "without form," probably refers to the work of the third day of creation, when the dry land was made to separate out of the waters— "and God called the dry land Earth" (Genesis 1:10).

In any case, the angelic rebellion in heaven could have had no effect on the earth and its supposed previous geologic ages. Even if, for the sake of argument, it is assumed that Satan's sin *did* cause a pre-Adamic cataclysm on earth, that still would not account for the geologic ages, with their evolutionary succession of identifying fossils, which had occurred *prior* to the cataclysm. The whole problem of aeons of suffering and death has still not been resolved, for all this occurred not only before Adam sinned but even, according to the gap theory, before Satan sinned!

3. *Scientific Problems with the Gap Theory*

The pre-Adamic cataclysm supposedly left the earth completely desolate and uninhabited, submerged in a universal ocean and universal darkness ("waste and void, with darkness upon the face of the deep"). There was no light of the sun, no land surfaces, no vegetation, no animal life, even in the seas. Yet, in the fossil-bearing rocks, there seems to be clear evidences that a great abundance of plant and animal life existed all over the pre-world, on both land and sea.

Such a sudden transition from a world teeming with life and activity to one which was utterly ruined and empty, buried in water and darkness, must have required a geological cataclysm of overwhelming magnitude. The whole earth literally must have exploded, perhaps in a great nuclear or volcanic holocaust, destroying all life, causing all land surfaces to slide into the ocean, and filling the skies with such clouds of smoke and debris as to actually blot out the sun and sky.

The problem is this: The pre-Adamic cataclysm has been postulated mainly as a means of reconciling the Bible with geology, but there is not the slightest evidence in the orthodox system of historical geology for such a cataclysm! No geologist accepts the gap theory for this very reason.

The whole system of modern geology has been built upon the dogma of uniformitarianism, not catastrophism. And it is the resulting system of geological ages which the gap theory attempts to pigeonhole between Genesis 1:1 and 1:2. One cannot have his cake and also eat it! The geological strata can be explained in terms either of global catastrophism or of uniformitarianism, but not both together. If they were formed by a universal pre-Adamic cataclysm, then there remains no evidence for the geological ages, and, therefore, no need for the gap theory as far as the antiquity of the earth is concerned. One cannot harmonize the geologic ages with the Bible by eliminating them.

It should be emphasized as strongly as possible that orthodox geology has no place for worldwide cataclysms. The strata are supposed to be explained by uniformity, by continuity of the processes of the past with those of the present. A worldwide cataclysm that could lead to the condition described in Genesis 1:2 simply does not exist in the standard system of geological ages, and it is unrealistic to identify the ice age or any other such local or regional geologic feature with a cataclysm of such universal scope. Such a destructive cataclysm would have completely devastated and disintegrated the sedimentary strata and fossils which are used as the evidence proving the geologic ages.

If, for the sake of argument, it is supposed that there *was* such a cataclysm but that by some miracle it left the previously deposited strata intact and undisturbed, one still faces the formidable problem of the relation between the fossil world and the present world. That is, the animals and plants preserved as fossils from the world before the cataclysm are in many cases practically identical with those in the present world. In fact, most of the kinds of organisms found in the world today have also been found in the fossils (often larger and more highly developed than their modern counterparts but nevertheless of the same basic kinds). This is true even of human fossils, and of the various hominid forms suggested as possible precursors of man. This is one reason various writers on the gap theory have postulated the existence of pre-Adamite men.

The problem is to explain why God would allow a cataclysm

to destroy all life on the earth and then proceed to restock it with the same basic forms of life He had just destroyed. The God of the Bible is not capricious.

There *is* a great worldwide cataclysm described in the Bible and that, of course, is the Flood of Noah. This cataclysm is described in considerable detail and is frequently mentioned in later parts of the Bible, whereas the supposed pre-Adamic cataclysm is never described at all. The reasons, causes, and effects of the Flood are given. The Flood does provide a satisfying explanation for the fossils and therefore eliminates any real scientific need for the geologic ages.

Catastrophism *does* provide the key to the geological ages—not an imagined cataclysm before Genesis 1:2 which supposedly allows us to retain the geologic age system—but rather the very real Noachian cataclysm which destroys it.

4. *Biblical Problems with the Gap Theory*

The Biblical problems which the gap theory entails are no less damaging than the scientific difficulties. The summary statement of Genesis 2:1-3 seems clearly to include the whole universe—"the heavens and the earth . . . all the host of them . . . all His work which God created and made." Or at least it comprehends the same universe as Genesis 1:1—"the heavens and the earth." In fact, no reference to the creation of the heavens occurs in the entire chapter except in Genesis 1:1, which therefore is included in the summary of Genesis 2:1.

This fact is made even clearer in Exodus 20:11: ". . . in six days the Lord made heaven and earth, the sea, and all that in them is, . . ." If this verse means what it says, then the creation of the heaven and the earth was included within the work of the six days. Therefore, the initial creative act of Genesis 1:1 was a part of God's work on Day One, and there is no time for any significant "gap" before Genesis 1:2.

If anyone is impressed by the fact that "made" (Hebrew *asah*) is used in Exodus 20:11 instead of "created" (Hebrew *bara*), the phrase "all that in them is" should make it plain that the whole earth structure—not just the earth's surface—is included in the entities that were "made" in the six days. The gap theory, on the other hand, attributes most of the earth's crust, including the sedimentary rocks and their fossil contents, to the pre-world, and assumes they remained in place during the great cataclysm and the subsequent six-day period of "re-creation." This view obviously contradicts the comprehensive statement of Exodus 20:11, regardless of whether or not *asah* is used in this verse (as it often is when God is the subject) to express essentially the same meaning as *bara*. In any case, it does not mean "re-made," as the gap theory requires.

Similarly, God's evaluation of "all that He had made" as "very good" (Genesis 1:31) is strange and grotesque if the sedimentary rocks under the feet of Adam and Eve were at the same time filled with the fossilized remains of billions of years of suffering and death, so that almost everywhere man would look on the earth he would encounter this vast graveyard. It could hardly look "very good" to men; how could it be pronounced "very good" by God?

The exegesis required by the gap theory for the six days' work of Genesis 1 must also be strained and forced, rather than natural and normal. Thus, "Let there be light," in verse 3 must be interpreted as "Let light pierce through the atmospheric debris following the cataclysm and again reach the earth's surface." Similarly, the simple statement of verse 16, "And God made two great lights . . . the stars also," must be understood as saying "God removed all the clouds still remaining from the cataclysm so that now the sun, moon and stars could be seen again on earth." Similar strained renderings are needed for other passages.

Furthermore, the translation required by the gap theory for Genesis 1:2—"The earth *became* (instead of 'was') waste and void"—is itself highly questionable. There is admittedly a difference of opinion among Hebrew scholars whether or not this is a permissible translation, but it should be noted that practically all the generally recognized and standard Old Testament translations render the verb "was" instead of "became." It is the regular Hebrew verb of being (*hayetha*) instead of the verb which is normally used to denote a change of state (*haphak*). Although *hayetha* can, under some circumstances, be translated as "became" instead of "was," such a meaning must be clearly required by the context. In at least 98 percent of its occurrences in the Pentateuch it is properly translated as "was." The question then is whether the internal context in Genesis 1:1-5 requires or justifies this unusual translation. Advocates of the gap theory have not yet shown this to be the case. In fact, use of the connective "and" (*waw*) between Genesis 1:1 and 1:2 seems to imply that the state described in the second verse followed immediately upon the action described in the first verse. Verse 2 clearly consists of an explanation as to how the earth *was* at creation, not how it became later.

It is recognized that a few Hebrew scholars argue vigorously that "became" should be used in verse 2. When experts and specialists disagree, it should perhaps be left an open question. Even if there *is* such a "gap" between the two verses, there is no contextual justification for understanding it as a gap of long duration. It could just as well have been, say, a minute or an hour, as five billion years.

Similarly, there is nothing in verse 2 to imply a great cataclysmic judgment from God. The initial aspect of creation as described in that verse was not "perfect," in the sense that it was "complete," until God pronounced it complete and "very good" at the end of the six days of creative work. But it was perfect for His immediate purpose.

One would be justified in concluding, therefore, that the "gap" exegesis of Genesis 1:1,2 is very tenuous.

5. *Critique of Proof-Texts for the Gap Theory*

Although Genesis 1:1,2 does not lend itself well to the gap theory in its immediate context, there are several suggested proof-texts for the theory that have been found in other parts of the Bible. These must now be examined.

Regardless of these proof-texts, one should not forget the overwhelming scientific and theological difficulties inherent in the idea that the geological ages occurred between the two verses and that these ages terminated in a global cataclysm. This theory must not be used to explain the geological ages or to justify a great age for the earth. The gap theory creates many serious scientific problems and solves none.

With this warning in mind, let us see whether the proof-texts really do *require* a gap interpretation. The first of these is Genesis 1:28, where God told Adam and Eve to "... Be fruitful, and multiply, and replenish the earth. ..." The verb translated as "replenish" is the Hebrew *male*, which means simply "fill" or "be filled" or similar expression in all the many other places where it is used, with only a few very questionable exceptions.

Jeremiah 4:23 is frequently cited: "I beheld the earth, and lo, it was without form, and void; and the heavens, and they had no light." This is quoted in a context of divine judgment, and so it is said that Genesis 1:2 likewise reflects such a judgment. It is quite certain, however, that the divine judgment described in Jeremiah 4:23 has nothing to do with Genesis except similar rhetoric. It is a prophecy of a coming judgment on the land of Israel (see Jeremiah 4:14,22,31), not a history of past judgment on the earth. The words "earth" and "land" are the same in Hebrew. One can translate the verse correctly as follows: "I beheld the land, and lo it was waste and empty, and the sky and it had no light." This will be fulfilled during the coming "day of Jacob's trouble" (Jeremiah 30:7).

Another proof-text is Isaiah 24:1: "Behold, the Lord maketh the earth empty, and maketh it waste, and turneth it upside down, and scattereth abroad the inhabitants thereof." Again, in the context, this verse is quite obviously a prophecy of the coming judgment upon the land and the people of Israel, not on a hypothetical race of pre-Adamites.

The most important proof-text is Isaiah 45:18: "For thus saith the Lord that created the heavens; God Himself that formed the earth and made it; He hath established it, He created it not in vain (the phrase 'in vain' is the Hebrew *tohu*, same as 'without form' in Genesis 1:2), He formed it to be inhabited. . . ."

The argument goes that, since the above verse says that God created not the earth *tohu*, and since the earth of Genesis 1:2 was *tohu*, therefore the latter could not have been the earth as it was created in Genesis 1:1. The inference is that the earth became *tohu* by the pre-Adamic cataclysm.

Again, this interpretation requires lifting the verse out of its context. The verses before and after indicate that the subject at hand is Israel and God's purposes and promises to His people. That is, just as the Lord had a purpose in creating the earth, so has He a purpose for Israel. In Isaiah 45:17, the preceding verse, He said: ". . . Israel shall be saved in the Lord with an everlasting salvation: ye shall not be ashamed nor confounded world without end."

In support of this tremendous promise, God reminds the Israelites of His mighty creation itself, which was not without purpose. He "formed it to be inhabited," and He accomplished that purpose, creating and redeeming a race of men in His own image. Just so, He will accomplish His purpose for His special people, Israel.

The fact that His full purpose in creation was not completed on the first day of creation is irrelevant. He "created it not in vain, He formed it to be inhabited," and He accomplished that purpose. The word *tohu* takes several shades of meaning, depending on context. It occurs 20 times and is translated 10 different ways in the King James translation. The context in Isaiah 45:18 justifies the translation "in vain" or "without purpose." The context in Genesis 1:2 warrants "without form" or "structureless."

There is no conflict between Isaiah 45:18 and the statement of an initial formless aspect to the created earth in Genesis 1:2. The former can properly be understood as follows: "God created it not (to be forever) without form; He formed it to be inhabited." As described in Genesis 1, he proceeded to bring beauty and structure to the formless elements and then inhabitants to the waiting lands.

It should be remembered that Isaiah 45:18 was written many hundreds of years after Genesis 1:2 and that its context deals with Israel, not a pre-Adamic cataclysm. Such an isolated and incidental verse, which is easily capable of an alternate interpretation, is hardly an adequate base on which to build a theory of such tremendous import as that of the primeval cataclysm.

Two verses in the New Testament have occasionally been used to support the gap theory. One is II Corinthians 4:6: ". . . God, who commanded the light to shine out of darkness, hath shined in our hearts . . ." The darkness in the heart is due to sin and is illuminated by the entrance of Christ. Just so, it is said, the primeval darkness must also have been due to sin.

The analogy breaks down, however. The gap theory postulates a perfect world in the beginning, plunged into darkness, and then illuminated again when God commanded the light to shine out of darkness. A soul in darkness, however, is *born* in darkness. The true analogy would be with a world which was also born in darkness. Darkness is not evil in itself since it was created by God. "I form the light, and create darkness . . ." (Isaiah 45:7). Perhaps this analogy even suggests the reason why God first created the world in darkness, so that the work of creation might serve as a pattern and type of the work of the "new creation" (II Corinthians 5:17) created by the Holy Spirit in the receptive heart.

The other verse is II Peter 3:6: ". . . the world that then was, being overflowed with water, perished." Although some have taken this as a reference to a pre-Adamic cataclysm, it is obvious that it refers instead to the Flood of Noah. The very word "overflowed" indicates this. It is the Greek word *kataklusmos*. In its noun form, it occurs four times (Matthew 24:38,39; Luke 17:27; II Peter 2:5), referring always to the Flood of Noah. There has been only one cataclysm in earth history, not two, and that was the great Flood described in Genesis 6-9.

One other interesting argument has been advanced. The phrase "foundation of the world" (Matthew 13:35 and nine other places) can be translated "casting-down (Greek *katabole*) of the world," and the idea is that it may refer to the primeval cataclysm. A foundation is "cast down" or "laid down," so the word is used properly to mean "foundation," as Greek scholars uniformly agree. There is nothing in the context of any of the ten occurrences to suggest such a novel interpretation as that of a primeval cataclysm. The phrase means "*foundation* of the world" and nothing more.

The lack of any clear Biblical evidence for the gap theory, along with the highly equivocal nature of all its supposed proof-texts—in the context of its scientific fallacies and its serious theological problems—is adequate justification for rejecting it altogether. God does not speak in uncertain sounds.

6. *The Pre-Genesis Gap Theory*

Dr. Merrill F. Unger, formerly of Dallas Seminary, has proposed a modified gap theory.[1] Convinced that the Hebrew construction of Genesis 1:1,2 precludes a gap *between* these two verses, Unger suggests placing the angelic sin and pre-Adamic cataclysm *before* Genesis 1:1. In this view, the statement, "In the beginning God created the heavens and the earth," refers to a *re-creation*, following the geological ages.

---

[1] *Unger's Bible Handbook* (Chicago: Moody Press, 1966), pp. 37-39.

There is no Biblical basis for this view. Unger is frank in saying that its basis is the necessity to accommodate the geologic ages.

However, all the same scientific and theological objections to the gap theory that have already been detailed apply with equal force to Unger's modification of the theory. The geological ages which the theory tries to adopt are based upon the system of evolutionary uniformitarianism which Unger professes to reject. There is no room at all for the imaginary pre-Adamic cataclysm in the standard concept of geological ages.

Similarly, the existence of evil, suffering and death in the world prior to the six days of creation week and even prior to Satan's rebellion—as required by the very concept of geological ages—seems explicitly precluded by the nature of God as a God of order, purpose, efficiency, and love, as well as such Scriptures as Genesis 1:31 ("very good") and Romans 5:12 ("death by sin").

The Framework Hypothesis

It has been seen that the geological ages cannot be placed before the six days of creation (gap theory), during the six days of creation (day-age theory), or after the six days (which, since they antedate man, no one suggests at all). The only remaining possibility is that either the six days or the geological ages had no existence in the first place.

To someone who is firmly committed to the geological ages (and therefore to evolution), there is no alternative but to give up belief in Genesis as an actual historical record of the events of creation. This is what all liberal theologians have done long ago, and what increasing numbers of evangelicals are doing today.

Many of these latter wish to retain some kind of confidence in the divine inspiration of Genesis rather than to reject it completely. Accordingly, they have tried to consider the creation story as some kind of literary device rather than actual history. The "framework hypothesis" of Genesis 1-11 views these chapters as essentially a rhetorical framework within which are developed the grand spiritual themes of "creation" (the divine source and meaning of reality), of man's "fall" (man's ever-recurring experience of spiritual and moral inadequacy), and of reconciliation (the broad currents in history through which man is seeking to understand and appropriate spiritual meaning in life).

The particular "framework" in which these ideas are developed varies according to the particular expositor.[1] Some speak of Genesis as "allegorical," others as "liturgical," others as "poetic," others as "supra-historical." All agree, however, in rejecting it as "scientific" or "historical." They concur that Genesis teaches the *fact* of "creation" and the "fall," but deny that it has anything to say concerning the *method*. They hope to retain whatever theological significance it may have while, at the same time, avoiding scientific embarrassment.

This type of Biblical exegesis is out of the question for any real believer in the Bible. It is the method of so-called "neoorthodoxy," though it is neither new nor orthodox. It cuts out the foundation of the entire Biblical system when it expunges Genesis 1-11. The events of these chapters are recorded in simple narrative form, as though the writer or writers fully intended to record a series of straightforward historical facts; there is certainly no internal or exegetical reason for taking them in any other way.

Each chapter of Genesis 1-11 leads naturally into the next chapter. In the same way Genesis 11, which gives the genealogy of the Messianic line down to Abraham, is followed logically by Genesis 12, which gives the first recorded events in the life of Abraham. The latter events are within the period of recorded history and are now almost universally accepted as factual. The life of Abraham, as the founder of the chosen nation Israel and the ancestor of Jesus Christ, is suspended without background or foundation if Genesis 1-11 is only an allegory.

Furthermore, the later writers of Scripture refer again and again to these early chapters of Genesis, always accepting them as both factual history and authoritative doctrine. Moses refers to the six-literal-day creation in Exodus 31:17 and to the division of the nations at Babel in Deuteronomy

---

[1] One example is N. H. Ridderbos, *Is There A Conflict Between Genesis 1 and Natural Science?* (Grand Rapids: Eerdmans Publ. Co., 1957).

32:8. Joshua 24:2 accepts the account in Genesis 11 of Abraham's ancestors. Although the later historical books are naturally more occupied with the histories of their own times, they occasionally refer back to earlier times. Hezekiah speaks of the creation (II Kings 19:15) and I Chronicles 1:1-28 repeats the genealogies of Genesis 5, 10, and 11. After the captivity, Nehemiah likewise refers to the creation (Nehemiah 9:6). Job several times refers to both creation and the Flood (9:5-9; 12:15; 26:7-13; 31:33; 38:4-7; etc.).

The book of Psalms abounds in references to the creation. Psalm 8:3-8 speaks of God giving dominion over the earth to man. Psalm 33:6-9 emphasizes the instantaneous creative acts of God in the beginning. Psalm 90:2,3 speaks of creation and the fall of man. Psalm 148:1-5 tells of the creative acts of God. There are many other such references. Psalms 29 and 104 describe graphically the events during and following the great Flood. Even Proverbs (8:22-31) refers to the creation.

The prophetical books likewise refer often to the early chapters of Genesis. Isaiah refers both to the creation (40:26; 45:18) and to the Flood (54:9). Jeremiah 10:11-13; 31:35, and 51:15,16 all refer to different aspects of the creation. Ezekiel refers to Noah in 14:14,20, and Amos also mentions the Flood, in both 5:8 and 9:6. Micah 5:6 mentions the "land of Nimrod," as does Zechariah 5:11, who speaks of the "land of Shinar," both passages obviously referring to Genesis 10:10.

It is the New Testament that contains the clearest and most numerous references to Genesis 1-11. The Apostle Paul mentions Adam and Eve several times in a manner demonstrating that he regarded them as real people, the first man and first woman on earth. Note the important discussions in Romans 5:12-19; I Corinthians 11:7-12, 15:21,22, 38-41, 45-47; II Corinthians 11:3,8 and I Timothy 2:13-15. The effects of the great Curse on the earth are discussed in a classic passage in Romans 8:18-25.

The book of Hebrews contains an important passage dealing with the completeness of the creation and God's seventh-day rest (Hebrews 4:1-11). Abel, Enoch and Noah are listed as the first three of the great heroes of faith in Chapter 11. Abel is again mentioned in 12:24.

The Apostle Peter places great emphasis on the Flood (I Peter 3:20; II Peter 2:4,5; II Peter 3:5,6). John refers to Cain and Abel (I John 3:12). Jude also refers to Cain (verse

11), as well as to the sinning angels of Genesis 6:1-4 (verse 6) and to Enoch, as the seventh in the line of patriarchs from Adam listed in Genesis 5 (verse 14).

Most significantly of all, the Lord Jesus Himself frequently cited these early verses of Genesis in support of some of His most important teachings. His doctrine of marriage was based explicitly on a combined quotation from the first two (supposedly contradictory!) chapters of Genesis (Matthew 19:3-6; Mark 10:2-9; compare with Genesis 1:27 and 2:24). He compared the days of Noah, just before the universal Flood, with the last days prior to His own return in world-wide judgment (Matthew 24:37-42; Luke 17:26,27). He even referred to Abel as the first martyr and first prophet (Matthew 23:35; Luke 11:51). He mentioned "the beginning of the creation which God created" (Mark 13:19). He called Satan the father of liars, no doubt referring to his lie to Eve in the garden of Eden (John 8:44).

Likewise, the preaching of the Gospel by the early church in the book of Acts included references to these first Scriptures. Stephen (Acts 7:2-4) mentions Abraham's background as given in Genesis 11:26-32. Paul preached from the witness of creation in Acts 14:15 and 17:24, mentioning also the first establishment of the nations in 17:26.

The fullest references to the beginning of things are found in the book of Revelation, which describes the restoration and consummation of all things. In the letter to the apostate church at Laodicea, Jesus Christ reminds them that He is ". . . the beginning of the creation of God" (Revelation 3:14). Frequent stress is placed on God as the Creator of all things (Revelation 4:11; 10:6; 14:7). In Revelation 14:7, the "everlasting Gospel" is said to include recognition of Him ". . . that made heaven, and earth, and the sea, and the fountains of waters."

The great protevangelic promise of Genesis 3:15 is expanded and expounded in Revelation 12, which also includes reference to Satan as the serpent (verse 9) who had deceived all men. The prophecy of the development and fall of the final Babylon (chapters 17 and 18) undoubtedly is built upon the foundation furnished by the first Babylon of Genesis 10 and 11.

The last two chapters of the Bible, Revelation 21 and 22, describe the creation of the new heavens and new earth, just as Genesis 1 and 2 describe the creation of the first heavens and earth. In these last two chapters—as in the first two—reference is made to the Bride; the personal presence of God; the Curse, in its fourfold aspect; the end of death; the removal of the Curse; the ending of darkness; and the restoration of the tree of life and the river flowing out of the midst of paradise.

Modern theologians who would eliminate the first eleven chapters of Genesis from the realm of true history are guilty of removing the foundation from all future history. They, in effect, reject the teachings of Peter and Paul and all the other Biblical writers as naive superstition and the teachings of the infallible Christ as deceptive accommodationism. The "framework hypothesis" of Genesis, in any of its diverse forms, is nothing but neo-orthodox sophistry and inevitably leads eventually to complete apostasy. It must be unequivocally rejected and opposed by Bible-believing Christians.

Gaps in Human Chronology

The genealogical lists in Genesis 5 give the age of each man in the line from Adam to Abraham at the birth of the son who is next in the line. When these are added, they give a total of 1656 years from Adam to the Flood. A similar list for the postdiluvian patriarchs in Genesis 11 gives 368 years from the Flood until Abraham migrated into Canaan. Abraham's time is well within the period of recorded history. Although a number of detailed chronological questions for the post-Abrahamic period are not settled, there is general agreement that Abraham's migration occurred no earlier than 2000 B.C.

Therefore, the date of the creation, as obtained by simple addition of the figures given in the Bible, was about 2024 years prior to Abraham's journey from Haran to Canaan, or around 4000 B.C. The date of the Flood on this basis was around 2350 B.C.

Dates such as these are considered by modern anthropologists to be quite absurd. These scholars believe man to have been on the earth for at least a million years. The Flood is rejected altogether, except perhaps as an old tradition of a Euphrates flood occurring sometime around 3000 B.C.

The sharp disagreement of the Genesis chronologies of human pre-history, with these speculations of evolutionary anthropology and archaeology, is a matter of serious concern. This problem has led to various theories about imaginary "pre-Adamite" men and has been one of the main reasons why so many modern theologians have relegated Genesis 1-11 to the realm of mythology, rejecting its historical content altogether.

1. *Accuracy of Transmission*

For those who take these chapters historically, there seem to be three possible approaches to consider: first, it may be possible that the numbers in Genesis 5 and 11 have been corrupted by faulty transmission. The Massoretic text, on which the figures cited above were based, differs from the Septuagint and Samaritan texts. The Samaritan text would add 301 years and the Septuagint 1466 years to the period calculated above from the creation to Abraham.

This would only extend man's creation back to about 5500 B.C. at most, and this is only a drop-in-the-bucket compared to the demands of evolutionary chronology.

2. *Genealogical Gaps*

A second approach is to assume there are certain gaps in the genealogies of Genesis 5 and 11, with the term "begat" implying ancestry rather than immediate parental relationship. At least one such gap is specifically suggested by the genealogy in Luke 3, which inserts the name Cainan between Arphaxad and Salah. This name is actually found in the Septuagint translation of Genesis 5, with an additional increment of 130 years. Also a gap is perhaps implied at the time of Peleg (Genesis 10:25 and 11:18). The life spans of Peleg's ancestors were: Shem, 602; Arphaxad, 438; Salah, 433; Eber, 464. Peleg himself lived only 239 years. His immediate descendants were: Reu, 239; Serug, 230; Nahor, 148; Terah, 275. There is thus a rather sharp decline in longevity between the time of Eber and Peleg, and this may well be because an unknown number of intervening generations have been omitted. On the other hand, it was in the days of Peleg that the earth "was divided" and this division, whatever it was, may itself have suddenly decreased man's longevity.

This "genealogical gap theory" is Biblically permissible if kept within reasonable bounds. There are a number of other instances in Scripture where similar gaps can be found (e.g.,

Matthew 1). Thus the Flood may possibly be dated considerably earlier than the previously calculated 2350 B.C., and
the creation considerably earlier than 4000 B.C. If such gaps
are allowed, however, there seems no exact way of determining these dates from Biblical considerations alone.

In any case, this device does not correlate the Biblical
chronology with the standard evolutionary chronology of
human history. There are 20 names in the patriarchal list
from Adam to Abraham, with the total time indicated as
about 2000 years. To correlate this with the evolutionists'
chronology of approximately 1,000,000 years of human
history requires an average "gap" between each adjacent
pair of names in the genealogical lists of almost 50,000 years!
This is obviously absurd, and makes Genesis 5 and 11 look
ridiculous. One would have to read Genesis 5:6, for example,
in some such fashion as: "Seth lived an hundred and five
years, and begat (a son whose remote descendant, 50,000
years in the future, would be) Enos." The same flexibility
has to be assumed for all other links in the chain. Actually
only 15 possible gaps exist, since the connection of Seth to
Adam, Noah to Lamech and to Shem, Shem to Arphaxad,
and Terah to Abraham, are spelled out in such a way as to
preclude the possibility of intervening generations in those
cases. Furthermore, Jude 14 agrees with Genesis 5 that
Enoch was the "seventh from Adam," so this eliminates five
more possible gaps. Thus, the average gap really has to be
100,000 years! Since all known and recorded human history
extends back only about 4000 years, the average gap in
every case must be about 25 times longer in duration than
all known history!

Preservation of the patriarchal names and ages and historical events by any kind of tradition over such long ages is
a patent impossibility. It could only have been given by
direct dictation to Moses if meaningful and accurate information of this kind were to be conveyed for inscripturation in
God's Word. That being the case, there is no reason why the
names of Cainan, Mahalaleel, Serug, *et al*, were included in
the list at all. No other information is given concerning
them, and the 20,000 or so names that were omitted in the
lists were just as vital in transmitting the patriarchal seed
as these.

Lamech, the father of Noah, was still keenly aware of the

terms of God's Edenic Curse (Genesis 5:29), which would be highly unlikely if the Curse had been pronunced half a million years before his time. Job, who lived in the early centuries after the Flood and long before the book of Genesis had been compiled by Moses, was well aware of Adam and the events of patriarchal history, as we have already seen.

Furthermore, it is significant that the same genealogical lists of Genesis 5 and 11 are repeated in I Chronicles 1:1-4, 24-27 and Luke 3:34-38, with no indication that either the ancient Jewish historians or the early Christians had any inkling these lists were so fantastically fragmentary.

It must be concluded that the Biblical record cannot be harmonized at all with the standard evolutionary reconstruction of human history as promoted by modern anthropologists and archaeologists. To the extent that *sound* archaeological research may *require* dating of early human settlements at dates earlier than the traditional Ussher chronology allows, the Bible does indicate the possibility of minor gaps in the genealogies (especially between the Flood and Abraham) which may correlate with such dates.

3. *Revision of Secular Chronology*

On the other hand, it should be realized that the archaeological dating of prehistoric human sites is a highly uncertain process, involving a great number of unverifiable assumptions (as in the radiocarbon technique) and subjective evaluations (as in pottery correlations), all of which to some degree are based on evolutionary presuppositions. In the absence of actual *proof* to the contrary, the dates of creation and the Flood are quite reasonably placed within the past several thousand years.

The Local Flood Theory

The great Flood of Genesis 6-9 is of critical importance to the true understanding of earth history. It has been seen that sound Biblical exegesis will not permit placing the geological ages either before or during the six days of creation. Neither can the six days of creation be interpreted as non-historical or allegorical. The only other alternative is to reject the standard system of geological ages altogether.

This is of course a drastic suggestion—orthodox geologists indeed reject it out of hand. However, there is no other alternative. If the Bible is the Word of God—and it is—and if Jesus Christ is the infallible and omniscient Creator—and He is—then it must be firmly believed that the world and all things in it were created in six natural days and that the long geological ages of evolutionary history never really took place at all.

This position forces one to find another explanation of the great sedimentary beds of the earth's crust, as well as the fossil record contained in them. All of the geologic strata and formations, the great coal and oil deposits, the volcanic and glacial beds, the mountain ranges and geosynclines, and all the multitudinous phenomena of historical geology, interpreted for over a hundred years in terms of uniformity and evolution, must be re-evaluated in terms of the Biblical framework of history. Furthermore, its integral association with the fossil record indicates that the whole geological column must have been formed after the fall of man. Fossils clearly speak of death, and the Scriptures teach plainly that, "by man came death" (I Corinthians 15:21).

The only possible explanation for the geologic column and fossil record, consistent with Scripture, must therefore be sought in terms of the Noachian Deluge. This tremendous worldwide cataclysm does provide a satisfactory framework within which to reinterpret these data.

If the Flood was really of the magnitude and intensity the Bible indicates, then the entire case for evolution collapses. Evolution depends entirely on the fossil record interpreted in terms of vast geologic ages. If these did not take place, evolution is impossible.

It is not surprising, therefore, that orthodox geologists strongly oppose the idea of a worldwide Flood. In view of this intense and almost unanimous opposition, many evangelicals insist that Genesis be reinterpreted in terms of a local flood.[1] It is actually very common, as could be

---

[1] The local-flood theory, in one form or another, has been advocated by such evangelical writers as Russell Mixter, Harry Rimmer, Arthur Custance, Bernard Ramm, William LaSor, and many others. One of the best expositions is found in *The Christian View of Science and Scripture*, by Bernard Ramm (Grand Rapids: Eerdmans Publ. Co., 1954), pp. 229-249.

expected, to find the local flood view combined with either the day-age theory or the gap theory. Since both of the latter theories seek to salvage the geological ages, and since a universal Flood would eliminate the entire basis for them, it is obvious that the concept of a global deluge is incompatible with either theory.

It is not easy in the academic world to maintain a so-called "flood theory of geology." There are, no doubt, certain geological problems in such a position, but a far more real problem is the "flood" of scholarly wrath and ridicule that descends upon those who hold it—and that is no theory! The Genesis Flood is the real crux of the conflict between the evolutionist and creationist cosmologies, and evolutionists invariably concentrate their strongest attacks at this point. By the same token, this is where Christians should also marshall their strongest and most vigorous campaign. Unfortunately, their strategy until recent years has almost completely ignored it.

If the system of flood geology can be established on a sound scientific basis, and be effectively promoted and publicized, then the entire evolutionary cosmology, at least in its present neo-Darwinian form, will collapse. This, in turn, would mean that every anti-Christian system and movement (communism, racism, humanism, libertinism, behaviorism, and all the rest) would be deprived of their pseudo-intellectual foundation.

These are the stakes involved and it is no wonder that evolutionists have so opposed the historical fact of the global cataclysm known as the Genesis Flood.

It almost seems frivolous to try to show that the Bible teaches a worldwide Flood. This fact is obvious in the mere reading of Genesis 6-9 and one who does not see it there will hardly be influenced by other reasoning. For the record, however, a few of the many possible formal arguments are summarized below:

1. *The Height and Duration of the Flood*

The record says the Flood covered the tops of the highest mountains (Genesis 7:19,20) and that this situation prevailed until ten months (8:5) after the Flood began. If the mountains were the same elevation then as now, which the local-flood theory assumes, the waters were at least 17,000 feet high (Mount Ararat, on which the Ark rested, is this high) for a period of at least nine months. To require such a condition to be a "local" flood imposes impossible hydraulic demands on the water involved. One has to assume a sort of egg-shaped flood three miles high!

2. *The Need for an Ark*

The requirement for Noah to build a gigantic barge to "keep seed alive upon the face of all the earth" (Genesis 7:3) was unnecessary, to say the least, if it were only to be a local flood. The Ark had a carrying capacity at least equal to that of 522 standard railroad stock cars, as can be quickly calculated from its recorded dimensions (Genesis 6:15). This is more than twice as large as necessary to accommodate two of every species of known land animal that ever lived. If the Flood were only a local or regional flood, it would be folly to spend 120 years to prepare an ark large enough to carry animals from the whole world. Its size was absurdly out of proportion for a mere regional fauna. Even the latter could easily have escaped a local flood by the obvious expedient of migrating to higher ground elsewhere.

3. *Destruction of the Earth*

The Biblical description of the unique and overwhelming physical aspects of the Flood precludes a mini-flood. God said, in fact, He was going to "destroy the earth" (Genesis 6:13). The 40-day downpour (the "windows" of heaven were literally "floodgates"), the simultaneous cleavage of the vast "fountains of the great deep" (7:11), the absence of rain before the Flood (Genesis 2:5), the establishment of the rainbow after the Flood (9:13), and the fact that the waters "overturned the earth" (Job 12:15) all are understandable only in terms of a unique worldwide cataclysm.

4. *God's Unbroken Promise*

God's unequivocal promise never again to send the Flood (Genesis 9:11) has been broken repeatedly if that Flood were only a local flood. Thus the local-flood theory not only repudiates the plain meaning of the Biblical record of the Flood, but even charges God with breaking His promises!

5. *Testimony of Christ and the Apostles*

The Lord Jesus Christ Himself, as well as Peter (II Peter 2:5; 3:6) and Paul (Hebrews 11:7) confirmed that the Flood at least destroyed all mankind. Christ said, "the Flood came, and destroyed them all" (Luke 17:27). The modern system of geology and archaeology, which the local-flood theory tries to accommodate, certainly includes a worldwide distribution of mankind long before any possible Biblical date for the Flood. A flood which was anthropologically universal would certainly have to be geographically universal.

These and numerous other reasons that could be listed clearly prove that the Biblical record teaches a worldwide Flood. One could, in fact, prove this directly, merely by the experiment of a slow, thoughtful reading of Genesis 6-9, trying to understand each verse as a description of a "local" flood. It will soon be realized what distortion of the plain sense of the inspired text this requires.

The Tranquil Flood Theory

Strangely and almost unbelievably, there have been a few competent geologists (Charles Lyell in the last century, J. L. Kulp,[1] Davis Young and others in the current generation) who have gone on record as believing in a worldwide *tranquil* cataclysm! At least they acknowledge the compelling witness of Scripture to a universal Noahic Flood, but then they abandon physical reality by imagining that such a flood may have been mild and gentle, geologically impotent, leaving no physical evidence that it ever happened.

Even on the basis of uniformitarian considerations (the relatively small local floods of the present are often tremendously destructive, leaving great gullies and thick deposits of sediment) it should be obvious that a global *kataklusmos*, such as the Bible describes, with its torrents of water from the skies, its erupting reservoirs from the depths, its universal destruction, its violent tidal actions, its great wind, its rising mountains and sinking basins, and other non-tranquil phenomena must surely have accomplished far more geologic work than a great number of local floods could ever do.

---

[1] This theory is advocated, for example, by Dr. J. Laurence Kulp, one of the nation's leading geologists specializing in geochronometry, in his article "Flood Geology" in the *Journal of the American Scientific Affiliation*, Vol. 2 (January 1950), pp. 1-15.

How it is that the usual slow, uniform processes of nature could leave permanent records in the form of great sedimentary strata and fossil graveyards all over the world and through all the ages, while a uniquely powerful worldwide hydrodynamic convulsion—which destroyed all living land animals and the earth itself—would leave no discernible records whatever, poses a unique geological conundrum. The idea of a worldwide, year-long "tranquil" flood is hydrologically and geophysically absurd.

Summary and Conclusion

There seems to be no possible way to avoid the conclusion that, if the Bible and Christianity are true at all, the geological ages must be rejected altogether. Neither the day-age theory, the gap theory, nor any other theory is capable of reconciling them with Genesis. In their place, as the proper means of understanding earth history as recorded in the fossil-bearing sedimentary rocks of the earth's crust, the great worldwide Flood so clearly described in Scripture must be accepted as the basic mechanism.

The detailed correlation of the intricate geophysical structure of the earth with the true Biblical framework of history will, no doubt, require a tremendous amount of research and study by Bible-believing scientists. Nevertheless, this research is urgently needed today in view of the world's increasing opposition to the Biblical Christian faith.

The vast complex of godless movements spawned by the pervasive and powerful system of evolutionary uniformitarianism can only be turned back if their foundation can be destroyed, and this requires the re-establishment of special creation, on a Biblical and scientific basis, as the true foundation of knowledge and practice in every field. This therefore must be a primary emphasis in Christian schools, in Christian churches and in all kinds of institutions everywhere. It is hoped that this book will provide the information necessary to undergird and energize this movement.

APPENDIX
BIBLIOGRAPHY ON CREATIONISM

The books and periodicals listed below are recommended for all school libraries in order to provide students and teachers access to a fair sample of the available literature on scientific creationism. All books listed are believed to be currently in print.

I. *Books by Creationist Scientists Emphasizing the Scientific Aspects of Creationism.*

Anderson, J. Kerby and Harold G. Coffin, *Fossils in Focus* (Grand Rapids: Zondervan, 1980), 96 pp.

* Andrews, E.H., *God, Science and Evolution* (Welwyn, Hertfordshire, England: Evangelical Press, 1980), 129 pp.

Arndts, Russell and William Overn, *Isochron Dating and the Mixing Model (Minneapolis: Bible-Science Assoc., 1983), 36 pp.*

* Austin, Steven A., *Catastrophes in Earth History* (San Diego: Institute for Creation Research, 1984), 318 pp.

* Aw, S.E., *Chemical Evolution: An Examination of Current Ideas* (San Diego: Creation-Life, 1982), 206 pp.

* Barnes, Thomas G., *Origin and Destiny of the Earth's Magnetic Field* (San Diego: Institute for Creation Research, 1983), 132 pp.

* Barnes, Thomas G., *Physics of the Future* (San Diego: Institute for Creation Research, 1983), 208 pp.

* Bowden, Malcolm, *Ape-Men: Fact or Fallacy* (Bromley, Kent, England: Sovereign Publications, 1977), 258 pp.

Camp, Robert S., Ed., *A Critical Look at Evolution* (Atlanta: Religion, Science and Communication Research and Development Corp., 1972), 212 pp.

Clark, Harold W., *Fossils, Flood and Fire* (Escondido, CA: Outdoor Pictures, 1968), 239 pp.

Clark, Harold W., *New Creationism* (Nashville: Southern Publ. Assoc., 1980), 128 pp.

* Clark, Marlyn E., *Our Amazing Circulatory System* (San Diego: Institute for Creation Research, 1976), 64 pp.

Clark, Robert E.D., *Darwin: Before and After* (Chicago: Moody Press, 1967), 192 pp.

Coffin, Harold G., *Creation: Accident or Design?* (Washington: Review and Herald, 1969), 512 pp.

Cook, Melvin A., *Prehistory and Earth Models* (London: Max Parrish Co., 1966), 353 pp.

Coppedge, James, *Evolution: Possible or Impossible?* (Grand Rapids: Zondervan, 1973), 276 pp.

257

Cousins, Frank W., *Fossil Man* (Hants, England: Evolution Protest Movement, 1971), 138 pp.

Daly, Reginald, *Earth's Most Challenging Mysteries* (Nutley, NJ: Craig Press, 1972), 403 pp.

Davidheiser, Bolton, *Evolution and Christian Faith* (Nutley, NJ: Presbyterian and Reformed, 1969), 372 pp.

Dewar, Douglas, *The Transformist Illusion* (Murfreesboro, TN: DeHoff Publ., 1955), 306 pp.

Dillow, Joseph C., *The Waters Above* (Chicago: Moody, 1981), 479 pp.

Enoch, H., *Evolution or Creation* (Madras, Union of Evangelical Students of India, 1966), 172 pp.

Frair, Wayne and Wm. P. Davis, *A Case for Creation* (Chicago: Moody Press, 1983), 155 pp.

* Gish, Duane T., *Evolution: The Fossils Say No!* (San Diego: Institute for Creation Research, 1979), 198 pp.

* Gish, Duane T., *Speculations and Experiments on the Origin of Life* (San Diego: Institute for Creation Research, 1972), 41 pp.

* Gish, Duane T. and Donald Rohrer, *Up With Creation* (San Diego: Creation-Life, 1978), 341 pp.

* Gish, Duane T. and Henry M. Morris, *The Battle for Creation* (San Diego: Creation-Life, 1976), 321 pp.

Hedtke, Randall, *The Secret of the Sixth Edition* (New York: Vantage, 1983), 136 pp.

Howe, George, Ed., *Speak to the Earth* (Phillipsburg, NJ: Presbyterian and Reformed, 1975), 463 pp.

Klotz, John W., *Genes, Genesis and Evolution* (St. Louis: Concordia, 1970), 544 pp.

Lammerts, W.E., Ed., *Scientific Studies in Special Creation* (Philadelphia: Presbyterian and Reformed, 1971), 343 pp.

Lammerts, W.E., Ed., *Why Not Creation?* (Philadelphia: Presbyterian and Reformed, 1970), 388 pp.

Lester, Lane P., *Cloning: Miracle or Menace?* (Wheaton, IL: Tyndale, 1980), 156 pp.

Lester, Lane P. and Raymond G. Bohlin, *The Natural Limits to Biological Change* (Grand Rapids: Zondervan, 1984), 207 pp.

* Lubenow, Marvin, *From Fish to Gish* (San Diego: Creation-Life, 1983), 304 pp.

Mandock, R.L.N., *Scale Time Versus Geological Time in Radioisotope Age Determination* (San Diego: Institute for Creation Research, 1983), 160 pp.

Marsh, Frank L., *Life, Man and Time* (Escondido, CA: Outdoor Pictures, 1967), 238 pp.

Marsh, Frank L., *Variation and Fixity in Nature* (Mountain View, CA: Pacific Press, 1976), 150 pp.

* Moore, John N., *How to Teach Origins without ACLU Interference* (Milford, MI: Mott Media, 1983), 382 pp.

Moore, John N., *Questions and Answers on Creation and Evolution* (Grand Rapids: Baker, 1976), 110 pp.

* Morris, Henry M. *Evolution in Turmoil* (San Diego: Creation-Life, 1982),

190 pp.

* Morris, Henry M., *The Scientific Case for Creation* (San Diego: Creation-Life, 1977), 87 pp.

* Morris, Henry M., *The Troubled Waters of Evolution* (San Diego: Creation-Life, 1974), 217 pp.

* Morris, Henry M., *The Twilight of Evolution* (Grand Rapids: Baker, 1964), 103 pp.

* Morris, Henry M., Wm. W. Boardman, and Robert F. Koontz, *Science and Creation* (San Diego: Creation-Science Research Center, 1971), 98 pp.

* Morris, Henry M. and Gary E. Parker, *What is Creation Science?* (San Diego: Creation-Life, 1982), 306 pp.

* Morris, Henry M. and Donald Rohrer, *Creation: The Cutting Edge* (San Diego: Creation-Life, 1982), 240 pp.

* Morris, Henry M. and Donald Rohrer, *The Decade of Creation* (San Diego: Creation-Life, 1980), 316 pp.

* Morris, Henry M. and John C. Whitcomb, *The Genesis Flood* (Philadelphia: Presbyterian and Reformed, 1961), 518 pp.

Morris, Henry M., et al., *A Symposium on Creation* (Grand Rapids: Baker, 1968), 156 pp.

* Morris, John D., *Tracking Those Incredible Dinosaurs, and the People Who Knew Them* (San Diego: Creation-Life, 1980), 240 pp.

Mulfinger, George, Ed., *Design and Origins in Astronomy* (Norcross, GA: C.R.S. Books, 1984), 150 pp.

* Parker, Gary E., *Creation: The Facts of Life* (San Diego: Creation-Life, 1980), 163 pp.

Patten, Donald W., Ed., *Symposium on Creation II* (Grand Rapids: Baker, 1970), 151 pp.

Patten, Donald W., Ed., *Symposium on Creation III* (Grand Rapids: Baker, 1971, 150 pp.

Patten, Donald W. Ed., *Symposium on Creation IV* (Grand Rapids: Baker, 1972), 159 pp.

Patten, Donald W., Ed., *Symposium on Creation V* (Grand Rapids: Baker, 1975), 135 pp.

Pitman, Michael, *Adam and Evolution* (Hutchinson, 1984), 268 pp.

* Read, John G., *Fossils, Strata and Evolution* (Culver City, CA: Scientific Technological Presentations, 1979), 64 pp.

Setterfield, Barry, *The Velocity of Light and the Age of the Universe* (Brisbane, Australia: Creation Science Publishing, 1981), 48 pp.

Shute, Evan, *Flaws in the Theory of Evolution* (Philadelphia: Presbyterian and Reformed, 1966), 286 pp.

Siegler, H.R., *Evolution or Degeneration—Which?* (Milwaukee: Northwestern Publ. House, 1972), 128 pp.

* Slusher, Harold S., *Age of the Cosmos* (San Diego: Institute for Creation Research, 1980), 76 pp.

* Slusher, Harold S., *Critique of Radiometric Dating* (San Diego: Institute for Creation Research, 1981), 58 pp.

* Slusher, Harold S., *Origin of the Universe* (San Diego: Institute for Creation Research, 1980), 90 pp.

* Slusher, Harold S. and Thomas Gamwell, *Age of the Earth* (San Diego: Institute for Creation Research, 1978), 77 pp.

* Slusher, Harold S. and Stephen Robertson, *Age of the Solar System* (San Diego: Institute for Creation Research, 1982), 131 pp.

Taylor, Ian T., *In the Minds of Men: Darwin and the New World Order* (Toronto: TFE Publ., 1984), 498 pp.

Thaxton, Charles B., Walter L. Bradley and Roger L. Olsen, *The Mystery of Life's Origins* (New York: Philosophical Library, 1984), 228 pp.

Tinkle, William J., *Heredity* (Grand Rapids: Zondervan, 1970), 182 pp.

Utt, Richard H. Ed., *Creation: Nature's Designs and Designer* (Mountain View CA: Pacific Press, 1971), 182 pp.

Van Dolson, Leo R. Ed., *Our Real Roots* (Washington: Review and Herald, 1979), 189 pp.

Von Fange, Erich, A., *Time Upside Down* (Ann Arbor, MI: Author, 1981), 41 pp.

* Whitcomb, John C. and Donald B. DeYoung, *The Moon: Its Creation, Form and Significance* (Winona Lake, IN: BMH Books, 1978), 180 pp.

White, A.J. Monty, *What About Origins?* (Devon, England: Dunestone, 1978), 170 pp.

* Wilder-Smith, A.E., *Man's Origin, Man's Destiny* (Wheaton, IL: Harold Shaw Co., 1968), 320 pp.

* Wilder-Smith A.E., *The Creation of Life* (Wheaton, IL: Harold Shaw Co., 1970), 269 pp.

* Wilder-Smith, A.E., *The Natural Sciences Know Nothing of Evolution* (San Diego: Master Books, 1981), 166 pp.

Williams, Emmett L. Ed., *Thermodynamics and the Development of Order* (Atlanta: Creation Research Soc. Books, 1981), 141 pp.

* Wilson, Clifford D., *Monkeys Will Never Talk—Or Will They?* (San Diego: Creation-Life, 1978), 183 pp.

* Wysong, R.L., *The Creation-Evolution Controversy* (East Lansing, MI: Inquiry, 1976), 455 pp.

Zimmerman, Paul A., Ed., *Darwin, Evolution and Creation* (St. Louis: Concordia Publ. House, 1959), 231 pp.

II. *Books by Evolutionists Containing Valuable Critiques of Aspects of Evolutionary Theory or Practice.*

Ager, Derek, *The Nature of the Stratigraphical Record* (New York: John Wiley, 1981), 122 pp.

Barzun, Jacques, *Darwin, Marx, Wagner* (New York: Doubleday, 1958), 373 pp.

Berggren, W.A. and John A. Van Couvering, Eds., *Catastrophes and Earth History* (Princeton: Princeton Univ. Press, 1984), 464 pp.

Blum, Harold F., *Time's Arrow and Evolution* (Princeton: Princeton Univ. Press, 1968), 232 pp.

Campbell, Jeremy, *Grammatical Man* (New York: Simon and Schuster, 1982), 319 pp.

Clube, V. and B. Napier, *The Cosmic Serpent* (London: Faber, 1982), 299 pp.

Corliss, William R., *Ancient Man: A Handbook of Puzzling Artifacts* (Glen Arm, MD: Sourcebook Project, 1978), 786 pp.

Corliss, William R., *Incredible Life: A Handbook of Biological Mysteries* (Glen Arm, MD: Sourcebook Project, 1981), 1018 pp.

Corliss, William R., *Unknown Earth: A Handbook of Geological Enigmas* (Glen Arm, MD: Sourcebook Project, 1980), 833 pp.

DeBeer, Sir Gavin R., *Homology, an Unsolved Problem* (London: Oxford Univ. Press, 1971).

de Grazia, Alfred, *Chaos and Creation* (Princeton, NJ: Metron, 1981), 336 pp.

Fix, William R., *The Bone Peddlers* (New York: Macmillan, 1984), 337 pp.

Goodman, Jeffrey, *The Genesis Mystery* (New York: Times Books, 1983), 304 pp.

Grasse, Pierre P., *Evolution of Living Organisms* (New York: Academic Press, 1977), 297 pp.

Greene, John C., *Science, Ideology and World View* (Berkeley, Univ. of California Press, 1981), 202 pp.

Gribbin, John and Jeremy Cherfas, *The Monkey Puzzle* (New York: Pantheon Books, 1982).

Haller, John S., *Outcasts from Evolution* (Urbana: Univ. of Illinois, 1971), 228 pp.

Heribert-Nilsson, N., *Synthetische Artbildung* (An English Summary) (Victoria, B.C.: Evolution Protest Movement, 1973).

Himmelfarb, Gertrude, *Darwin and the Darwinian Revolution* (London: Chatto and Windus, 1959), 422 pp.

Hitching, Francis, *The Neck of the Giraffe* (New York: Tichnor and Fields, 1982), 288 pp.

Ho, M.W. and P.T. Saunders, *Beyond Neo-Darwinism* (New York: Academic Press, 1984).

Hoyle, Sir Fred, *The Intelligent Universe* (New York: Simon and Schuster, 1984), 256 pp.

Hoyle, Sir Fred and Chandra Wickramasinghe, *Evolution in Space* (New York: Simon and Schuster, 1982).

Keith, Arthur, *Evolution and Ethics* (New York: Putnam, 1947), 239 pp.

Kerkut, G.A., *Implications of Evolution* (London: Pergamon Press, 1960), 174 pp.

MacBeth, Norman, *Darwin Retried* (Boston: Gambit, Inc., 1971), 172 pp.

Mackal, Roy, *Searching for Hidden Animals* (New York: Doubleday, 1980), 294 pp.

Matthews, L. Harrison, *Introduction to "Origin of Species"* (London: J.M. Dent & Sons, Ltd., 1971).

Moorhead, P.S. and M.M. Kaplan, Eds., *Mathematical Challenges to the Neo-Darwinian Interpretation of Evolution* (Philadelphia: Wistar Institute Press, 1967), 140 pp.

Nelson, Gareth and Norman Platnick, *Systematics and Biogeography*

(New York: Columbia Univ. Press, 1981), 567 pp.

Rifkin, Jeremy, *Algeny* (New York: Viking Press, 1983), 305 pp.

Rifkin, Jeremy, *Entropy—A New World View* (New York: Viking Press, 1980), 305 pp.

Salet, G., *Hasard et Certitude* (Paris: Tequi-Diffusion, 1972), 456 pp.

Taylor, Gordon Rattray, *The Great Evolution Mystery* (London: Secker and Warburg, 1983), 277 pp.

Thompson, Adell, *Biology, Zoology and Genetics* (Washington: Univ. Press of America, 1983), 134 pp.

Velikovsky, Immanuel, *Earth in Upheaval* (New York: Dell, 1955), 288 pp.

Watson, Lyall, *Supernature* (London: Hodder and Stoughton, 1973).

Zirkle, Conway, *Evolution, Marxian Biology, and the Social Scene* (Philadelphia: Univ. of Pennsylvania Press, 1959), 527 pp.

III. *Books by Creationist Authors, both Scientists and Theologians, Discussing Relation between Science and the Bible.*

* Bowden, Malcolm, *The Rise of the Evolution Fraud* (San Diego: Creation-Life, 1982), 227 pp.

Camping, Harold, *Adam When?* (Alameda, CA: Frontiers for Christ, 1974), 297 pp.

Chittick, Donald E., *The Controversy: Roots of the Creation-Evolution Conflict* (Portland, OR: Multnomah Press, 1984), 280 pp.

Clark, Harold W., *The Battle Over Genesis* (Washington: Review and Herald, 1977), 239 pp.

Clark, R.T. and James D. Bales, *Why Scientists Accept Evolution* (Nutley, NJ: Presbyterian and Reformed, 1966), 113 pp.

Coder, S. Maxwell and George F. Howe, *The Bible, Science and Creation* (Chicago: Moody Press, 1965), 128 pp.

Culp, G. Richard, *Remember Thy Creator* (Grand Rapids: Baker, 1975), 207 pp.

Custance, Arthur C., *Evolution or Creation?* (Grand Rapids: Zondervan, 1976), 329 pp.

Custance, Arthur C., *Genesis and Early Man* (Grand Rapids: Zondervan, 1975), 331 pp.

Custance, Arthur C., *Noah's Three Sons* (Grand Rapids: Zondervan, 1975), 368 pp.

Fields, Weston, *Unformed and Unfilled* (Nutley, NJ: Presbyterian and Reformed, 1976), 245 pp.

Geisler, Norman, *The Creator in the Courtroom* (Milford, MI: Mott Media, 1982), 242 pp.

Hall, Marshall and Sandra Hall, *The Truth: God or Evolution?* (Nutley, NJ: Craig Press, 1974), 184 pp.

Kang, C.H. and Ethel R. Nelson, *The Discovery of Genesis* (St. Louis: Concordia, 1979), 139 pp.

Keith, Bill, *Scopes II: The Great Debate* (Lambertville, NJ: Huntington, 1982), 193 pp.

Kofahl, Robert and Kelly Segraves, *The Creation Explanation* (Wheaton, IL: Harold Shaw, 1975), 255 pp.

* Morris, Henry M., *Biblical Cosmology and Modern Science* (Nutley, NJ: Craig Press, 1970), 146 pp.

* Morris, Henry M., *Evolution and the Modern Christian* (Philadelphia: Presbyterian and Reformed Publ., 1967), 72 pp.

* Morris, Henry M., *History of Modern Creationism* (San Diego: Creation-Life, 1984), 382 pp.

* Morris, Henry M., *King of Creation* (San Diego: Creation-Life, 1980), 239 pp.

* Morris, Henry M., *Many Infallible Proofs* (San Diego: Creation-Life, 1974), 386 pp.

* Morris, Henry M., *Men of Science—Men of God* (San Diego: Creation-Life, 1982), 128 pp.

* Morris, Henry M., *The Beginning of the World* (Denver, Accent Books, 1977), 160 pp.

* Morris, Henry M., *Studies in the Bible and Science* (Philadelphia: Presbyterian and Reformed Publ., 1966), 186 pp.

* Morris, Henry M., *The Bible and Modern Science* (Chicago: Moody Press, 1968), 128 pp.

* Morris, Henry M., *The Biblical Basis for Modern Science* (Grand Rapids: Baker, 1984), 516 pp.

* Morris, Henry M., *The Genesis Record* (Grand Rapids: Baker, 1976), 716 pp.

* Morris, Henry M., *The Remarkable Birth of Planet Earth* (San Diego: Institute for Creation Research, 1972), 114 pp.

Morris, John D. and Tim F. LaHaye, *The Ark on Ararat* (Nashville: Thomas Nelson, 1976), 275 pp.

Morton, Jean, *Science in the Bible* (Chicago: Moody Press, 1978), 272 pp.

Mulfinger, George and Donald E. Snyder, *Earth Science for Christian Schools* (Greenville, SC: Bob Jones Univ. Press, 1979), 469 pp.

Nelson, Byron C., *The Deluge Story in Stone* (Minneapolis: Bethany Fellowship, 1968), 204 pp.

Newton, Brian, *Monsters and Man* (Devon, England: Dunestone, 1979), 133 pp.

Patten, Donald W., *The Biblical Flood and the Ice Epoch* (Seattle: Pacific Meridian, 1966), 336 pp.

Pinkston, William S., Jr., *Biology for Christian Schools* (Greenville, SC: Bob Jones Univ. Press, 1980), 741 pp.

Rehwinkel, Alfred A., *The Flood* (St. Louis: Concordia, 1951), 372 pp.

Rendle-Short, John, *Man: Ape or Image* (Sunnybank, Queensland, Australia: Creation-Science Assoc., 1981), 195 pp.

Richardson, Don, *Eternity in Their Hearts* (Ventura, CA: Regal, 1981), 176 pp.

Rushdoony, Rousas J., *The Mythology of Science* (Nutley, NJ: Craig Press, 1967), 134 pp.

Steidl, Paul B., *The Earth, the Stars and the Bible* (Phillipsburg, NJ: Presbyterian and Reformed, 1979), 250 pp.

Taylor, Charles V., *The Oldest Science Book in the World* (Slacks Creek,

Queensland, Australia: Assembly Press, 1984), 140 pp.

Thompson, Bert, *Theistic Evolution* (Shreveport: Lambert, 1977), 235 pp.

Tinkle, William J. *God's Method in Creation* (Nutley, NJ: Craig Press, 1973), 93 pp.

* Whitcomb, John C., *The Bible and Astronomy* (Winona Lake, IN: BMH Books, 1984), 32 pp.

* Whitcomb, John C., *The Early Earth* (Nutley, NJ: Craig Press, 1972), 144 pp.

* Whitcomb, John C., *The World That Perished* (Grand Rapids: Baker, 1973), 155 pp.

Williams, Emmett L. and George Mulfinger, *Physical Science for Christian Schools* (Greenville, SC: Bob Jones Univ. Press, 1974), 628 pp.

CREATIONIST PERIODICALS

* *Acts and Facts* (San Diego, Institute for Creation Research, published monthly).

Bible-Science Newsletter (Minneapolis, Minn., Bible-Science Association, published monthly).

Creation (Middlesex, England, Creation Science Movement, published semi-annually).

Creation Research Society Quarterly (Ann Arbor, Michigan, Creation Research Society, published quaterly).

Creation Social Science and Humanities Quarterly (Wichita, Kansas, Creation Social Science and Humanities Society, published quarterly).

* *Ex Nihilo* (Sunnybank, Queensland, Australia, Creation Science Foundation, published quarterly).

Origins (Loma Linda, California, Geoscience Research Institute, published semi-annually).

Origins Research (Goleta, California, Students for Origins Research, published semi-annually).

*Available from Master Books, P.O. Box 1606, El Cajon, CA 92022.

INDEX OF SUBJECTS

INDEX OF NAMES[1]

---

[1]This Index does not include the names of authors alphabetically listed in the Bibliographies, pp. 257-264.

276

INDEX OF SCRIPTURES